World War II Memory and Contested Commemorations in Europe and Russia

World War II Memory and Contested Commemorations in Europe and Russia

By

JENNIFER A. YODER

OXFORD

UNIVERSITY PRESS

OXFORD
UNIVERSITY PRESS

Great Clarendon Street, Oxford, OX2 6DP,
United Kingdom

Oxford University Press is a department of the University of Oxford.
It furthers the University's objective of excellence in research, scholarship,
and education by publishing worldwide. Oxford is a registered trade mark of
Oxford University Press in the UK and in certain other countries

Published in the United States of America by Oxford University Press
198 Madison Avenue, New York, NY 10016, United States of America

British Library Cataloguing in Publication Data

Data available

Library of Congress Control Number: 2023942409

ISBN 9780198894162

DOI: 10.1093/oso/9780198894162.001.0001

Printed and bound by
CPI Group (UK) Ltd, Croydon, CR0 4YY

Links to third party websites are provided by Oxford in good faith and
for information only. Oxford disclaims any responsibility for the materials
contained in any third party website referenced in this work.

For my children, Clio, Jess, and Cole

Preface

This study springs from my longtime interest in postwar German efforts to reckon with the Nazi and Communist pasts. Instead of focusing on the East–West German divide over interpretation of the twentieth century, this study widens the lens to include other countries that fell on either side of the Cold War divide. It is very much a study that, while ostensibly tied up with "history" and interpreting the past, is about power, persuasion, and identity in the present.

In this book, I seek to contribute a comparative politics perspective to the relatively new and highly multidisciplinary field of memory studies. The dictatorships, wars, genocides, occupations, collaborations, expulsions, and Cold War division that are part of Europe's "ravaged century," as the late historian Robert Conquest called the twentieth century, are now several decades in the past, yet their meanings and legacies continue to spark political and cultural debate, pose challenges for official practices of remembrance and public education, and affect feelings of belonging and purpose. Where and why do such debates and challenges arise? How do we make sense of them? Are they perhaps the result of unexamined or repressed trauma? Or are they better understood as instrumental memory games stemming from other causes? While both of these may be at work, this book mainly examines the latter, the manipulation of the past for political gain.

These questions have been on my mind for some time, but I would be remiss if I did not recognize the impact of several recent and ongoing events on my thinking about the political uses of the past. As I researched and wrote this book, the United States was in the throes of a memory war over how—or even whether—to remember its difficult history of encounters with Native peoples and the enslavement of people from Africa. Accusations of "CRT" (Critical Race Theory) being used by schools to indoctrinate American children to hate their country abounded in print and social media, interrupted the work of school boards, and were hurled like bombs by politicians at the local, state, and national levels. The Trump Administration withdrew federal funding for diversity, equity, and inclusion training of employees in federal agencies and threatened to cut funding to public schools that used Nikole Hannah-Jones'

"1619 Project" in their lessons. Book-banning in public school districts was a daily topic in the news. Under the guise of "patriotism" and "national unity," memory was wielded as a weapon to silence and divide.

Memory wars did not die down during the global covid-19 pandemic. Protests against public health-related restrictions occurred in many corners of the globe, but those in Germany were particularly alarming. First, on August 29, 2020 a group, including the far-right, anti-government Reichsburger, sought to storm the Reichstag, the building that houses the German national parliament, and the symbolic site of German democracy. That same building was the site of a bloody riot in 1920 and the infamous fire on February 27, 1933 used as a pretext by the Nazis to suspend civil liberties and arrest political opponents. In the months that followed the 2020 attack, the ugly past returned repeatedly; this time as protestors of pandemic restrictions donned yellow Stars of David with the word "unvaccinated," insinuating that *they* were victims of tyranny. Other protestors in concentration camp uniforms held signs saying "Vaccinations make you free" or claiming that the German government sought to perpetrate a "holocaust" with its public health policy. One protestor even compared herself to Sophie Scholl, the young woman killed by the Nazis for her resistance activities. This jarring appropriation and trivialization of symbols of the Nazi dictatorship was not limited to Germany, however, it was particularly jarring in a country so sensitive to its history.[1]

As I neared completion of the book, Russia invaded Ukraine. Like some of his Soviet predecessors, Vladimir Putin brazenly used distortions and lies to justify murderous policies and illegal territorial claims and to convince his people of the existential necessity of those actions. Putin claimed that the war against Ukraine is a continuation of the Great Patriotic War's fight against Nazism. He appropriated the label "Nazi" to delegitimize and vilify Ukraine's leaders, including its president, Volodymyr Zelenskyy, who is of Jewish heritage, and accused Ukrainians of perpetrating a "genocide" against ethnic Russians in the Donbas. In doing so, he employed a key strategy of memory manipulation, historical equivalence: Ukrainians seeking to preserve their country's independence were equated with Nazis, and disputes over language policies in schools and public places were equated with genocide. At the same time, Putin ignored the unmistakable historical echoes of Nazi Germany's Anschluss of Austria and occupation of the Sudetenland, or the actual genocides perpetrated by the Nazis against European Jews in the Holocaust

---

[1] The Anti-Defamation League identified similar appropriations of Nazi symbols in numerous countries. See https://www.adl.org/resources/blog/shocking-rise-holocaust-trivializing-yellow-stars-across-europe.

and attempted by the Soviet Union with a forced famine, the Holodomor, in Ukraine in the early 1930s. Putin's rhetoric obscured many more inconvenient truths about Soviet policy in the 1930s and 1940s, such as the USSR's cooperation with Nazi Germany, its occupation of the Baltic states and Poland against the wishes of those countries, and the many Soviet war crimes that could not be included in the Nuremberg Trials. In addition to his distortions and omissions, Putin frequently revised history to justify the invasion of Ukraine by dismissing the country's claim to sovereign statehood. In his speech on February 21, 2022, he claimed that "Ukraine actually never had stable traditions of real statehood . . . It is an inalienable part of our own history, culture and spiritual space . . . Since time immemorial, the people living in south-west of what has historically been Russian land have called themselves Russians." These instrumentalizations of the past have two related goals: to undermine the legitimacy of Ukraine's sovereignty and its democratic system and to draw a connection between Russia's aggression today and its role in the Great Patriotic War.[2]

In short, the phenomena I describe and analyze in this book should, unfortunately, sound familiar to observers of local, national, and certainly world affairs. While the cases presented in the following chapters may be less familiar to some readers, their impacts are often as significant for domestic politics as the memory wars in the United States. Putin's war against Ukraine, furthermore, is a stark reminder of the potential for conflict in memory battles between states.

I am grateful to have had a number of students assist me in preparation of this book. Ethan vanderWilden and Danny Hoenig provided superb research assistance and Haydn Sage contributed valuable "technical support" in the final stages of manuscript preparation. I thank the reviewers of the manuscript for their helpful feedback. Finally, I wish to thank OUP publisher Dominic Byatt for his enthusiasm for this project and Phoebe Aldridge-Turner, the Title Manager of this book, for her generous assistance.

[2] See Timothy Snyder's June 29, 2021 piece in the *New York Times Magazine* titled "The War on History Is a War on Democracy," https://www.nytimes.com/2021/06/29/magazine/memory-laws.html.

Contents

List of Figures and Tables

Figures

Tables

1

Introduction to the Politicization of World War II in Europe and Russia

Actors and Strategies in Recent Memory Wars

This study begins with the simple question: Why is the wartime past still present and, more curiously, why is it still being contested? After eight decades, several generations, and tens of thousands of books (fifty thousand "histories of World War II" available on Amazon), disputes still arise within and between countries about what happened, why it happened, and what meaning the wartime past has for the present. The discourses, symbols, and rituals associated with the memory of World War II vary across time and space. A particular day or event in the war is likely to be remembered very differently by a country on the winning side than one on the losing side, or by a country to the west of the postwar Iron Curtain than one to the east of it. Generations, too, remember the war differently, depending on whether they lived through the war or not and, if not, how much distance there is between a specific generation and the war.

Occasionally, differences in wartime remembrance arouse intense emotions within societies; they can also have consequences for relations between countries. A highly visible example of the latter occurred in 2012, when then President Barack Obama made a reference to "Polish death camps" in a ceremony to award posthumously the Medal of Freedom to Polish resistance fighter Jan Karski. For the American president, or at least his speech writers, and for many Americans, the use of the modifier "Polish" before "death camp" may seem unproblematic: most camps were in Poland. Some Americans might not know how Poles were affected by the war, the Nazi occupation, or the death camps. Poles, however, certainly do know, and they are concerned that confusing Poland's role in the war, even if by mistake or ignorance, not only casts Poland in a bad light—as perpetrators of the Holocaust—but fails to recognize their own victimhood at the hands of Nazis. Obama's gaffe caused a tremendous uproar in Polish society, along with demands by the Polish government

World War II Memory and Contested Commemorations in Europe and Russia. Jennifer A. Yoder, Oxford University Press.
© Jennifer A. Yoder (2024). DOI: 10.1093/oso/9780198894162.003.0001

for an apology. Eventually, the Polish legislature passed a law criminalizing the defamation of the country's wartime role.[1]

A more recent example is President Putin's use of the label "Nazi" for Ukrainian President Volodymyr Zelenskyy and other resistors of Russia's invasion of Ukraine. Putin claims Ukraine must be "de-Nazified" to protect ethnic Russians living there and to bring Ukraine under Russian rule. Unlike Obama, however, Putin's language is not an ill-informed gaffe but a calculated weaponization of a term that people all over the world associate with anti-Semitism, racial fascism, and aggressive war. Much less dramatic than these two examples are the many occasions when an event, figure, or consequence of the war is invoked to influence how the wartime past is remembered and what its meaning holds for present-day politics and identity.

This book examines the contestation over the wartime past in Europe and in Russia and uses several key concepts drawn from the multi-disciplinary field of memory studies. Memory, particularly the collective memory of groups, nations, or countries, can be a tool or weapon wielded by anyone. The politicization of the past, however, is most potent and, potentially, harmful when it is wielded by actors with authority and when such memory actors claim to champion the narrow interests of one constituency at the expense of another or at the expense of a more complete accounting of events and their consequences. "Mnemonic manipulations" (Braslava 2017) or "moves" invoke the past to achieve particular ends, such as provocation or mobilization of action. Often they aim to shift praise toward, and blame away from, themselves or groups with which they identify. This book is concerned with a particular kind of mnemonic move, one that seeks to disrupt the status quo or, more precisely, to oppose or revise a dominant memory narrative about the war. By dominant memory narrative I mean the fundamentals of what happened during the war, by whom and to whom, and with what consequences as generally agreed upon by professional historians and articulated by official institutions, through laws, public school curricula, or days of remembrance.

The main subjects of this study are what I will call *memory challengers*—political leaders, parties, interest groups, social movements, or groups of intellectuals or prominent members of a society—who wield the past for political gain. Their challenges to the dominant memory narrative can be lodged in almost any public space, including the media, public venues, or in official institutions or speeches. In this book, I investigate commemorations—days and

---

[1] The Polish government also requested that the UNESCO World Heritage Committee change the name of Auschwitz-Birkenau to "the Former Nazi German Concentration and Extermination Camp of Auschwitz," which it did in 2007.

rituals of remembrance related to World War II—that have been instrumentalized by memory challengers to further their own political agendas, which, as I have already suggested, typically entail assuaging the memory and upgrading the status of some while explicitly or implicitly downgrading that of others. The aim of this book, then, is to develop a framework for understanding what motivates memory challengers and what mechanisms they use to manipulate the past. I seek to identify whether or not there are particular factors that facilitate or constrain memory challengers and determine their strategies for contesting the dominant memory narrative associated with wartime commemorations. I also am interested in whether and how memory challenges in one country might affect memory politics in other countries.

The cases of memory contestation examined here span Western and Eastern Europe and include Russia. As explained later in this chapter, I distinguish between Western and Eastern European mnemonic regions, since very different interpretations of the war and patterns of memory politics developed on the two sides of the Iron Curtain. I feel it is important to include Russia, primarily because, technically, its predecessor, the Soviet Union, profoundly influenced the politics of memory in what are now the former Soviet republics and satellite countries; Russia continues to play a significant role in those countries' self-understandings and their domestic and foreign policies. And, despite being wartime allies, the West and Russia developed very different narratives about the war and their respective roles during and after it. Ironically, some of the memory challengers in Western Europe find common cause with, and derive financial support from, the most powerful memory challenger in Russia, President Putin. Before delving further into regional differences in wartime remembrance, I elaborate my approach to analyzing memory challengers' motivations and their mechanisms for contestation. I first discuss the role and types of grievances that likely motivate memory challenges and then explain why wartime commemorations are important sites of memory talk and ritual. After that, I will describe the range of approaches to challenging the memory of the wartime past and suggest how a memory challenger's toolkit may be affected by local, national, or transnational institutional and/or cultural factors.

Antagonistic Memory Motivated by Grievance

Studying the politics of the twentieth anniversary of the fall of communism in Eastern Europe, Michael Bernhard and Jan Kubik (2014) identified four ideal-types of mnemonic actors. Of the four types, Bernhard and Kubik's "mnemonic warriors" are the most relevant for the current study of memory challengers, since they adopt an antagonistic, Us *versus* Them, approach to the representation of the past. Mnemonic warriors "espouse a single, unidirectional, mythologized vision of time. In this conception, the meaning of events is often determined by their relationship to some 'paradise lost' or—negatively—an 'aberrant past'" (Bernhard and Kubik 2014, 13). This type of memory actor is not interested in a pluralistic vision of the past that legitimizes others' experiences; rather, memory warriors prefer a monist vision that legitimates their own interests, identity or claim to power. Mnemonic pluralists, in contrast, allow for a memory that recognizes an Us *and* Them, appreciating that different actors may have different memories of the past, but "within an agreement on the fundamentals of mnemonic politics" (15). Bernhard and Kubik's other two ideal-types are not relevant to this study, since they either discount the salience of memory (mnemonic abnegators) or prefer to look forward rather than back (mnemonic prospectives).

If the intentions of memory challengers are, by definition, antagonistic, it is important to reflect on why that is the case. It is reasonable to assume that memory challengers have some grievance regarding the dominant, or official, memory of the war. This study will probe the nature of those grievances. Perhaps the dominant narrative, or a particular element of it, causes memory challengers *discomfort*, possibly arising from the lingering pain of traumatic or humiliating wartime experiences, or from the dissonance between their own perception of their own, their group's, or country's wartime role and the representation of that role in the dominant narrative. Another source of grievance may arise from memory challengers' *frustration* with a dominant narrative they believe to be partial, neglecting their own role as victim, hero, innocent bystander, etc. Memory challengers in that case are likely motivated by a desire to "correct the record" and to receive the honor or sympathy that they feel they are due. Another possibility is that memory challengers believe the dominant narrative to be biased and factually wrong; they seek to *fundamentally change* it by inverting roles or distorting, even denying, facts in a way that upgrades their own status and downgrades that of others. The examination in the following chapters will pay close attention to the source of grievances and the extent to which the grievances determine the means by which memory challengers try to achieve their mnemonic goals.

Other scholarship on collective memory offers additional clues as to the motivations of the memory challengers that interest us. In describing populist-nationalist actors in Europe, Anna Cento Bull stressed the antagonistic mode of remembrance as a "counter-hegemonic project" (2016, 215). Like many populists, the memory challengers examined in this book tend to oppose a reflexive, contrite memory culture. In their antagonistic politics, memory challengers often assume a moralistic tone that interprets the past as well as the present in dichotomous terms: Us/Them, insiders/outsiders, authentic/inauthentic. These memory actors try to impose a different, often narrower and more monist memory, denying those they see as Others access to memories of victimhood or heroism and, thereby, closing Them off from the community, from Us. Like Bernhard and Kubik's mnemonic warriors, memory challengers typically oppose the very idea of pluralistic memory. They are skeptical or even offended by the notion of the past having a universal rather than particularistic, or inclusive rather than exclusive, meaning. Anna Cento Bull and Hans Lauge Hanson explain that:

> Across Europe, populist nationalist and/or radical right movements have developed counter-memories in a strongly antagonistic mode, re-imaged territory in exclusionary terms and constructed rigid symbolic boundaries between "us" and "them." In direct opposition to current processes of self-reflection on past conflicts and injustices, these movements promote memories which essentialize, as opposed to problematizing, a collective sense of sameness and we-ness, with accompanying sentiments of they-ness.
>
> (Bull and Hanson 2016, 393)

The antagonistic memory politics that Bull and Hanson describe opposes what is called a "cosmopolitan" mode of remembrance that is associated with Holocaust memory. Cosmopolitan memory has a narrative style that is reflexive, mournful, and regretful. It is associated with remembrance and meaning-making that eschews narrow understandings of agency and belonging; instead it draws attention to the importance of recognizing and protecting basic human rights and the consequences of not doing so. In other words, it focuses attention on the universal lessons of the war and of the Holocaust. Cosmopolitan memory was a reaction, or correction, to the antagonistic mode of remembering that was common in the first few decades of the postwar period and that focused narrowly on the criminal actions of a few while overlooking or minimizing the harm caused by collaboration and even by the silence of bystanders. Antagonistic memory has been reclaimed in recent years by nationalists and populists and redeployed to challenge the cosmopolitan memory narrative where it is dominant, in Western Europe; where it is nascent, in post-communist Eastern Europe; and where it is very weak, in

Russia. More will be said below about each of these clusters of countries, or mnemonic meso-regions.

As a general mode or disposition, antagonistic memory can be harnessed to distract or deflect from a painful past by whitewashing unpleasant memories of perpetration or complicity. It can also be used to shift blame or to identify a scapegoat for grievances by maligning ideological adversaries or by distorting inconvenient memories.[2] Kristen Ghodsee uses the term "blackwashing" to describe the tendency in post-communist countries to "paint the communist era as unequivocally evil, to ignore or belittle inconvenient historical facts that might explain (or at the very least complicate) the actions of the communist governments that came to power after WWII."[3]

The Study of Commemorations: Memory Talk and Ritual

Antagonistic memory that is motivated by grievance can be expressed in many different places and arenas, using a variety of modes of remembrance, such as speeches, memorials and museums, and place names. The largely unexplored mode of remembrance of the commemoration is a ceremony where, typically, a person, a group, or an event is remembered. The commemorations of interest here involve wartime events and actors. Please see Figure 1.1.

Since commemorations say and do things to guide a target audience to remember the past in particular ways, memory challengers may find it tempting to try to influence what is said and done at wartime commemorations. The scholarship tells us that memory actors engage in "strategic narratives" (Jones 2017), "mnemopolitical discourse" (Mälksoo 2009), or simply "memory talk" (Korycki 2017). These terms suggest the importance of the story told about an event. Our interest is in the story that memory challengers tell, how they tell it, and to whom. What do they include, emphasize, embellish, as well as omit, neglect, or distort about the people or events recalled? Do they access language, symbols or tropes from the past? Are there particular phrases, songs, documents that are recited or read each year, and why have they been chosen? Who recites them, and who do they claim to represent?

---

[2] I recognize that the terms "whitewashing" and "blackwashing" have different meanings in contemporary American popular culture, where the terms are often applied to the television and film industries. In this study, they are imperfect terms used to connote the construction of an exculpatory narrative about the past and its opposite, the construction of a defamatory or calumnious one.

[3] "Blackwashing History," *Anthropology News* (2013) at https://scholar.harvard.edu/files/kristenghodsee/files/blackwashing_history.pdf. See also her book *Red Hangover: Legacies of Twentieth Century Communism* (Duke University Press 2017).

**DAYS OF REMEMBRANCE AS THEY
FALL ON THE CALENDER**

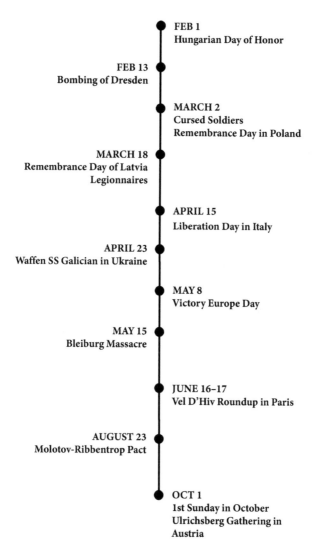

Figure 1.1 Days of remembrance
Source: Author.

Similarly, this study pays attention to what memory challengers *do* at commemorations. To understand that, it is important to recognize that commemorations typically have a structure, temporal and spatial, which entails rituals that can both bind participants to the past and to each other and also blind participants to the more complete, complex story of what occurred in the past and its meaning in the present. Calendric memory, days of remembrance, can have a deep, lasting impact on people's understanding of the past and the meaning of the past for their own relationship to historical events and their legacies. More so than discrete speeches or official statements delivered in far-away capitals or via media, members of the public are likely to have opportunities to engage with the past through the annual consumption of information—stories—connected with a commemoration, and they are more likely to be part of making meaning of the past through participation in commemorative rituals. Rituals can include gatherings, processions, laying of wreaths, lighting candles, partaking in special foods, wearing special clothing, reenactments, observing silence or a group recitation of special texts or songs. Rituals are carefully developed with particular ends in mind.

Emotion and connection are central to rituals at commemorations. Aline Sierp observes that, "anniversaries of historical events mark and produce memory," and as rituals "of joy and triumph or rituals of trauma and mourning [they] firmly fasten the cultural memory of the past to the future by committing future generations to it" (2014, 19). Sierp continues, "[e]xperience that might have lost its personal reference is thus transferred to the abstract group collective; it is symbolically condensed and enables future generations to grow into a shared memory even though they have no direct relationship with the experience" (Sierp 2014, 20). Connecting the past to the present and future as well as connecting the people in attendance at a commemoration to one another are important elements of days of remembrance and their rituals. Who or what is *not* included in a commemorative ritual is possibly as important as who or what is bound by it.

Commemorations are meant to illustrate to domestic and sometimes international audiences which moments in history are important to the group, or community, and what role those moments continue to play in a community's historical consciousness. As such, they perform identity, very often national identity, and signal to a target audience that there is a community in the offing. Commemorations and their associated rituals and symbols "activate a type of emotional code" that "standardizes and synchronizes public modes of thought" (Ariely 2019, 1393). As "socially standardized" events (Pavlaković 2010, 2), commemorations help produce and maintain "standardized group identity" (Sierp 2014, 20). Commemorations are thus part of the "imagined community" of nations (Anderson 1991). As powerful tools for constructing and maintaining group identity, commemorations are, moreover, mechanisms of political power. In her study of commemorations, Rebecca Clifford's observes, "the battles over what should be publicly commemorated are really battles over what should comprise a nation's collective identity. Commemorative ceremonies are vectors through which the relationship between the nation's past and national identity in the present is reworked and redefined" (2013, 13).

Lyn Spillman's work on American and Australian centennial and bicentennial commemorations explores elites' efforts to construct national identity in two regionally and ethnically diverse settler societies (1997). In those cases, the target audiences of commemorations were broad, in an effort to construct national identity where spatial and other divides were significant. Most countries have official national holidays marking important events in their histories, such as their independence, the founding of their democratic systems, or their victories in war. Most also have days of remembrance for soldiers who died in service to the country. War commemoration and memorialization of the noble dead are traditional vehicles for national identity building and, in the extreme, for fomenting hyper-nationalism. More recently, countries have established commemorations to mark darker events, memorializing victims of state violence or genocide and, occasionally, recognizing a country's own role in such atrocities. Such commemorations are usually a top-down, officially sanctioned way of communicating the importance of a past event to the community. With calendric memory, commemorative dates are often deemed official holidays or days of remembrance, sometimes with a holiday from work or school. Occasionally, non-state groups become memory entrepreneurs by introducing new commemorations and rituals, or by seeking to disrupt and alter established commemorations. In the commemoration of war-related events described in the following chapters, war veterans and their advocacy groups often play important roles in shaping the meanings and rituals associated with days of remembrance.[4]

Commemorations, then, "create a representation of a historical event" and "remind communities of their identity" (Clifford 2013, 12). This is especially true where days of remembrance are marked by participation in some sort of performed memory, such as wearing a symbolic article of clothing, gathering for speeches by individuals, partaking in a group recitation, or walking a particular route to a particular, historically relevant destination site. A commemoration is a "performative act of remembrance" and also a

---

[4] For more on the role of war veterans as memory actors, see Benjamin Ziemann, *Contested Commemorations: Republican War Veterans and Weimar Political Culture* (Cambridge University Press 2013).

form of "performed identities."[5] The selection of events to be commemorated and the ritual behaviors associated with them say something about a
nation's self-image and the image it seeks to convey to others (Sierp 2014, 21).
Commemorations are expression of values, and they define the community
through symbols, codes, and shorthand meanings that are widely known
and shared. Commemorations, it follows, are important parts of a society's
memory regime, its official or institutionalized memory, and thus can be
seen as agents of socialization. They focus the attention of a community and
often invite engagement of some kind, whether thinking and reflecting or
doing/performing something in the same or similar way.

Because of the functions played by commemorations, they are often sites
of contestation and attractive targets for memory challengers seeking to reinterpret the meaning of the date, change the associated rituals and symbols,
and/or affect the composition of the community, of Us. It is also reasonable to
assume that commemorations are susceptible to politicization, because they
tend to be less institutionalized and centralized than other forms of remembrance, thereby providing more opportunity for reinterpretation of the past
and insertion of new meanings for the present. They are also susceptible to
politicization because of the popular dimension: they are part of a shared calendar that guarantees attention (especially if a work holiday), and they invite
participation, unlike other forms of remembrance. Finally, we expect commemorations to be most susceptible to politicization when they are focused on
a particular site, where it is possible for local interests and civil society actors
to influence the meaning of symbols and to mythologize independent of the
dominant memory regime.

The Memory Challengers' Toolkit

Memory challengers, we have established, are motivated by grievances they
harbor about the dominant interpretation of the wartime past, and commemorations offer them an easy target for manipulating memory to serve their
political agenda. We now turn to the question of how they do that: do memory
challengers use certain discursive and performative approaches to construct
and promote their interpretation of the wartime past? In Table 1.1, I identify
a range of approaches, in order of how much they manipulate the past, from

---

[5] See Winter 2010. Hurd and Werther note that "Memory is then anchored in bodily experiences of
symbolically meaningful spaces" (2016a, 344).

Table 1.1 Range of approaches to challenging memory of the wartime past

Approach	Features
Manipulation of emotions	Performative identity, rituals that bind, empower, uplift, such as gathering, marching, reciting or singing, lighting candles, laying wreaths Emphasis on trauma, victimhood, martyrdom, or heroism and glory Use symbols, tropes, even clothing that signifies belonging, continuity with the past
Obfuscation	Whitewashing—filters out negative, uncomfortable memories or details Use of a screen memory to deflect attention from unflattering or painful past What-aboutism to downplay negative memory by drawing attention to supposedly similar situations as a strategy to lessen the uniqueness of an unflattering past Yes, but . . . attempts to downplay the negative memory by balancing the bad with the good
Construction of binaries	Simplistic distinctions to distract from complexity, critical thinking, such as inside/outside, pure/artificial, innocent/guilty
Symmetric approaches	Construction of a duality or symmetry, often suggesting equivalence of type or effect (e.g., between Nazism and Stalinism or Auschwitz and the Gulag in the Double Genocide theory). Competitive martyrology or competitive victimhood to elevate one's status or downgrade that of others Use of metaphor and analogy to distort Appropriation of terminology, symbols with clear meaning (e.g., Holocaust, Hiroshima)
Revisionism	Whitewashing Blackwashing—as with Whitewashing, this form of revisionism tends to ignore historical context (e.g., many communists were anti-fascists and victims of Nazis, while anti-communists were often Nazis or collaborators) Inversion of guilt/innocence, victim/perpetrator Distortion of magnitude of atrocity, pain, and suffering, usually by inflating casualty numbers to increase claim to victimhood or deflating them to diminish another group's claim to victimhood and/or to diminish one's own role as perpetrator Conspiracy thinking/theorizing
Denialism	Short of complete denial that an event occurred or occurred as the historical record shows, softer forms of denialism are trivialization and exculpation

Source: Author.

manipulating emotions or producing a slight shift in emphasis, to discursive strategies of denial and exculpation.[6]

Manipulation of emotions through symbols, rituals, myths. Typically, memory challengers appropriate existing modes of remembrance, such as symbols, rituals, and myths, then try to impose their preferred representation of what happened in the past, along with their interpretation of its significance in the present. The goal is either to bind people together to strengthen their common identity and fate, or to blind them to the original or dominant meaning of the symbol, ritual, or myth.

Obfuscation, possibly using a "screen memory," filters out negative, uncomfortable memories or details. It can also be used to try to balance the bad with the good. It is a form of "yes, but" or "what about-ism," used to distract or deflect from a painful or embarrassing memory. Dovid Katz has written about Holocaust obfuscation. Among the behaviors he considers obfuscation is the glorification of Holocaust perpetrators as national, that is, anti-Soviet, heroes.[7]

Construction of binaries over-simplifies truth and meaning with Manichaen thinking and imagery. Simplistic distinctions between good and evil, insiders and outsiders distracts from the more complicated nature of wartime events and their meanings. This can include paranoid, magical thinking to sow doubt, fear, create anger, and spark action against a perceived competitor or foe.

Symmetric approaches use comparison and equivalences to distort the truth and construct a particular meaning and memory of the past. An example of this was the German *Historikerstreit* (historians' debate) of 1986, when prominent conservative historians compared Nazism with communism in order to suggest that one was a reaction to the threat of the other, creating a moral equivalence, that is, actually suggesting that Asiatic communism was more ruthless. In much the same way, memory challengers in post-communist countries compare and often equate fascist and communist totalitarianism, promoting a Double Genocide Theory. While comparison is often used by scholars to deepen and expand understanding, the opposite is true of memory challengers; they use comparison and, most often, equivalence to avoid

---

[6] This list is broader than that of Manfred Gerstenfeld, which he explained in his article "The Multiple Distortions of Holocaust Memory," in *Jewish Political Studies Review* (2007). His detailed list specifically classified Holocaust distortions: 1. Holocaust promotion; 2. Holocaust denial; 3. Holocaust deprecation; 4. Holocaust deflection; 5. prewar and wartime Holocaust equivalence; 6. postwar Holocaust equivalence; 7. Holocaust inversion; 8. accusations of Jewish Holocaust-memory abuse; 9. obliterating the Holocaust memory; 10. Holocaust-memory silencing; and 11. universalizing/trivializing the Holocaust (page 36).

[7] See Katz's "Review Article: Detonation of the Holocaust in 1941: A Tale of Two Books," *East European Jewish Affairs*, Vol. 41, No. 3 (December 2011) 207–21.

careful examination and analysis in order to achieve other goals. Not only are perpetrators compared in symmetric strategies, so too are victims: competitive martyrology/victimhood is an attempt to distract from responsibility for crimes as perpetrators, collaborators, or even by-standers, by claiming the mantle of innocent victim under one or both forms of domination and tyranny. Although less blatant, the use of analogy and metaphor is also used by memory challengers to construct a meaning about events or actors in World War II and the Holocaust. Jan-Werner Müller suggests that historical analogies are mis-used to "reduce complexity and short-circuit critical reflection" (2002, 27). Christian Karner and Bram Mertens ask "how, where, and for what purposes are memories and narratives of World War II selected and articulated?" More specifically, "what forms of politics are facilitated by analogical thinking?" and how are they connected "with contemporary debates about migration, multiculturalism integration, and identity politics?" (2013, 17–18). The table of equivalences that these authors suggest are being constructed by memory challengers goes something like this: liberal democracy = anti-nationalism = threat to national identity and culture. The appropriation of terminology, such as holocaust or genocide, can also be considered a symmetric approach used by memory challengers.

Revisionism infers that memory challenges can be in the form of casting doubt on widely held understandings of the past or even replacing the consensus about the past and its meaning with a wholly different narrative. Whitewashing downplays guilt, while blackwashing vilifies another, casting them as solely responsible, or as evil in intent and consequence. Inversion of the roles of victim and perpetrator, of who is innocent or guilty, is another common form of revisionism. An example is the historical inversion constructed by far-right, pan-Germanic fraternities in Austria, who compared protests against their annual ball in Vienna's Hofburg to the Nazi pogroms of 1938. The leader of the far-right Freedom Party of Austria, Heinz-Christian Strache, took the analogy further, saying "we are the new Jews" (Karner 2013, 193). The purpose of these mnemonic moves is to transform oneself or one's group from victimizer into victim, thus turning the real victim into the enemy. This is a form of scapegoating that absolves memory challengers from the taint of guilt or culpability. Conspiracy thinking and theorizing similarly casts the dominant narrative about the past and those who support it as part of a plot to do harm. Widely recognized victim groups may also be blamed by conspiracy theorists as being party to a plot to cause harm, particularly by manipulating memory. In many instances, contention over the number of casualties is part of the revisionism.

Denialism, the most extreme form of revisionism, is often discussed as it pertains to the Holocaust. Deborah Lipstadt describes hardcore Holocaust denial as denial of the facts of the Holocaust. In this category, I would include trivialization of the crimes of the Holocaust or other wartime atrocities, as well as the exculpation of those who perpetrated atrocities. Lipstadt disguished hardcore from softcore denialism, which does not outright deny that the Holocaust happened but rather "creates a moral equivalency with other events," much like the previous two categories of manipulation noted here (2020, 76).

Opportunities and Constraints

Do memory challengers face any constraints in their efforts? Of relevance here is Bernhard and Kubik's identification of structural and cultural constraints that influence the choices available to mnemonic actors who seek to influence the memory regime in their societies. Bernhard and Kubik were most interested in the institutional constraints, or the legacies, of communism in each country, such as the relative power of political actors or parties or the salience of the Left–Right political cleavage. More relevant here are the constraints of domestic political regimes that have become relatively institutionalized as well as the constraints of EU membership and other transnational commitments. Where public and private media outlets uphold professional journalistic standards and a code of ethics, memory challengers are likely to find those doors closed to their often flagrant distortions of the past. Relatively unregulated social media, however, offers memory challengers the opportunity to articulate an unmediated narrative about the wartime past and to disseminate it through networks that are undetected, difficult to police, or are tolerated by the authorities. Legal restrictions on hate speech or incitement, where they exist and where they are enforced, present another constraint on the memory talk and rituals at commemorations. In such cases, memory challengers are likely to attempt to bypass official and conventional channels for disseminating their memory narrative and search for alternative platforms, such as on the dark web, or by creating their own platforms. In post-communist Europe and Russia, the independent media are younger than in Western Europe, so it may be a weaker institutional constraint on memory challengers. In countries like Hungary under Viktor Orban, Poland under the Law and Justice Party, or Russia under Vladimir Putin, the independent media have been curbed and, in some cases, brought under political control, providing national-conservative memory challengers with both legitimacy and a wide audience.

Cultural constraints, Bernhard and Kubik write, consist of historically formed repertoires of cultural forms and themes (2014, 22). Societies tolerate, expect, and socialize their members to use language in certain ways, to have common understandings of tropes or symbols. Much depends on the religious, ethnic, linguistic cleavages and other culturally conditioned codes in a society (2014, 24). Memory challengers at commemorations may purposely break taboos in their memory talk and rituals, seeking to provoke either domestic or international audiences, or both. On the other hand, they can be expected to use language, symbols, and codes that are familiar to those whose opinions and loyalties they wish to sway.

It seems logical that the more cultural and legal constraints there are in a society, the more difficult it will be for memory challengers to employ the higher forms of manipulation, denial and exculpation. We would expect to see greater institutional and cultural constraints in countries with stable political systems, particularly in older, liberal democracies. Such systems often feature longstanding norms and laws fostering human rights, respect and tolerance for minorities as well as educational institutions and other agents of socialization that emphasize a cosmopolitan mode of remembrance. Such countries typically enjoy strong media independence and well-developed civil societies that can foster critical and pluralistic perspectives, and they may have laws against hate speech and Holocaust denial. In those cases, we would expect memory challengers to be limited to approaches on the lower end of the memory manipulation spectrum.

Where a country's borders or political system have been less stable, where political and legal institutions are less well established and more vulnerable to ideological shifts or personalism, a cosmopolitan memory is less likely to be well established. Likewise, where there are fewer cultural constraints from education, socialization, media, or civil society, and where traditions of minority protection and tolerance for difference is weaker, the ground is likely to be more fertile for memory challengers. We might expect countries in Eastern Europe where liberal democratic norms have been challenged, as in Hungary and Poland, or certainly in Putin's Russia, to pose fewer institutional and cultural constraints on memory challengers. With fewer or weaker cultural and institutional constraints, memory challengers are likelier to employ approaches on the higher end of memory manipulation, such as outright denial of well-established facts about World War II and the Holocaust, possibly even articulated by political officials, state institutions, including museums and memorials, and public media.

The Triangle of Wartime Memory: Encounters between the Mnemonic Meso-Regions

By examining memory eruptions at a number of wartime commemorations across Europe and Russia, it may be possible to discern patterns of memory challengers' emergence and activity and also to identify the ways in which the manipulation of the wartime past in one country affects remembrance in other countries. To provide some context for this analysis, it is useful to describe briefly the mnemonic landscape as it has evolved over the decades since the end of World War II. In this section, I will first examine several assumptions about wartime memory and then provide an overview of the conditions that led to significant divergence of national memory construction after 1945 and throughout the Cold War. That divergence is important to acknowledge, as it has become a source of conflict between regions since the end of the Cold War, conflict that often finds expression in commemorations of the war.

Assumptions about Wartime Memory

While the construction of memory occurs at various levels—individual, group, national, and even transnational, it is national, country-level memory that concerns this study, since it is at that level, arguably, where the war and its meaning have been made most visible in political and cultural institutions, symbols, and discourses. All countries or nations have meta-narratives about the past that include founding myths and significant events. A meta-narrative informs what is often called "collective identity" by telling a story about who "we" are based on past experiences and, as a result, what "we" stand for in the present. Another relevant term is "national memory culture," which includes commemorative rituals, memorialization practices, symbols and tropes for interpreting the past that are commonly understood in a society. Similarly, each country develops a "memory regime," comprising the top-down, or official, and institutionalized practices of articulating the past. With its patterns of memory politics and by articulating the meaning of the past through institutions like schools, museums, or laws, a memory regime lends internal legitimacy to the political system as well as external legitimacy in foreign relations.[8] Since most of the countries in Western and Eastern Europe

---

[8] For the role of memory regimes in internal legitimacy, see Bernhard and Kubik 2014. For a discussion of the role of memory in external legitimacy, particularly in the case of Germany, see Jenny Lind 2008 and Thomas Berger 2012.

belong to the European Union, and since the European Union has sought to articulate elements of a European identity and memory culture, this study also makes references to the European Union as a memory actor with a dominant narrative about the war.

The first assumption this study makes is that wartime memory has been constructed differently across each country. World War II became a signifi- cant element of the meta-narratives in the countries it affected; in the decades following the war, each country developed a "dominant" memory narrative of that war. That development moreover occurred in each country in distinc- tive steps or phases, with distinctive influences and outcomes (Berger 2012; Gudehus 2008; Caramani and Manucci 2019; Lebow, Kansteiner, and Fugo 2006).

The second assumption is that wartime memory is not fixed but rather reconstructed by new generations and by new actors. Memory, as is well established, is selective and can change according to the needs of a society or group in the present. Following World War II, the needs of groups and societies varied, but all shared a desire to rebuild and return to some sort of normalcy. For the vanquished, these goals were accompanied by the desire for reputational recovery and reintegration into regional and international communities. Daniele Caramani and Luca Manucci refer to the process of meaning-making after the war as the "re-elaboration" of the fascist period and World War II, which was a kind of story-telling of the nation about itself (2019, 1164). Insights from psychology suggest that there are a range of ways that individuals may deal with trauma or shame. Similarly, societies—or more pre- cisely, their political and cultural leaders—exhibit a wide range of approaches to making sense of the dark past, from facing it readily and openly to repressing it as much as possible. Between remembering and forgetting are many more approaches to re-elaboration that distort the past in order to avoid discomfort, as well as reconcile the contradictory past with the desired present and future.[9]

A third assumption is that wartime memory has profound effects on how a society sees itself and defines its values and policies. The war's physical and material effects were visible for many years and its political-cultural consequences divided the continent for half a century; but arguably, it is the psychological and identitive effects that persist well beyond the rebuilding of cities and towns and, later, the end of the Cold War. Memory of World War II remains relevant to national identity, the definition of a society's core values,

---

[9] See for example the "Four formats of memory" discussed by Aleida Assmann (2004) or the typology developed by Caramani and Manucci (2019, 1164).

including attitudes about difference and about the treatment of minorities, and even guiding some kinds of domestic and foreign policy. As Caramani and Manucci have noted, World War II is "a common European-wide defining moment" and "[i]n the 1930s and 1940s, every country was confronted, more or less directly, with fascist regimes and had later to take a position, which crystalised into a collective memory of the country's role during that historical juncture" (2019, 1163–4). The current study expands Caramani and Manucci's notion of World War II as a confrontation with fascism to include the Eastern European confrontation with communism and Soviet imperialism.

Because of the centrality of memory to national identity and culture, a related assumption is that memory of major events in the past, such as World War II, can be contentious within and between societies. Memory of the war, specifically narratives about what it was about and what it means for the present, can lead to competition and even conflict. Many years after the events of war, one might assume that the facts about who did what to whom, why and how they did it, and with what consequences have been well established by historians and thus agreed upon by successive postwar governments and their citizens. However, memory eruptions, like that sparked by Obama's "Polish death camps" remark, or sustained memory wars within and between countries suggest that the representation of the facts of Europe's ravaged century and the construction of their meaning have never been uniform. They moreover remain subject to disagreements and shifts over time.[10] Even where some consensus about the representation and meaning of a past event emerges, there may be moments when that past is revisited, when the past is *mobilized* in order to create a rupture with its accepted representation.

Our interest here is not with *any* contest or eruption of memory where facts about past events have been uncovered or rediscovered. Rather, it is with cases where facts are challenged and often manufactured or manipulated with the intention of reinterpreting the meaning of events for political advantage, what Bill Niven calls the "political functionalization of memory" (2006). In an era of "fake news," where political actors and occasionally even national leaders question the reliability of democratic elections, the independence of the media,

---

[10] I borrow the term "memory eruption" from Nelly Richard, *Eruptions of Memory: The Critique of Memory in Chile, 1990–2015* (Polity 2019). I deliberately use the term memory eruption rather than memory event, as the latter is, as Aline Sierp suggests, "a revisiting of the past that creates a rupture with its accepted representation." See Sierp 2017, 441. While that is an element of what I seek to examine here, a memory eruption is more dramatic, with more political intentionality and, importantly, greater capacity for political contestation and controversy.

the veracity of scientific studies, and the work of professional historians, the spectacle of playing politics with the past may seem almost normal, but it is not; distorting the past can be harmful to individuals, marginalized groups, and, eventually, democracy. While individual politicians may distort their own record or that of an opponent's for immediate political gain, those distortions are not what motivate this study; rather it is the mnemonic ruptures (Subotic 2018) that occur from attempts to alter the dominant narrative about World War II that are of concern in the chapters that follow.

The way in which the wartime past is remembered in a society is the product of an idiosyncratic set of choices and experiences. For the purposes of this study, we can think of the process as having two steps: first the construction of a postwar national memory, then the confrontation and rectification of national memory with the more universal and "cosmopolitan" meaning of the war and the Holocaust that eventually emerged in the West and became dominant in European institutions. The universal meaning of the Holocaust includes the idea that education about and remembrance of the events leading to and including the Holocaust will help to prevent future genocide and ethnic cleansing. The first step in constructing a dominant, or official, collective memory about the war moreover unfolded in the broader context of the ideological division of Cold War Europe. Decades later, the collapse of communism, the break-up of the Soviet Union, and the implosion of Yugoslavia profoundly affected that process, essentially restarting it again. For Western Europeans, the construction of a national memory of the war developed during the decades after the war, eventually converging on a Holocaust-centered memory of the war. For Eastern Europeans, constructing autonomous national memories was not possible until the end of communism and Soviet imperialism. As such, post-communist countries encountered the Holocaust-centered memory narrative much later, less endogenously, and more abruptly. Russia, in contrast to Western and Eastern European countries, was affected relatively little by encounters with Holocaust-centered memory of the war.

Postwar Memory Divides

At the risk of simplification, we can categorize wartime memory in geographic terms, suggesting that the three meso-regions of Western Europe, Eastern Europe, and the Soviet Union constructed very different meanings of the war.[11,12] In Western Europe, the process of reckoning with the traumas and atrocities of World War II began in the immediate postwar years, largely in response to pressure from the victorious powers of the war. Initially, the Allies focused their punitive, "corrective justice" efforts on identifying the organizations responsible for waging aggressive warfare, war crimes, and a new charge, crimes against humanity. The International Military Tribunal at Nuremberg did not consider other crimes committed by Nazis and their collaborators against civilians, such as rape, looting, destruction of property, and wanton killing. Charges of atrocities against the Red Army were out of the question, since the USSR sat among the four powers presiding over the trials. "Inconvenient facts" of French collaboration and war crimes committed by the Allies were thus repressed in the official memory of World War II, viewed as irrelevant or undeserving of recognition in the face of the magnitude of atrocities committed by the German Nazis. Later, domestic pressure for a more truthful, critical examination of the past emerged in some countries, but by and large, postwar leaders focused on rebuilding and moving forward, ends best achieved by emphasizing unity and healing.

The Nuremberg Trials and the vetting of personnel, the short-lived de-Nazification, resulted in limiting guilt to top-ranking German leaders and organizations, allowing the rest of German society as well as former allies and collaborators of the Nazi regime to evade responsibility. These evasions and deflections were repeated in political speeches, official documents, or other forms of mythologizing by the early postwar governments of West Germany, Austria, Italy, and France.[13] They would set the tone for at least a generation of war remembrance.

Each nation experienced the war and its traumas differently, but the two main victors—the United States and the Soviet Union—were able to dominate the overarching narratives of the war (Krzeminski 2005). A West European narrative of the war cast Germany as the main villain, whose rehabilitation was possible and necessary, with the United States as the main hero. According to this narrative, the war began in September 1939 when Germany invaded Poland and ended on May 8, 1945, when Germany surrendered at Reims.

---

[11] For an insightful reflection on divided memory after 1945, see Tony Judt's Epilogue, "From the House of the Dead: An Essay on Modern European Memory" (2005).

[12] For example, different versions of World War II are discussed by Adam Krzemsinski in "As Many Wars as Nations: The Myths and Truths of World War II" (2005), Maria Mälksoo's "The Memory Politics of Becoming Europen" identifies four "mnemonic communities" of the war (2009), and Timothy Snyder identifies three narratives of dictatorship in "The Historical Reality of Eastern Europe" (February 2009).

[13] See examples in the case studies in Richard Ned Lebow, Wulf Kansteiner, and Claudio Fugo, The Politics of Memory in Postwar Europe (2006).

While there were millions of victims in the war, the genocide of Europe's Jews, symbolized by Auschwitz, eventually became a central symbol in the Western European memory of World War II. That Holocaust-centered narrative imparted a strong warning against nationalism and other exclusivist ideologies and implied a commitment to universal principles of tolerance and human rights. In contrast, the Soviet narrative of the war cast the USSR as both the hero and the main victim of the war against Nazism. This narrative carefully ignored the 1939 Non-Aggression Pact between Hitler and Stalin and marked the start of the war in 1941, with the Nazi invasion of the USSR. The Soviet narrative also ignored the identity of Nazism's main targets for annihilation, namely Jews and Roma. The "Great Patriotic War" is central to Soviet and now Russian national memory and identity as a heroic, sacrificing country. The war's end in 1945 is commemorated in Russia as May 9, marking Germany's surrender to Stalin.

While the Allies dominated the early processes of reckoning and remembrance, the memories of Eastern European countries brought unwillingly into the USSR or turned into satellite "people's democracies" are distinctive from both the Western European and Soviet narratives. Their narratives of Europe's ravaged century focus on moments of victimhood and betrayal, such as the Molotov-Ribbentrop Pact of 1939 and the Yalta Conference of February 1945, when their fates were sealed by others. Under the Cold War domination of Eastern Europe by the USSR, this distinctive memory could not be openly discussed, except by émigrés like Milan Kundera, whose essay from 1984, "The Tragedy of Central Europe," bitterly but eloquently describes the countries of the region as "victims and outsiders." The postwar division of Germany and Europe gave the communist leadership in Eastern European countries no choice but to adopt a variation of the Soviet narrative. This entailed what Adam Krzeminski describes as a "staged version of the gratitude of the liberated nation" toward the USSR and which served as cover for Soviet aspirations in the region (2005, n.p.). That version of wartime memory also entailed a refusal to take any responsibility for the crimes of the Nazis in the East German state, the German Democratic Republic (GDR), much less for homegrown fascists and Nazi collaborators in other communist states. With its focus on class struggle, communist ideology interpreted the war as a battle against fascism, which itself was a product of capitalism. If not ignored entirely, anti-Semitism and Jewish suffering were subordinated to the suffering of communists during the war; suffering, in general, was superseded by the victory of communism over fascism. Until its dismantling in 1989, the Iron Curtain sealed off this interpretation of the war from the Holocaust-centered memory in the West.

The case of divided Germany offers an interesting microcosm of broader European developments and, as such, will be referenced at several points in the study. Owing to its communist ideology, the GDR denied the need to reckon with the Nazi past. The Western state, the Federal Republic of Germany (FRG), paid reparations to Israel and, eventually, embarked on processes of reconciliation with wartime foes. Beginning with the Nuremberg Trials, West Germany traveled a long and winding road toward what Jeffrey Olick has called a "politics of regret" (2013). After an initial period of Allied-led transitional justice, the preferred memory frame cast Hitler and his henchmen as the sole perpetrators and the majority of Germans as victims: of wartime violence and deprivation; of a totalitarian regime that limited their choices and shielded them from what was happening to their Jewish neighbors or to Jews and others in occupied territories; and, finally, of expulsions from the east and mass rape by Red Army soldiers. Over time, coupled with pressure from the postwar "68er" generation and then from historians and public intellectuals, West Germany engaged in memory work that would imprint its domestic and foreign policies. The (official) West German culture of remembrance, maintained in unified Germany, focused on "negative memory" of the World War period and the Holocaust.[14] It has included a wide range of memory practices of memorialization, rehabilitation, reparation, special relationships, educational exchanges, and joint-textbook commissions.

Occasionally political figures in Germany, including the chancellor from 1982 to 1998, Helmut Kohl, sought a less restrictive memory culture, hoping that Germany might be treated by other countries as "normal" and that Germans could feel pride in their country's accomplishments. When Kohl accompanied US President Reagan to the Bitburg Cemetery in 1985 and was photographed laying a wreath at a tomb that included members of the SS, the German media and public were astounded. That memory eruption contributed to a public debate between historians on the right and left about the uniqueness of the Holocaust and whether that chapter of the national past should continue to impact the identity and culture of Germany in the present. Conservative historian Ernst Nolte sparked the debate when he published an opinion piece in the *Frankfurter Allgemeine Zeitung* on June 6, 1986, reacting to the Bitburg controversy. In his article, "The Past That Will Not Pass," Nolte argued against the key premise of the Holocaust-centered memory that had emerged in West Germany over the previous decade and had begun to

---

[14] The term "negative memory" comes from Reinhart Kosseleck, *Verbrechen erinnern. Die Auseinandersetzung mit Holocaust und Völkermord* (2002) cited in Gudehus 2008.

spread throughout Western Europe: that the Holocaust was unique and so was Germany for having perpetrated it. Nolte argued that German Nazism was a reaction to the threat of communism. "Wasn't the gulag archipelago more original than Auschwitz? Wasn't Bolshevik 'class murder' the logical and actual predecessor to National Socialist 'race murder'?"[15] Nolte argued that communism was the more deadly ideology, a claim echoed by some historians, in *The Black Book of Communism*, published in 1997, as well as many on the far-right.[16] The implication of Nolte's relativization was that Germans should not bear particular guilt or responsibility for the war and Holocaust, and they should be able to feel and express a "normal" pride in their country. The rebuttal on the left came first from philosopher Jürgen Habermas, followed by other prominent German historians, such as Jürgen Kocka, Hans Mommsen, Martin Broszat, Hans-Ulrich Wehler, and Heinrich August Winkler. The *Historikerstreit* continued for three years, ultimately resulting in a reaffirmation of a culture of remembrance and contrition. While smaller-scale debate crops up in Germany from time to time, a rather serious version of the debate has emerged in post-communist countries that seeks to place Nazism and communism on equal footing in the European mnemonic landscape.

The construction of wartime memory that included a "politics of regret" emerged more slowly in other countries that had been wartime allies of Nazi Germany. Postwar Austria clung to its narrative of having been Germany's first victim; it avoided serious reflection on its wartime past until the Waldheim Affair erupted in 1985. Kurt Waldheim had long denied any part in wartime atrocities, but his record as a military officer and member of the *Sturmabteilung* (SA) raised doubts among some university students and critical journalists. His candidacy for Austria's presidency sparked a bitter public debate about his—and Austria's—complicity in the Holocaust. Many credit this memory eruption with heralding in a new period of national self-reflection

---

[15] Ernst Nolte, "Die Vergangenheit, die nicht vergehen will. Eine Rede, die geschrieben, aber nicht gehalten werden." Frankfurter Allgemeine Zeitung, June 6, 1986.

[16] Critics of the Black Book have pointed especially to Stephane Courtois' claim that Nazi methods of mass killing were borrowed from the Soviets and that the term "genocide" applied to the Soviet Union's crimes against some of its ethnic groups. Finally, the Black Book ascribed 100 million deaths to communism, which it compared to the 25 million attributed to Nazism. For a discussion of the Black Book's comparison of communism and Nazism, see Vladimir Tismaneanu's remarks of 2001 at https://www.wilsoncenter.org/publication/241-understanding-radical-evil-communism-fascism-and-the-lessons-the-20th-century. The claims about communism being more deadly than Nazism have also been made by Holocaust deniers like Mark Weber of the far-right Institute for Historical Review. See the Southern Poverty Law Center's bio of Weber at https://www.splcenter.org/fighting-hate/extremist-files/individual/mark-weber

and memorialization of the Holocaust in Austria.[17] The electoral fortunes of the far-right Austrian Freedom Party and its participation in a governing coalition in (1999/2000) prompted further critical reflection about Austrian culture and identity as it relates to the past and how others perceive the country. The Vichy Syndrome was identified in the early 1990s by historian Henry Rousso, who diagnosed France's inability to look truthfully at its own wartime role, particularly its collaboration and anti-Semitism, as a cause of malaise and national identity crisis. It was not until the mid-1990s that a French President, Jacques Chirac, publicly acknowledged the French role in the persecution of Jews and fully embraced a Holocaust-centered memory of the war. While a Holocaust-centered memory was recognized as important for Germany and for Europe, Italy remained divided over how it should remember the war, and far less critical reflection has taken place (Foot 2009).

The End of the Cold War: A New Stage in Memory and Meaning-Making

For four decades, Eastern Europe's Soviet-backed communist regimes carefully crafted narratives of the past that placed all responsibility for fascism and Nazism on European countries' capitalist systems, while expressing gratitude to the USSR for liberating them from fascism and making possible the development of "people's democracies." Through official ideology transmitted by mass organizations and state media organs, communist regimes proscribed a limited view of the past; their roles in the war were interpreted either as heroic anti-fascist resisters or as innocent victims of Western imperialist schemes. Dan Stone described the Cold War as a freezer, which, once it ended in 1989–1991, led to the thawing out of many long-buried memories (2013, 174–5). In Western Europe, especially Germany, some long-repressed memories included the rape of many women by the Red Army, or the violence against eastern expellees. In Eastern Europe, what thawed were memories of local participation in wartime atrocities. After the Cold War and after over forty years of communist socialization, East Europeans' exposure to the Western European Holocaust-centered memory "put national versions of the war into perspective" (Krzeminski 2005), a perspective that created a great deal of discomfort and resistance.

---

[17] See Pelinka (2017), Uhl (2017), and also Beniston (2003), who also attributes the Waldheim Affair to a nationalist, anti-Semitic backlash in Austria that benefited the far-right FPÖ.

In the immediate post-Cold War years, the past that East Europeans most urgently wished to confront was the communist/Soviet imperialist one. Transitional justice efforts focused on the "lustration" of former secret police collaborators and the trials of communist leaders rather than on reckoning with events that had occurred before 1945. At the same time, into the vacuum left by the implosion of communist ideology emerged ethnic nationalism and what Vladimir Tismaneanu (2009) called "fantasies of salvation" from Soviet imperialism, born of the shame and humiliation of subordination. Rather than reckon with uncomfortable truths about the World War period, numerous political parties and leaders in post-communist Eastern Europe attempted to bolster their legitimacy through nationalist credibility—by pushing back on the dominant, that is, Western Holocaust-centered narrative, claiming it neglected important aspects of their experience—particularly their own victimhood under communism. A Holocaust-centered memory moreover ran counter to efforts to restore the national past and rehabilitate figures like Admiral Horthy in Hungary, General Ion Antonescu in Romania, or Stepan Bandera in Ukraine. During the decade prior to the EU accession of post-communist countries, it became clear that the construction of memory in Eastern Europe not only differed in significant ways from that of Western Europe but also seemed to compete with it.[18]

The unification of Germany provided a preview of the encounter between Western and Eastern European wartime memory narratives. Forty years of different trajectories had resulted in distinctive Eastern and Western Germans cultures and identities. For many Eastern Germans, it was liberating to express national German pride and identity during and after the peaceful revolution of 1989: the initial slogan of demonstrators in the autumn of that year "we are the people" quickly gave way to "we are one people." That expression of solidarity was also a protest against the communist regime and its refusal to reform, even as the Soviet Union under Gorbachev was engaging in *glasnost* and *perestroika*. Expressions of national pride, something many West Germans had qualms about, were less taboo for East Germans, whose wartime memory culture focused on resistance to fascism rather than the Holocaust. With the fall of communism, almost every aspect of East Germans lives changed rapidly. Transitional justice in this case was swift and relatively thorough: there were trials, the vetting of personnel, public access to secret police files, and a special commission charged by the parliament with investigating the nature of

---

[18] See Blacker, Etkind, and Fedor 2013; Verovšek 2016; Mälksoo 2009; Himka and Michlic 2013; Luthar 2017; Stone 2013; Pakier and Stath 2010; Sindbæk and Törnquist-Plewa 2016; Miller and Lipman 2012.

the "SED dictatorship."[19] In contrast to other post-communist societies, transitional justice and the eventual process of making sense of the communist past in Eastern Germany took place in a unique setting: transformation by accession to a ready-made democratic system and a well-established culture of remembrance. As such, Eastern Germans were not fully autonomous in their construction of memory about the GDR, the Cold War, or the legacies of World War II. While it is difficult to measure what the impact of their intense encounter with the Western memory regime have been, there were signs of frustration with it, if not outright resentment, already brewing among Eastern Germans by the 1990s. While the frustration initially seemed to come from former "winners" of the GDR system, such as communist apparatchiks and secret police informers, new far-right groups mobilized broader discontent with German democratic leaders, institutions, and policies by the second decade of unification. Many factors surely have led to the emergence of far-right protest in unified Germany, but the general sense of grievance over the course of political change across the last three decades and the sense of loss felt by some East Germans found expression in the Monday "evening strolls" of the Pegida movement in places like Dresden and in the election campaigns of the far-right Alternative for Germany. AfD posters in eastern states presented the party as heir of the "peaceful revolution" of 1989, appropriating the slogan "we are the people" (Yoder 2020).

Competition among Memory Narratives

Western Europe

By the end of the Cold War, there was a general consensus in Western Europe about the facts surrounding World War II and the lessons arising from it. Germany bore most of the guilt for the traumas related to the war, but others acknowledged playing a role directly or indirectly. The centrality of Holocaust consciousness became part of a consensus within countries and undergirded cooperation between them. The World War period was a collective trauma to be remembered in order to avoid its repetition: in short, "never forget" in order to ensure "never again." That dark past provided the impetus for cooperation in the present as well as an emphasis on mutual interests and common values

---

[19] The SED, the Socialist Unity Party of Germany, was the East German communist party. The term "SED dictatorship" was controversial among many East Germans, who perceived its use as a strategy to equate the SED regime with that of the NSDAP (Nazis).

over narrow national ones. For the European Union, the Holocaust served as a "negative founding myth" (Leggewie 2010), a metaphor for the evils of tribalism and nationalism, supplying an impetus for new forms of cooperation and greater integration of policies. Several high-profile developments helped to solidify the dominance of Holocaust-centered memory in Europe.

In 2000, Sweden hosted the Stockholm Forum on the Holocaust from which the International Task Force on Holocaust Education, Remembrance and Research emerged.[20] In 2005, the European Parliament adopted a Resolution on the Holocaust, establishing January 27 as European Holocaust Remembrance Day. The European Parliament passed a number of resolutions and other types of "soft law" addressing Holocaust commemoration, highlighting the connections between Holocaust remembrance and human rights.[21] The European Union invested resources in constructing a transnational memory of the past by creating the European House of History, along with a variety of educational and cultural programs under the umbrella of Europe for Citizens. In her exploration of the European Union's efforts to construct a European narrative, Ann Rigney attributed Germany's "repentance-based identity" as an influence on other European societies: "Even where European don't share a common narrative, they increasingly share a common memory culture" (Rigney 2012, 614). She adds, "From the outset, the project of a specifically European memory, like that of European integration, was linked to a desire for reconciliation and to the possibility of generating new alliances and identities based on what Graham Dawson has called 'reparative remembering'" (612).

Eastern Europe

The integration of post-communist countries into the European Union disturbed the consensus around Holocaust-centered memory by bringing into contact significantly different memories of the twentieth century and, importantly, different memory agendas.[22] The memory agenda of "Westropeans," as Jerzy Jedlicki calls them, emphasized the common values of tolerance,

---

[20] Allwork (2015) describes the work of the Forum as promoting Holocaust remembrance as a "civil religion" for the European Union.

[21] See the European Parliamentary Research Service Briefing "The European Union and Holocaust Remembrance" (February 2020) at https://www.europarl.europa.eu/RegData/etudes/BRIE/2018/614662/EPRS_BRI(2018)614662_EN.pdf

[22] Dan Stone calls the emergence of this divide between Western and Eastern European countries a "breakdown of the post-war (anti-fascist) consensus" (2013, 176–8). Memory challengers in post-communist countries tend to downplay or simply deny their own role as fascist perpetrators and

transparency, and human dignity, linking them to lessons of World War II and the Holocaust. In contrast, many "Eastropean" leaders sought to use the past to strengthen national identity and their regimes' or governments' legitimacy (2005, 45). Following their experiences with fascist and then communist dictatorships, Eastern Europeans could, at long last, exercise national sovereignty and celebrate distinctive histories, cultures, and identities. Some have thus been reluctant to subordinate national interests and memory narratives to transnational ones and have argued loudly in favor of integrating their own national or regional memories of the World War period into the memory culture of Europe, especially in the context of the European Union.[23]

Jelena Subotic observes that, soon after the two eastern enlargements of the European Union in 2004 and 2007, "East Europeans forged alliances with the West European right, most directly the European People's Party in the European Parliament, in pushing for EU resolutions and proclamations that would de-centralise the Holocaust from pan-European memory and add crimes of Stalinism as the second leg of this memory stool" (2018, 302). The European Parliament's 2008 Prague Declaration was the most visible effort to integrate the Eastern European memory agenda into the European consciousness. Kristen Ghodsee argues that Nolte's conservative *Historikerstreit* arguments laid the intellectual foundations for the Prague Declaration (2017, 142). Ghodsee and others (Dujisin 2021) analyze how a group of anti-communist members of the European Parliament (MEPs) from Eastern Europe mobilized support among fellow conservatives from Western European countries for their memory politics. Anti-communists are not only opposed to giving positions of power to former communists and their successor parties, which often includes social democrats on the mainstream left; they actively seek to "expose" their past affiliations and alleged crimes, turning the public against them and, often, stoking fears of a counter-revolution. The anti-communist political agenda includes construction of a narrative of equivalence between "Two Totalitarianisms," Left and Right, Communist and Fascist, and their role in perpetrating "Double Genocide" via the Holocaust and the Gulag.

The MEPs who promoted the Two Totalitarianism and Double Genocide theories proposed the introduction of a new day of remembrance, the Day of Remembrance for the Victims of Totalitarian Regimes, to be observed on

collaborationists, refusing to accept responsibility for the injustices of the past. See also Uhl 2009; Blacker, Etkind and Fedor, 2013; and Kattago 2009.

[23] For an excellent analysis of Western and Eastern Europeans' different relationships to European Holocaust memory, see Marek Kucia, "The Europeanization of Holocaust Memory and Eastern Europe," *East European Politics and Societies*, Vol. 30, No. 1 (February 2016): 97–119.

August 23, the date of the Molotov-Ribbentrop Pact of 1939. This new day of remembrance was meant to be on par with International Holocaust Remembrance Day on January 27, marking the liberation of Auschwitz-Birkenau. Also in 2009, the European Parliament passed the "Resolution on European Conscience and Totalitarianism," which, according to Zoltan Dujisin, "was the first time the EU opened the door to a potential equalization of communism and Nazism" (2021, 66). There were several rhetorical mnemonic moves in the resolution, such as referring broadly to "communist crimes" instead of "Stalinist crimes," implying "that terror was communism's central organizing feature, which then makes it easily narratively equated with fascism" (Subotic 2019, 39), and by claiming that both communism and fascism exterminated whole nations and groups. Ghodsee uses the term "blackwashing" to describe this kind of characterization of the communist era as evil and par with Nazism.[24] While asserting their own suffering at the hands of the Soviets and introducing this experience to the European memory narrative, Eastern European memory actors, intentionally or not, deflected from their countries' roles in the war. They neglect to point out that some of their national heroes and ordinary citizens were fascist collaborators and perpetrators of atrocities.

Fueling this mobilization of memory among the newer members of the European Union were their own national official and cultural memory practices in the 1990s. The politics of post-communist transformation, including whether and how to carry out transitional justice measures (trials, lustration, restitution, etc.) created deep divisions in society and a powerful anti-communist cleavage in politics. In Poland, transitional justice was comparatively limited in the 1990s, a fact that became a rallying cry for the anti-communist, nationalist Right, which complained about an "unfinished revolution" of 1989. Many East European countries have elected parties and governments intent on exposing and marginalizing former communists as well as setting the record straight about the horrors of communism. To achieve those goals, several countries developed government-funded National History (or "Memory") Institutes. The degree of independence accorded such institutes has varied and changed over time, depending on the country.[25] What they have in common is the insistence on the comparability of fascism (specifically Nazism) and communism, of the Holocaust and the Gulag. They also

[24] See Kristen Ghodsee on "blackwashing" in *The Red Hangover: Legacies of Twentieth-Century Communism* (Duke University Press 2017).

[25] See Georges Mink, "Institutions of National Memory in Post-Communist Europe: From Transitional Justice to Political Uses of Biographies (1989–2010)," in Georges Mink and Laure Neumayer, eds. *History, Memory and Politics in Central and Eastern Europe* (Palgrave 2013) 155–70.

share a tendency toward obfuscating the dark past of culpability in favor of a heroic past or one of innocence and victimhood. In practice, this has led to the construction of official narratives, found in museums, monuments, or educational materials, that erase or minimize the distinction between perpetrators and victims and play up the victimization of one's own group or society, while forgetting or downgrading the role of the suffering of others and, significantly, their own role therein.

The periods when new member states from Eastern Europe held the rotating presidency of the European Union's Council of Ministers, such as the Czech Republic's presidency in January–June 2009, offered unique opportunities for highlighting the comparability of fascism and communism as totalitarian systems and suggesting the comparability of their lethality. Eruptions of memory inside several post-communist countries closely tracked this transnational debate, injecting notions of competitive victimhood and moral equivalence.[26] Disputes erupted across post-communist countries—sometimes among scholars but often in the wider sphere of politics and publicized by the media—as to which memories should be prioritized and what consequences the past holds for the present. The national history and memory institutes noted above recommended policies such as the renaming of streets and towns, the removal of communist-era monuments, and the drafting of "memory laws" to criminalize speech that cast the national past in a negative light. The national-populist Law and Justice Party in Poland passed such a law in the aftermath of the "Polish death camp" controversy. A 2015 Ukrainian law forbade the questioning of the "criminal character of the communist totalitarian regime of 1917–1991 in Ukraine," implying that the actions of Ukrainian fascists were courageous, while those of the 1.5 million Ukrainians who fought against Hitler in the Red Army were not (Ghodsee 2017, 130).

The Soviet Union/Post-Soviet Russia

In Russia, the loss of the Soviet empire was experienced as a national trauma, while the instability of the 1990s and the Yeltsin years were a national nightmare. To assuage the pain and humiliation of collapse and to strengthen unity after years of tumult and doubt, President Vladimir Putin recentralized power. He also led a return to the cult of World War II. Putin's memory politics

[26] One of the most heated debates, one that stretched across the Atlantic as well as across Europe, surrounded the American historian of Europe, Jan Gross, and his 2001 book *Neighbors* about the massacre of Jews by their Polish neighbors in the town of Jedwabne in 1941.

focus on Russian heroes and sacrifice in the service of nationalism and neo-imperialism. In that memory narrative, there is no place for regret over Stalin's atrocities or those of anyone else in the USSR; neither is there room for recognizing the Jewish victims of Nazism or Stalinism. In this and many other ways, the Russian memory narrative finds common cause with the Western European far-right.

Responding to the European Union's Prague Declaration and the anti-Soviet narratives of its former republics and satellite countries, Putin has become obsessed with refuting narratives involving the Double Genocide and comparing the Soviet system with the Nazi dictatorship. As later chapters will show, Putin's refutations often include revisionist accounts of the war, whipping up the Russian nationalism that concerns European countries, particularly the Baltics and Poland. Coupled with the neo-imperial ambitions of his regime, Putin's revisionist narratives about the war are viewed by many Eastern Europeans as dangerous provocations and part of a hybrid warfare waged against them by the Kremlin.

The framework for analysis described here directs our attention to differences across the mnemonic meso-regions; we will also be attentive to similarities, if present. Are there any circumstances, types of actors, or strategies and tactics that memory challengers across the three mnemonic meso-regions share? If so, what might account for those similarities?

The Return of the Nation: Challenges to Holocaust-Centered Memory

Over the last decade or so, the tension between a narrowly defined, exclusivist interpretation of a national past, on one hand, and a more broadly inclusive and critical interpretation of past, on the other, have become more visible around the globe. Efforts to examine the legacies of slavery, colonialism, and imperialism in many places have led to a rethinking of memorialization practices, including calls for the removal of monuments honoring individuals linked to slavery, like Confederate General Robert E. Lee in the American South, or Edward Colston in Bristol, England or nineteenth-century imperialists like Cecil Rhodes, whose statue at Cape Town University was removed in 2015. The Contested Histories Project of the Institute for Historical Justice and Reconciliation identified more than a hundred cases across the five continents where controversies over memorialization in public spaces has occurred in recent years.[27] Attempts to face the difficult past truthfully and critically are often contested, typically by nationalist-conservative intellectuals and media, affiliated political parties and movements.[28]

Similarly, efforts by historians, activists, journalists, or even political leaders to pierce the armor of denial or innocence and to center the Holocaust in wartime memory have, themselves, sparked memory challenges. Many of the cases examined in this study are reactions to efforts to reckon with the past and to uncover long-buried truths denied or silenced by official interpretations of the past. Such attempts at the pluralization, or unsettling of memory, sparked angry defenses of the mnemonic status quo. In these cases, the memory challengers are reactionary; they prefer a narrower, exclusive interpretation of the past positioning others as guilty, morally deficient, and a threat to the community—most often, the ethnically pure nation, while the in-group is innocent, virtuous, and under threat.

Opposition to national and European memory that is Holocaust-centered usually comes from the far-right, from old and new nationalist parties and, since 2019, from a new far-right party grouping inside the European Parliament called Identity and Democracy. Less institutionalized challenges to Holocaust-centered memory cultures and practices come from the New Right, a loose group of individuals and networks that include Identitarians, Q-Anon supporters, Three Percenters, and any number of other "movements" that communicate in chat rooms. They occasionally mobilize protest movements, such as Pegida in Germany or, in rare cases, terrorist movements like the National Socialist Underground, also in Germany. The Identitarian Movement exists in a number of European countries, affiliated with right-wing publishing houses and think tanks. During the covid-19 pandemic, groups opposed to their governments' pandemic restrictions and anti-vaxxers found common cause with the anti-establishment agenda of the New Right. Rather than seeing Europe as a community of values of equality, tolerance, and

---

[27] See the description of the project at https://www.ihjr.org/ethics-and-legacy/.

[28] One of the most visible cases of backlash erupted in 2017 in Charlottesville, Virginia when the Unite the Right rally protested—among other things—the removal of Confederate monuments, including Robert E. Lee, from a public park in that city. Other efforts to more fully and critically examine the dark past come from public intellectuals, like Nikole Hannah Jones, whose long-form journalism articles in the *New York Times* and podcast, called "The 1619 Project," sought to "reframe the country's history by placing the consequences of slavery and the contributions of Black Americans at the very center of the United States' national narrative." See https://www.nytimes.com/interactive/2019/08/14/magazine/1619-america-slavery.html. Attacks on The 1969 Project from the nationalist right quickly emerged, including from then US President Donald Trump, who responded by creating "1776 Commission" to support "patriotic education."

human dignity, as the European Union asserts, New Right groups like the Identitarians define Europe as a white, Christian (though they say "Judeo-Christian") civilization that must be defended from foreign civilizations, namely Islam, seeking to "replace" white Europeans.

Holocaust remembrance identifies clear victims and perpetrators, implies shame for perpetrators, and implies a duty for all to guard against a repeat of the past, to uphold human dignity, and to protect the vulnerable, such as minorities, migrants, and refugees. Holocaust commemoration is thus antithetical to exculpatory narratives about the past which are often part of the far-right's exclusionary, nationalist project.[29] Active opposition to Holocaust remembrance or, at the very least, attempts to downgrade its importance, have become a strategy for nationalist-populist and far-right actors to attack their rivals in mainstream governments, political parties, and cultural institutions, to mobilize resentment among their target audience. Two well-known examples from Germany illustrate this strategy. In 2017, a leader of the extremist wing ("Der Flügel," now banned) of the Alternative for Germany, called for "a 180-degree turnaround in our policy of memory," criticizing the Holocaust Memorial in central Berlin as a "memorial of shame."[30] Another leader discounted the role that the Nazi years should play in Germany as "a speck of bird shit" that should not affect German identity.[31] The clear implications of this discourse are that the German government, particularly former Chancellor Merkel, harm the country by giving credence to a Holocaust-centered memory, so Germany should downgrade "those twelve years" and focus on positive moments in history.

Rather than viewing efforts to construct a Holocaust-centered European memory culture as complementary to national forms of collective memory and identity, far-right parties and movements view such efforts as undemocratic (even "totalitarian") and unpatriotic ploys to replace or diminish national constructions. These groups prefer a selective national remembrance that upholds their own nation's heroism or victimhood, but denies its violent past and culpability. They prefer an idyllic past defined by tradition, homeland/place/belonging, and the sanctity of family and nation. Using culturalist rather than racist terms, they claim

---

[29] David Art explores this theme in *The Politics of the Nazi Past in Germany and Austria* (Cambridge University Press 2009) and in an excellent essay "Memory Politics in Western Europe" from 2010.

[30] Bern Höcke's 2017 speech is summarized at https://www.reuters.com/article/us-germany-afd/german-afd-rightist-triggers-fury-with-holocaust-memorial-comments-idUSKBN1521H3

[31] Alexander Gauland in 2018 https://www.dw.com/en/afds-gauland-plays-down-nazi-era-as-a-bird-shit-in-german-history/a-44055213

to defend their "heritage" and way of life, often engaging in nostalgia and, occasionally, in conspiracy theories about threats from outsiders and enemies.

The political right has, moreover, been traditionally concerned about the nation as a virtuous community, the nation-state as a natural unit, the primacy of national sovereignty, and the zero-sum nature of politics. The political right, particularly on the more extreme end of the spectrum, expresses concern about the defense of the Inside/nation from people, ideas, and cultural practices from the Outside. Throughout Europe and Russia, the Other often includes ethnic and religious minorities, LGBTQI∗ citizens, along with "cosmopolitan" journalists, human rights activists and organizations that shed light on those minorities' marginalized status. Historically, anti-Semitic tropes, symbols, and signals have been used to distinguish the "pure nation" from the Other, a practice substituted or sometimes complemented today by anti-Islam discourse. The right is more likely to want to distract or detract from painful memories of the war that bring national shame or remorse or that recognize the cosmopolitan/universal Holocaust-centered narrative about the war, its causes, and consequences. To protect and advance the integrity and strength of the nation, the right is more likely to seek to revise painful memories from the war to make them more benign or flattering. For these reasons, the right is more likely to emphasize heroic narratives of the past and encourage patriotism in mnemonic discourse and practices. Critical reflection on wartime motives or actions, moreover, are often viewed by the right, especially the extremists, as arising from self-hatred and ultimately as destructive.

In Eastern Europe, common targets of memory challengers on the political right, like residues of the communist past, competitors on the Left, and norms and institutions of EU governance are deemed threats to national sovereignty and identity. In Russia, the reassertion of a nationalist, exclusionist memory culture is part of a broader agenda to strengthen the state and its current president as well as reassert its interests abroad, especially in the "near abroad" former republics of the Soviet Union. Putin's domestic agenda holds significant implications for remembrance of the war: the crackdown on independent journalism and human rights organizations, such as Memorial; the rewriting of history textbooks; and the cultivation of Russian "exceptionalism" have all restricted the interpretations available to citizens about World War II, its causes, its victims, and its legacies. The lessons Russia draws from World War II are at odds with those of Western and Eastern Europe. In contrast to the Holocaust-centered memory dominant in the West, the Russian memory narrative emphasizes the importance of military strength, a geopolitical understanding of international relations, national-conservative values, and authoritarian leadership. Whereas Eastern Europeans recall bitterly their victimhood under Two Totalitarianisms, especially, the tyranny of the Stalinist years, Russians recall their bravery and sacrifices as Europe's liberators.

Three Mnemonic Patterns in Tension

Three broad mnemonic meso-regions emerged after the war, although the Eastern European remembrance was largely suppressed by the Cold War. Collapse of the Iron Curtain permitted the three mnemonic patterns to come into contact, sparking eruptions of long-repressed memory and, occasionally, challenges to the facts of the war or their meanings for the present. Starting in the 1990s and gaining momentum with EU enlargement, the Eastern and Western meso-regions came into contact, with significant efforts by Eastern Europeans to broaden European memory to include their own suffering under communism and Soviet imperialism. About the same time, Putin began to use memory politics to complement his domestic and foreign policy agendas. Ultranationalism and revisionism, both strong currents in the "memory turn" in Russia, became important tools in Putin's assertion of an alternative cultural and political model to that of the West.[32] Eastern European countries, Poland, and the Baltics were already well aware and deeply concerned about the "rebirth of Russian state power"; many in the international community only became attentive in 2014, when Russia annexed Crimea and invaded the eastern region of Ukraine.[33]

Since the end the Cold War division of the continent, national memory politics linked to World War II have rarely been isolated from international politics; shifts or eruptions in one country's memory politics often have effects in another. Beyond examining cases of memory manipulation in Western and Eastern European countries and in Russia as discrete occurrences, then, this study also considers the competition between the three mnemonic meso-regions and the feedback effects that changes in one region have in others.

---

[32] See Marcel H. Van Herpen, *Putin's Wars: The Rise of Russia's New Imperialism* (Roman & Littlefield 2014), particularly sections on the "New Ideological Triad: Orthodoxy, Power Vertical and Sovereign Democracy," p. 57, and "The Eurasian Union: Putin's Latest Imperial Project" pp. 75–85.

[33] For more on the "rebirth," see Van Herpen 2014, 118–19.

Plan of the Book

The first two substantive chapters are organized by mnemonic meso-region. Chapter 2 "Right-Wing Challenges to Cosmopolitan Memory in Western Europe" examines four cases of memory distortion masked as patriotism and efforts to "set the record straight" in Western Europe. Here I examine the contestation of commemorations of three key World War II events: the bombing of Dresden in February 1945; the liberation of northern Italy from Nazi control in April 1945; and the round-up of Jews in Paris by French authorities in July of 1942. It also includes a controversial commemoration not centered on a single event but rather on a specific group. The Ulrichsberg Gathering honors war veterans, including combat units in Nazi Germany's army, and takes place annually in Austria. All of these commemorations have been targeted by groups that oppose or wish to diminish the importance of the Holocaust-centered culture of remembrance in Western Europe. The four cases examined in this chapter illustrate how far-right actors use commemorations as a vehicle for externalizing guilt and for whitewashing their country's fascist or collaborationist past. Such acts of memory manipulation by far-right actors often contain an explicit electoral challenge to ruling parties and mainstream governments, coupled with an implicit challenge to liberal democratic values. Far-right memory challengers seek to strengthen particularistic national identity and memory by emphasizing themes of belonging, resistance to outside threats, and victimhood.

Chapter 3, addressing the "Restoration of Fallen Soldiers to the Pantheon of National Heroes: Commemorations in Eastern Europe," examines how and why fascist forces and Nazi collaborators, such as the Ustaše in Croatia and the Waffen-SS in Latvia and Ukraine, became the focus of efforts to reinterpret the past and construct an exculpatory, anti-communist memory narrative. I also consider examples of anti-communist forces, such as Poland's so-called "cursed soldiers" (referring to their status as traitors in the eyes of the communists), or resistors to the Red Army's siege of Budapest, who have recently been mythologized in the service of a national-conservative agenda. Among the memory challengers who insist on commemorating "fallen" and "cursed" soldiers are veterans' organizations, far-right organizations and political parties, and even some governing parties that increasingly adopt illiberal discourses and policies. The five commemorations discussed in this chapter illustrate revisionist strategies that both whitewash the history of Nazi collaboration/homegrown fascism and blackwash the history of communism. These memory challengers operate in a different environment than their Western

Europe counterparts, targeting dominant Holocaust-centered memory culture and official commemorations through right-wing mnemonic instrumentalization. In Eastern Europe, memory cultures are still in flux, moving away from Soviet and communist era narratives as they seek to accommodate their national pasts in the broader European mnemonic landscape.

The next two chapters consider interactions between mnemonic meso-regions around specific days of remembrance. In Chapter 4, "August 23, 1939: From a Non-Event to a Russian Weapon against Poland (and the West)," I examine the construction of memory and memory eruptions around the Molotov-Ribbentrop Pact between Hitler's Germany and Stalin's Soviet Union. Deliberately forgotten by the Soviets and their satellites during the Cold War, this event began to command attention in all three meso-regions of memory soon after the fall of the Iron Curtain, however it only became contentious in two: Eastern Europe and Russia.

The Baltic countries first revived the memory of August 23 in the early 1990s; it has become central not only to their commemorative calendars but also to the broader post-communist Eastern European memory. During the first decade of the new millennium, the new Central and Eastern European members of the European Union lobbied to place August 23 at the center of European war memory. In reaction to developments in Eastern Europe, Russian President Vladimir Putin reinterpreted the Molotov-Ribbentrop Pact, using deflection, disinformation, and distortion of the facts to construct a particular historical narrative inside Russia, thus provoking anger and fear outside of the country.

Chapter 5, "Commemoration of Victory Day: The Many Meanings of the War's End," considers Victory-Europe Day, a commemoration that illustrates the persistence of three distinctive strands of memory. While Western and Eastern Europeans and Russians agree that V-E Day marked the end of military conflict, strong disagreement persists about whether the date marks the liberation from fascism and the beginning of democratic renewal, or the colonization of Eastern Europe and another prolonged period of oppression. Should the event be commemorated as heroic or tragic? Efforts to deflect from the complexities of the war and to defend either a purely heroic or tragic narrative have provoked reactions from domestic actors and, especially, from other countries, serving to further divide the European mnemonic space.

Chapter 6 concludes by reflecting on the similarities and differences among memory challenges and challengers across the meso-regions. It reflects on the potential for wartime commemorations to become more than stages for memory challengers to bind and blind their target audiences and rather to serve as spaces for contestation where more pluralistic and diverse memories might be fostered. The feedback effect between the mnemonic regions—made easier by social media and the declassification of documents—offers opportunities not just for memory eruptions, but also for a more expansive understanding of the past and greater reconciliation between countries and regions.

2

Right-Wing Challenges to Cosmopolitan Memory in Western Europe

This chapter examines the contestation over commemorations of three World War II events: the bombing of Dresden in February 1945, the liberation of northern Italy from Nazi control in April 1945, and the roundup of Jews in Paris by French authorities in July 1942. I also include a controversial commemoration that is not about a single event but rather honoring war veterans, including combat units in the Nazi army, which takes place annually in Ulrichsberg, Austria. All four commemorations have been targeted by groups that seek to diminish or oppose the importance of the Holocaust-centered culture of remembrance in Western Europe. That narrative ascribes doubt, shame, or guilt to the nation or groups with which memory challengers identify, giving rise to mnemonic discomfort and frustration over misrepresentation or neglect, as they see it, in the grand narrative of the war. The Western European memory challengers described in this chapter use commemorations to externalize guilt and to whitewash the fascist or collaborationist past. In addition to their goal of "setting the record straight," these memory actors often use commemorations to challenge ruling parties, mainstream governments, and their liberal democratic values, particularly regarding the protection of human dignity and the treatment of minorities. The discourse and rituals of right-wing and far-right memory challengers at war commemorations are deployed to strengthen exclusivist national identity by emphasizing themes of belonging, resistance to outside threats, and victimhood.

The four West European countries discussed here were led by fascist governments during the war or, in the case of Vichy France, by a regime that collaborated with the Nazis. Each country has reckoned with its wartime role at different times, in different ways, and to varying degrees. Austria, France, and Italy shared an initial postwar pattern of externalizing guilt to Germany, a practice that delayed reckoning with their own roles in wartime atrocities. Memory challengers in those cases have resurrected the old habit of externalizing guilt. In all four of the cases, memory challengers employ

World War II Memory and Contested Commemorations in Europe and Russia. Jennifer A. Yoder, Oxford University Press.
© Jennifer A. Yoder (2024). DOI: 10.1093/oso/9780198894162.003.0002

nationalist-populist discourse to delegitimize European Holocaust memory as well as to tarnish the left and often the center-right as "totalitarian" threats to the nation. Memory challengers also seek to normalize the fascist past, cast fascist dictatorships as no worse than communist dictatorships, and suggest that fascists were defenders of Europe from communism, arguing that it is, therefore, just to honor veterans who fought on behalf of the Third Reich. With the fascists and their militaries whitewashed and normalized, an obstacle is removed for the normalization of far-right parties, easing their pathway into governments or, short of that, smoothing the way for the mainstreaming of their illiberal policy positions opposing the "Brussels dictatorship" and "protecting Europe" from migrants and multiculturalism.

For each case, I briefly review the facts of the events commemorated, the history of the commemoration, and its relationship to the dominant narrative. I examine the grievances that motivate memory challengers at each commemoration and explore the types of memory talk and rituals they wield, considering the institutional and cultural constraints on their efforts to manipulate the past. I conclude each case study by noting reactions to the memory challenges. At the end of the chapter, I reflect on the common features of the four cases of contested commemoration, the implications of their activities, and the factors that are likely to limit their success.

The Commemoration of the Bombing of Dresden, Germany

As noted earlier, the postwar Federal Republic (West Germany from 1949–1990), then unified Germany accepted responsibility for World War II and the Holocaust. Allied occupation authorities initially led the process of reckoning with the past that narrowly focused on identifying and removing Nazi officials from positions of power, a period that was short-lived. As the Cold War intensified, amnesties in the late 1940s and early 1950s allowed a number of former Nazis to assume positions of power and influence.[1] The mobilization of the student movement in the late 1960s and the coming of age of a generation socialized after the war contributed to more critical attitudes about the wisdom of silence about the Nazi period and a greater insistence on an endogenous process of examining the wartime past. The 1986 *Historikerstreit* accelerated this process of public and political reckoning. The unification of Germany and the end of the Cold War have not resulted in a weakening of

---

[1] For an excellent analysis of this, see Norbert Frei, *Adenauer's Germany and the Nazi Past: The Politics of Amnesty and Integration*, 2002.

the memory culture of contrition. One could argue that the chancellorship of Angela Merkel even strengthened that culture (Yoder 2019).

In addition to cultural constraints, Germany places a number of institutional constraints on individuals and groups that seek to manipulate history. Germany outlawed Holocaust denial in 1985, punishable with up to one year in prison and a fine. In 1994, amended legislation provided for a general anti-incitement law and increased the potential penalty to up to five years in prison. The law states, "incitement, denial, approval of Nazism, trivialization or approval, in public or in an assembly, of actions of the National Socialist regime is a criminal offense" (Bazyler, n.d.). Not only has Germany created institutional constraints; it also enforces them by investigating and prosecuting speech and behavior that runs counter to the law.

Germany's robust memory culture is visible across a rich landscape of memory sites and commemorations. Unlike most countries, monuments and memorials are not the responsibility of the national level of German government. During the Cold War, however, the GDR's Central Institute for Monument Conservation did have sole responsibility for public monuments and memorials. The sixteen federal states, often in cooperation with local-level authorities, have jurisdiction over cultural matters, including the development and conservation of memorial sites. Except for the federal holiday on October 3, Germany Unity Day, the sixteen federal states determine public holidays. Commemorations of significant anniversaries, such as the seventy-fifth anniversary of the end of World War II, are often observed at national, state, and local levels. The commemoration of the bombing of Dresden has taken place locally since 1948, though it receives national and international attention as a symbol of wartime destruction. More recently, it has received attention for being a site where various far-right groups converge to challenge Germany's memory of contrition.

Dresden was bombed not once but four times between February 13–15, 1945. As a result of the Allied bombings, some thirty-five thousand Germans lost their lives. Dresdeners annually commemorate the first attack, which occurred on February 13 at 10:00 p.m. While local in focus, the commemoration has an impact on the national memory culture; it has become a symbol in Germany and even worldwide of the destructiveness of war. The February thirteenth commemoration is interesting, because it has become a highly contested day of remembrance; "It frequently triggers vast political and media debates about the legitimacy of remembering German victimhood given Nazi responsibility for starting the war and the Holocaust" (Volk 2020, 1). The Dresden commemoration illustrates the evolution of a mode of remembrance during and after the Cold War, as well as the far-right's strategy of deflecting guilt through analogy, equivalence, and revision.

Although Dresden was one of fourteen cities bombed by the Allies in February of 1945, it became a focus of Nazi propaganda that claimed the bombing was strategically illogical and purposely inhumane and by exaggerating the death toll by ten-fold. These distortions were further developed by the East German communist regime and continued to be expressed by extreme right groups after the collapse of communism and the unification of Germany. Claudia Jerzak describes the regimes' processes of mythologizing Dresden as "the collective narration about bombings and destruction narrative elements like inflated mortality records, legends of unethical attacks, and assumptions about Allied bombing strategies that were intensified and disassociated from historical facts" (2015, 53).

The memory of the Dresden bombing constructed during the 1950s cast the Allies' bombing as a catastrophe that befell innocent and peace-loving Germans caught between "the two evils of allied bombing and persecution by the NS-regime" (Arnold 2003, n.p.). The communist regime of the GDR continued to frame the bombing as an extremist act, describing the bombing of Dresden as a war crime more lethal than the atomic bombing of Hiroshima and Nagasaki. Comparison and equivalence were important approaches in the GDR regime's strategy of separating itself from the Nazi period and from any responsibility for crimes against humanity. It attributed the bombing and the war, in general, to Allied imperialism, capitalism, and German fascism, the latter viewed as a by-product of capitalism and "superficial democracy" in Western Europe (Ten Dyke 2001, 41). Moreover, the regime placed the German victims of the Dresden bombing and the Jews of Europe in a single narrative of war victimhood, as was the norm in communist countries (Volk 2020, 2). This approach was on display at the Heidefriedhof, Dresden's largest cemetery, where victims of the firebombing were buried. Please see Figure 2.1.

In 1965 the GDR regime erected a memorial complex at the cemetery with a rondel comprised of fourteen steles, seven inscribed with the names of selected cities destroyed in World War II, including Dresden, and seven inscribed with the names of concentration and death camps.[2] These equivalences of capitalist democracies and Nazis, linking civilian casualties of bombings in Allied

[2] The seven cities are Coventry, Dresden, Leningrad, Lidice, Oradour, Rotterdam, and Warsaw and the camps are Theresienstadt, Sachsenhausen, Ravensbrück, Dachau, Buchenwald, Bergen-Belsen, and Auschwitz. Sites of Memory blog, http://sites-of-memory.de/main/dresdenheidefliegeropfer.html#:~:text=The%20seven%20on%20the%20right,%2C%20Oradour%2C%20Rotterdam%20and%20Warsaw.

Figure 2.1 The steles at the Dresden bombing memorial complex at the Heidefriedhof

Source: SLUB Dresden / Deutsche Fotothek / Erich Höhne & Erich Pohl (No. 70608124).

and Axis countries, and of bombing victims and Nazi concentration and death camp victims all served to deflect blame from East Germans and Soviets for war-related atrocities. East German communists need not feel responsible or contrite for anything, since communists were by definition anti-fascists. The equivalences also conveniently denied that the victims of Nazism were anything other than ideological enemies of fascism; in denying the Jewish, Roma, or homosexual identities of Holocaust victims, the GDR regime partook in a form of "soft" Holocaust denial (Lipstadt 2020).

The official commemoration of the Dresden bombing began with a ceremony at the Heidefriedhof cemetery in 1948, a year before the founding of the Federal Republic in the West and the German Democratic Republic in the East. Starting in the 1960s, local politicians as well as religious and civic groups made speeches and placed wreaths at the site on each anniversary of the bombing. On the thirteenth day of February people gathered and stood in silence for thirteen minutes. During the early years, commemoration was used by the GDR authorities to insert new meaning into the symbolism of Dresden, that of communism's commitment to peace. By using the commemoration to claim German civilians as the true victims of Nazism and by presenting the GDR as "a society which had uncompromisingly eliminated the social roots of war and whose main ideal was peace," the regime narrowed the memory of World War II and the Holocaust. In doing so, it distorted the war's meaning, using it to strengthen regime legitimacy (Rehberg and Neutzner 2015, 105).

As with many commemorative days, interest waxes and wanes, depending on the contemporary context and, often, the occasion of a significant anniversary. Official commemorative involvement fell off in the 1970s and early 1980s until it was re-established for the fortieth anniversary in 1985 (Petzold 2020, 445). In the meantime, the East German peace movement had emerged in the early 1980s and pushed back on the official narrative of a peace-loving regime. In 1982, peace activists initiated a separate silent vigil in front of the ruined Frauenkirche during the ringing of church bells that annually mark the time the bombings had begun in 1945 (445). The following year, the state staged its own elaborate commemoration in front of the Frauenkirche, rendering the church a new site in the battle between the official memory of a peace-loving GDR state and the nascent civil society that questioned the regime's commitment to peace and human rights. Despite their differences, both of these actors, official GDR memory actors and the local peace activists, upheld the ideas of Dresden as a "victim city" and Germans as victims of Western fascist qua capitalist imperialism. The commemoration continued to decontextualize the bombing of German cities from the wider history of the war and Third Reich's policies. Petzold explains, "This decontextualization was symbolized in the widespread use of the term '13. Februar' to refer to the anniversary, signifying a single historical event on a specific date that was separated from its historical context" (446).

The Dresden myth initially included the inflation of casualties, misinformation about the bombing's uniqueness, about the Nazi regime's level of preparedness for an attack, and the appropriation of the terms "genocide" and "Holocaust." The goal was to broaden and perpetuate the myth of both Dresden and Germany as innocent victims. The Red Cross estimated the death toll at twenty-five thousand, but the Nazis and subsequent revisionists claimed it was two hundred and fifty thousand. Revisionists framed Dresden as an

innocent city of culture, publicizing a list of the architectural and artistic trea-
sures destroyed by the bombing. Their framing ignored the fact that "The
Florence on the Elbe" had also been an important supply hub for the Germans on the eastern front, housed a major Gestapo headquarters and diverse
arms industries and military facilities.[3] Allies ordered the bombing of Dresden
as the war entered a new phase on the western front at the end of 1944. Due
to high levels of casualties there, the Allies shifted their target to the German
home front and their tactics to air warfare in an effort to lower the morale
of the German people and hasten an end to the war. Along with thirteen
other German cities, Dresden was heavily bombed, leaving just 24 percent
of its housing intact. Although Hamburg suffered even more casualties and
destruction, Dresden became the site of contested memory.

The most infamous challenger of the facts and meaning of the Dresden
bombing was David Irving, the British military historian and Holocaust
denier. His book, *The Destruction of Dresden* (1963), helped to weaponize
the memory of February 13, 1945, by popularizing the notion that Dresden
was uniquely victimized by the Allies. He described the Dresden attack as "the
greatest bloodbath in European history" (Rehberg and Neutzner 2015, 107).
He claimed that the number killed in the bombings stood at one hundred
and thirty-five thousand, though later he suggested it was over two hundred
thousand (Niven 2006, 113).[4] In addition to inflating casualty numbers, Irving's more serious memory challenge was in the moral equivalency implied
between the Allies and the Nazis: between countries at war waged by trained
soldiers and the deaths inflicted by state-organized forces inspired by a racist,
anti-Semitic ideology (Shermer and Grobman 2000, 104).

Four decades later, in 2002, German historian Jörg Friedrich published
Der Brand, in which he similarly cast Germans as victims of a cynical war
of annihilation by the Allies, especially the British (Pruesser 2007). Bill Niven
described Friedrich's approach as perpetuating a "commonality of perpetrator status linking Nazis and the Allies—while at the same time implying as a
corollary of this that the fate of Germans at the hands of the Allies was every bit

---

[3] https://www.dw.com/en/movie-about-dresden-bombing-confronts-taboos/a-1903823
[4] While Irving's writing on Dresden has garnered much media attention, other work by reputable
scholars reveals the complexity of the case of the Dresden bombing. See for example Eric Langenbacher's "The Anglo-American Aerial Bombing of Germany during World War Two," in Adam Jones,
ed. *Genocide, War Crimes and the West: History and Complicity* (London: Zed Books 2004). Lagen-
bacher examines the strategic and legal aspects of Allied bombing of cities, concluding "many in the
West acknowledged that excesses had been committed, and that the generous postwar policies toward
Germany can be partly explained as an informal way to provide a form of redress and to make amends"
(117). Also see Mary Nolan, "Germans as Victims during the Second World War: Air Wars, Memory
Wars." *Central European History* Vol. 38. No. 1 (2005): 7–40.

as terrible as that of the Jews at the hands of the Nazis" (2006, 13–14). Friedrich appropriated terms from the Holocaust of Jews describing Allied policy as the "politics of extermination" and underground cellars where German inhabitants sought shelter during the bombings as "crematoria" (Arnold 2014). Jörg Arnold and Bill Niven both describe Friedrich's approach, like Irving's in the 1960s, as historical decontextualization. *Der Brand* was popular in Germany, as was the 2006 German television series "Dresden—The Inferno," which aired on one of the main public stations (ZDF). *Der Brand* broke the taboo of portraying Germans as victims rather than as perpetrators or silent bystanders, while the series broke the taboo on treating the destruction of Dresden as a drama or as fiction rather than as a serious topic for documentary films.

"Hijacking" of the commemoration by the far-right

Given these postwar experiences of manipulating official commemorations and the popular memory of February 13, it was not surprising that far-right memory actors seized on the Dresden myth.[5] Its annual commemoration of German suffering could be weaponized for the far-right's purposes more easily than sites associated with Nazi power, many of which had been destroyed or were rejected by the wider German public (Rehberg and Neutzner 2015). In 1999, far-right and neo-Nazi groups began organizing "marches of grief" (*Gedenkmarschen* or *Trauermarschen*), attracting thousands of extremists dressed in black and carrying torches. Beyond using these emotional symbols of mourning, the far-right uses slogans like "Your sacrifice—our mission" and "Bomb Holocaust," making a claim to identify with victims of the bombings, but not with other victims of wartime violence, including genocide. Please see Figure 2.2.

Their appropriation of the term "Holocaust" implies opposition to the singularity of the Jewish Shoah and even its trivialization. Using this kind of memory talk and by appropriating familiar rituals of mourning, far-right groups used the commemoration to challenge democratic Germany's culture of contrition.

The hijacking of the commemoration took place against the backdrop of right-wing mobilization in Dresden, and to some extent, in unified Germany

---

[5] The headline of an article in the *Independent* on February 14, 2005 referred to a "hijacking" of the Dresden commemoration by neo-Nazis. https://www.independent.co.uk/news/world/europe/neo-nazis-hijack-dresden-ceremony-in-the-biggest-far-right-demonstration-since-hitler-483337.html, accessed April 26, 2021

Figure 2.2 Far-right participants in the "march of grief" in Dresden in February 2022. Their banner reads "You call it liberation. We call it mass murder. Bomb Holocaust Dresden February 13–15, 1945. Remember the 250,000 victims!"
Source: © PRESSESERVICE RATHENOW C/O FREIBEUTER EV GOETHESTR 40 14712 RN.

as a whole. In 2014, Dresden became the birthplace of Pegida, the Patriotic Europeans against the Islamicization of the West. Pegida's primary focus has been opposing immigration, especially of Muslims. The participants in Pegida's "evening strolls" on Mondays steadily grew in number, particularly after Chancellor Merkel's "open door," allowing refugees from Syria to apply for asylum in Germany in 2015. The movement echoes the populist, right-wing narrative about political elites and the policies they enact being threats to German culture and identity. Similarly, the movement stands in opposition to the memory culture of contrition and to Merkel's insistence that *Wir schaffen das!* (We can do it!) and that Germans *should* open the door to refugees and lead the way in humanitarianism given their troubled past.[6] Pegida, like other nationalist and nativist groups, connects damage allegedly inflicted on Germany by globalized migration and homogenization with Germany's commemorative culture, which it sees as harmful. Nationalist fraternities have also been regular participants in the challenges to the memory of February 13 in Dresden.

---

[6] See Jennifer A. Yoder, "Angela Merkel's Discourse about the Past: Implications for the Construction of Collective Memory in Germany." *Memory Studies* Vol. 12, No. 6 (2019): 660–76.

Long bastions of national-conservatism and often right-wing extremism, these secret societies dating back to the nineteenth century still have about eighty thousand members across seventy fraternities (Deutsche Welle 2018). The Junge Landsmannschaft East Prussia (JLO), a right-wing association obsessed with the former German region of East Prussia, has passed out leaflets at the Dresden commemoration claiming "In no other place is the mass death of innocent German people and the destruction of the German culture as concentrated as it is in Dresden" (Jerzak 2015, 63). The death of innocent Germans and exaggeration about the destruction of German culture act as a screen memory to obfuscate the mass perpetration of civilian death by Germans.

Far-right parties have been vociferous memory challengers in Germany; they have been particularly active in Dresden where they have won seats in local and state assemblies. The innocuous-sounding National Democratic Party of Germany (NPD), a neo-Nazi party formed in West Germany in 1964, uses a memory politics focused on German victimhood. While it never won enough votes to secure seats in the Bundestag during the Cold War, it did enter two western German state parliaments in the 1960s. It then began to fade away, until German unification. The NPD found a sympathetic ear in the eastern region of unified Germany, "where its provocative claims concerning Germans' suffering provided grist to the mills of many dissatisfied and disillusioned Ossis unhappy with the harsh post-unification reality," including the cuts to Germany's welfare system known as "Hartz IV" (Joel 2013, 242). The party won 9.2 percent of the vote in Saxony's state parliamentary election in 2004. Soon after, on January 27, 2005, which was the sixtieth anniversary of the liberation of Auschwitz, the twelve members of the NPD's state parliamentary group walked out of a plenary session during a minute of silence to mark the anniversary and to remember the victims of the Holocaust. The NPD members exited to protest that no minute of silence had been held for the victims of the Dresden bombing of 1945. Days earlier, NPD official Holger Apfel called for making February 13 the anniversary of what he described as "the terror attacks" on Dresden and "bombing Holocaust" perpetrated by American and British "mass murderers," a commemorative date on the same footing as January 27 (Joel 2013, 243). With this, the NPD's grievance was clear: it sought to downgrade the Holocaust-centered memory culture while also upgrading the memory of German suffering and innocence. To gain the attention the party believed German suffering was "due," the NPD used emotional appeals and moralistic claims, constructing an equivalence between the Holocaust and other crimes committed by the Nazis over twelve years and the Allied bombing of Germany.

Another far-right party functioning as a key memory challenger, the Alternative for Germany (AfD), emerged in 2013 when it barely missed winning enough votes to enter the Bundestag. It then won over 12 percent of the vote during the 2017 federal election, becoming the largest opposition party in the national parliament. An even higher proportion of east German voters, 20 percent, chose the AfD in 2017. The party now holds seats in every one of the sixteen state parliaments but remains particularly powerful in Saxony and its capital, Dresden. Begun by Western economists and former CDU members who opposed Germany's adoption of the European Union's single currency, the party has moved far to the right on cultural issues. It developed an extremist wing (der Flügel), now officially disbanded but still active, and a radical youth organization. In 2020 the party was put under surveillance by the German Agency for the Protection of the Constitution for suspected far-right extremism.

The memory politics of the AfD combine national-populist and anti-communist memory politics (Prosser 2018). The nationalist and revisionist tendencies of the party are most evident in the rhetoric of the party leadership, which often pushes back on the memory culture of contrition by claiming it unfairly and uniquely constrains Germans, a key grievance of the party. Several have made public statements about the damage done to German culture, identity, and interests by the dominant memory culture. In 2017, Björn Höcke, an AfD leader from the eastern state of Thüringen, gave a speech in which he called for a 180-degree turn from the tradition of remembering and atoning for the Nazi past. He complained bitterly about history education in Germany after the war, about which, claiming, "They wanted to cut off our roots and with the re-education that began in 1945, they nearly managed . . . our mental state continues to be that of a totally defeated people. We Germans are the only people in the world that have planted a monument of shame [the Holocaust memorial] in the heart of their capital."[7] Party chair from 2015–2017, Frauke Petry claimed "the negation of our own national interests is something that has become a maxim in Germany since World War II." Party leader Alice Weidel has characterized mainstream German leaders as "puppets of the victorious powers in WWII."[8] These statements demonstrate a main motivation behind

[7] Reuters, January 18, 2017 https://www.reuters.com/article/uk-germany-afd-idUKKBN1521HE

[8] Frauke's remarks are cited by Anton Troianovski, "The German Right Believes It's Time to Discard the Country's Historical Guilt," *The Wall Street Journal* (New York City), March 3, 2017, accessed April 28, 2021. Weidel's remarks are cited by Deutsche Welle, April 6, 2021 https://www.dw.com/en/germany-far-right-afd-alternative-for-germany-2021-election-results/a-57054532, accessed April 26, 2021.

the AfD's memory politics: opposing the established democratic political culture, political elites, and political institutions by opposing the memory regime that they support.

Using typical national-populist rhetoric, the AfD asserts itself as a protector of the people, not just against outside aggression but, importantly, against "establishment" German parties and elites it claims are self-hating in their identification with a memory culture of contrition. The AfD clearly pushes for a nationalist framing of the past rather than a memory narrative centered the Holocaust. It sees itself as the only "authentic" party that dares to oppose political correctness and insists on a memory politics in which, as Gauland suggested, "the twelve years" are reduced in importance, in favor of a longer, more positive history as the basis for collective memory. It is the only German party that does not mention the Holocaust in its official program.[9]

The anti-communist narrative that developed later was most visible in the party's 2017 campaign ads referring to the "unfinished revolution" of 1989; they insinuated that the Merkel government was comparable to the totalitarian state of the GDR. This element of the AfD's memory politics fixates on historical grievances rooted in the communist period. In addition to frequent references to Merkel as "Chancellor Dictator" and comparisons of her CDU party to the Socialist Unity Party, the AfD paints other institutions, such as the mainstream media, mainstream parties, and even churches as similar to those in the GDR.[10] For many Easterners, anti-communism is appealing. For many Westerners, it serves the purpose of distracting attention from the Nazi history.

The AfD's memory challenge goes beyond deflection; it seeks to replace the dominant memory narrative with one that focuses on positive dimensions of German history. The party program from 2017 states: "The current narrowing of the German culture of remembrance to the time of National Socialism should be opened in favour of a broader understanding of history, which also encompasses the positive, identity-establishing aspects of German history."[11] In 2017, the AfD in Baden-Würtemberg moreover made a motion to strike language in a bill funding educational visit to Nazi sites, referring instead to funding for field trips to "significant German historic sites." It stated further, "We strive for a balanced view of history . . . A one-sided concentration on

---

[9] See Monika Hübscher, "The AfD's Attitude towards National Socialism, the Holocaust and Antisemitism: A Facebook Analysis," November 2017, University of Haifa, p. 1.

[10] See Prosser 2018, 82 and 91.

[11] "Manifesto for Germany", April 2017, p. 46. https://www.afd.de/wp-content/uploads/sites/111/2017/04/2017-04-12_afd-grundsatzprogramm-englisch_web.pdf

12 years of National Socialist injustice is to be rejected."[12] In 2018, AfD leader Alexander Gauland famously told a conference of party youth, "Hitler and the Nazis are just bird shit among more than 1,000 years of successful German history."[13] In stark contrast to the post-World War II memory culture emphasizing German guilt and linking that guilt to moral responsibilities in the present, the AfD proposes to downgrade the Holocaust and re-nationalize memory about the war.

The AfD narrative regarding the Dresden bombing incorporates revisionist elements of both the Nazi and GDR regimes, including the inflation of casualties, criticism that Western allies acted inhumanely and unnecessarily, and casting Germans as victims without contextualizing their suffering. For example, Höcke, reflecting on his own family history, said in 2017:

> My father told me very early on—I come from a really politically and historically conscious family home—about what happened in Dresden at the end of the Second World War. The outcome of the war was already decided, the city was overflowing with countless refugees from the eastern German territories. . . . The bombing of Dresden and the subsequent firestorm destroyed the Florence of the Elbe and the people who lived there. The bombing of Dresden was a war crime.
>
> (Höcke cited in Petrovic 2018, 7)

Tino Chrupalla from Saxony, a co-leader of the national AfD party, claimed at the 2020 commemoration in Dresden that civilian casualties numbered one hundred thousand and that his grandmother had told him about the mountain of bodies she witnessed in the aftermath of the bombing.[14] The AfD has used the Dresden commemoration to relativize and normalize Nazi brutality to concentrate on German victimhood, breaking taboos in unified Germany's official memory culture of contrition. In 2020, the party set up an info-booth apart from the official commemoration in order to disseminate an alternative history of the event, one that presumably stripped away the universal, "cosmopolitan" meaning of war's destructiveness and made German suffering the focus. Jörg Urban, head of the AfD in Saxony explained: "The other events try to relativize this devastating bombing of Dresden, and put it into the context of what happened around the world . . . They talk about the civil wars that

---

[12] Troianovski (2017).

[13] Deutsche Welle, June 2, 2018, https://www.dw.com/en/afds-gauland-plays-down-nazi-era-as-a-bird-shit-in-german-history/a-44055213

[14] France24, February 13, 2020, https://www.france24.com/en/20200213-germany-dresden-bombing-world-war-two-nazis-afd-commemoration

happen around the world, saying that this kind of thing happens everywhere, and forget that we as a city had an individual fate. For Dresdeners, commemorating the victims has always been an identity-forming event. We want to keep it as a local Dresden event."[15] The party has proposed that February 13 become a "central commemorative event" and to mark the "senseless" killing of Germans by Allied bombing.[16]

The far-right's framing of the commemoration resonated with some Germans, as evidenced by the increasing numbers of demonstrators between 1999 and 2009. Sabine Volk attributed the increase, in part, to a lack of a coordinated civic response and to ideological differences among the political factions in the city council (2020). The mayor of Dresden responded in 2004 with the creation of a commission of historians to examine the myths surrounding the 1945 bomb campaign. The commission's final report of 2010 established the number of victims at twenty-five thousand and debunked the myths about strafing (they were not part of the attack) and its characterization as the deadliest attack during the war. The subsequent mayor established a working group to recommend an official commemoration of the war dead to counter the far-right extremists' appropriation of the event. Bringing together a broad spectrum of political and societal actors, the working group organized a human chain to place a symbolic protective shield around the city center, suggesting its impermeability to the perceived neo-Nazi threat to the commemoration and the broader memory culture.

The 2005 commemoration drew six thousand neo-Nazis, widely estimated to be the largest rally of the far-right in Europe since 1945. In the run-up to the commemoration, the NPD put out the call "60 years of liberation lies—down with the cult of guilt" (Joel 2013, 245). NPD members carried crosses with names of other cities or countries subjected to American bombing, including Hiroshima, Vietnam, Bagdad, and Dresden, which echoed a ritual at the fiftieth anniversary of the Dresden bombing where crosses bore names of cities bombed during World War II by Allies or Nazis. Tony Joel explains, "The NPD appropriated this same arresting imagery but changed the names in order to symbolize ongoing 'American imperialistic warmongering'" (2013, 258). NPD leader Holger Apfel gave a speech blaming US foreign policy "exclusively" for turning Dresden from a *Kulturstadt* to an *Opferstadt*

[15] DW February 13, 2020, https://www.dw.com/en/dresden-marks-wwii-bombing-in-far-right-stronghold/a-52368359

[16] Eliza Apperly, "The Far Right Is Taking on Cultural Institutions," October 28, 2019, https://www.theatlantic.com/international/archive/2019/10/germany-far-right-culture-war/598978/,   accessed April 28, 2021.

(2013, 258). Critics pointed to the absence of a vocal, official political response at the commemoration, particularly in light of efforts to link the anniversary with far-right extremism. In 2009, several individual political figures, including former Federal-President von Weizsäcker, Bundestag President Wolfgang Thierse, and national leaders of the SPD, Greens, and the Linke, joined local anti-racist activists (Petzold 2020, 454).

Observing the Dresden commemoration on February 10, 2018, Susannah Eckersley reported that far-right demonstrators included members of the AfD, NPD, Pegida, and at least two nationalist fraternities, the Dresden branch of Burschenschaft Arminia zu Leipzig and the Dresdener Burschenschaft Salamandria (2020, 215). She noted that these actors partook in the commemoration but remained apart from the official ceremonies. Moreover, they made a point of not pausing at or recognizing in any way the Holocaust memorial along the route. For them, the only victims worth commemorating were Germans, removed from the larger context and supporting the myth of innocent Dresden. Moreover, they linked victimization by Allies in World War II and contemporary "threats" to Germans from non-European, non-Christian refugees (222–3).

To summarize, the far-right actors who focus their memory challenge on the Dresden bombing commemoration use several approaches to deflect from German guilt for the past and responsibility in the present. As the history of the Dresden commemoration suggests, the far-right's instrumentalization of the commemoration borrows from and builds on earlier Nazi and GDR narratives of victimhood and a refusal to accept responsibility or to feel shame. However, because they operate in a context defined by deeply rooted cultural and institutional constraints, far-right memory challengers are limited in terms of the language and symbols they can use. They cannot deny the Holocaust outright, but they certainly do neglect to mention the crimes of Nazi Germany. The story they tell at Dresden commemorations is partial and distorted. Their toolkit for instrumentalizing the wartime past stays within the law, but it is multifaceted, blatantly negating the dominant narrative of contrition.

Starting with the manipulation of emotions, the German far-right frequently uses language, symbols, and rituals of mourning to create a sense of grievance against the Allies and the dominant narrative about German guilt; its representations emphasize national belonging based on innocence and victimhood of Dresden, and, implicitly, of Germany as a whole. The far-right routinely uses obfuscation by focusing on the Allies' guilt and German victimhood and by downgrading the experiences and legacies of "those twelve years" of Nazi rule. The screen memories of German suffering filter out the wider context,

Germans' initiation of World War II and the perpetration of countless crimes against humanity. The far-right renationalization of wartime memory focusing on German victims serves to narrow the relevance of the commemoration and refutes the universal significance of the Dresden bombing. German memory challengers also use the tool of obfuscation to shift attention to places bombed by the United States, rather than drawing attention to global patterns, such as the humanitarian costs of war or the need for greater tolerance and empathy for others. The far-right constructs a dichotomy between insiders and outsiders, authentic and inauthentic remembrance, claiming the commemoration as a space for local memory in Dresden and in Saxony. Comparison and equivalence are likewise tools for the far-right at the Dresden commemoration. They challenge a significant taboo of the German memory culture in that they compare the suffering caused by Germans to the suffering of Germans caused by others; they seek to place February 13 on the same footing as January 27, Holocaust Remembrance Day. The far-right uses appropriation, most obviously by frequent invocation of the term "Holocaust" to describe the bombing and, rejecting the official commemoration by holding their own "march of grief."

Finally, though it does not engage in overt Holocaust revisionism to further its cause, the far-right does promote revisionist history by erroneously positing high numbers of casualties and by denying through omission other facts about the context of the Dresden bombing.

Reactions to the Memory Challengers

Although other German political parties and the media condemn such far-right's memory games, the conservative CDU leadership in Saxony found itself in somewhat of an awkward position. The party's hesitance to respond in a vigorous way to the extremists' revisionism stood in stark contrast with the anti-racist protests from the left, described by Petzold as "responsible remembering" (2020, 459). Rather than an "apolitical commemoration" more typical of earlier years, the far-right's efforts to hijack the Dresden commemoration since the late 1990s have led to the commemoration becoming "a consciously political one" that pushes back on the victimhood narrative and makes clear how the past is relevant to the present—to anti-racism, democracy, and the tolerance of diversity. In other words, an attempt by the far-right to transform the Dresden bombing commemoration into an antagonistic one of insiders/outsiders and innocent/evil has ironically become even more closely linked with Germany's memory culture of contrition. Anti-fascist groups reclaimed places where the far-right extremists had placed wreaths or made stops during February 13th commemorations. A Memorial Tour of the Traces of the Perpetrators was organized to redirect attention to the significance of Dresden as a site of "war industries, as a place of suffering for thousands of forced laborers, and as a military headquarters for trailblazers of racist ideology" (Jerzak 2015, 63). In 2020, the seventy-fifth anniversary of the liberation of Auschwitz, the bombing of Dresden, and the end of the war, eleven thousand people participated in the new commemorative tradition, the human chain of peace and tolerance "protecting" the public event from far-right disruption. Federal President Frank-Walter Steinmeier gave a speech in which he warned against political forces that aim to "manipulate history and abuse it like a weapon." Instead, he suggested, "Let's work together for a commemoration that focuses on the suffering of the victims and the bereaved, but also asks about the reasons for this suffering." In these two passages, Steinmeier emphasized the importance of contextualizing the suffering of Germans in the bombing and for linking the past with the present:

> When we remember the history of the bombing war in our country today, then we remember both things—the suffering of Germany's urban population and the suffering that Germans caused others. We do not forget that it was Germans who started this brutal war and ultimately it was millions of Germans who waged it—not all, but many of them, out of conviction. It was the National Socialists and their willing enforcers who carried out the mass murder of European Jews. And it was the Nazi regime that did not stop the murders even when it knew the war had long since been lost. We do not forget German guilt. And we live up to our abiding responsibility.
>
> The bombing of Dresden reminds us of the destruction of the rule of law and democracy in the Weimar Republic, of nationalist hubris and contempt for human life, of anti-Semitism and racist barbarity. And I fear that these dangers are still with us. (Steinmeier, Dresden, February 13, 2020).

Public opinion in Germany supports the continued importance of Holocaust remembrance in Germany. In an infratest dimap poll commissioned by Deutsche Welle in 2018 and 2019 and reported in 2020, 55 percent of respondents said Germany's culture of remembrance pays "adequate attention" to the Nazi crimes, 17 percent said "too little attention" and 25 percent said "too much attention." Among AfD sympathizers, 50 percent said "too much attention," followed by the conservative CDU/CSU at 23, the liberal-centrist FDP at 22, Social Democrats at 14, Left Party 11, and Greens at 7. When asked if Germans should occupy themselves less with the Nazi era, 37 percent supported the idea of "drawing a line under the past," while 60 percent thought they should "remember the past." Broken down by party affiliation, downgrading the importance of the Nazi era by "drawing a line under the past" was favored by 72 percent of those who identified with the AfD, compared with 37 percent CDU/CSU, 30 percent FDP, 27 percent SPD, 18 percent Left, and 13 percent Greens. Finally, when asked how Germans should remember the Nazi-era crimes, 75 percent agreed that "visiting a concentration camp memorial site should be mandatory for school classes"; 61 percent felt that "Everyone should examine their own family's role/behavior at the time."[17]

The reaction to the far-right's hijacking of the Dresden commemoration has been fierce over the last few years, widely shared by Dresdeners, national elites, and more generally by the public in Germany. Yet, it is not certain that the memory challenge from the far-right in Dresden will cease. Memory politics are part of the AfD's "resistance" to establishment elites, institutions, and norms. The 2021 commemoration did not take place due to the covid-19 pandemic, but it seems likely that the far-right will resume targeting the Dresden bombing as part of its campaign to replace the dominant memory culture. In 2020–2021, the far-right was joined by conspiracy-theorist groups like Q-anon and anti-vaxers who appropriated the Star of David to draw attention to their "suffering" under government pandemic restrictions. The AfD may have seen a slight decrease in its vote share in 2021, but it retains seats in the Bundestag. The party's presence in elected offices at the state and local politics remains significant for memory and identity, since the German states are responsible for education and cultural policies. Moreover, localities are sites of memory where groups can have a great deal of influence on commemorations and their rituals, rhetoric, and meaning. Before turning to two further commemorations of wartime events, I examine a controversial commemoration in Austria.

The Ulrichsberg Gathering in Austria

Postwar Austria was much slower than Germany to develop a Holocaust-centered narrative, despite its homegrown Austrofascist tradition going back to 1933. Even though many Austrians had eagerly welcomed the annexation

[17] The polling results are reported by Deutsche Welle at https://www.dw.com/de/die-deutschen-wollen-keinen-schlussstrich/a-52094901, accessed April 28, 2021

by Hitler in 1938, the country adopted an exculpatory, victim-centered narrative of the war. Quite different from that which occurred in Germany, this process was encouraged by the Allies and their Moscow Declaration of 1943, which called Austria the "first victim" of Nazism, a phrase repeated in the country's Declaration of Independence of 1945. Despite the fact that many Nazi leaders and most concentration camp administrators had been Austrian, there was far less Allied-directed denazification or domestically driven reckoning with its past until the mid-1990s. When Kurt Waldheim, a former United Nations Secretary General, ran for president of Austria in 1986, investigative journalists brought his SS past under scrutiny, exposing his misrepresentation of his wartime activities. Protests by students and others brought about a long-delayed public debate about Austria's responsibility for wartime atrocities and the Holocaust. In recent decades, greater official attention has been focused on debunking the "victim myth" and assuming a more penitent culture of remembrance (Berger 2012; Uhl 2006). In 1992, Austrian lawmakers prohibited denial or gross minimization of the Holocaust.

In stark contrast to postwar Germany, Austria developed a strong culture of commemoration for fallen soldiers of the Wehrmacht. These soldiers were initially portrayed as victims, sacrificed to "Hitler's war." Soon, however, with the onset of the Cold War, anti-communism became a common concern of right and left parties. In addition, an amnesty for former Nazis to foster their reintegration into the democratic institutions facilitated a shift in the image of former Wehrmacht soldiers from victims of Nazism to protectors of the Austrian homeland. Heidemarie Uhl explains: "The intention to present the commemoration of wartime heroes as a *narrative dispositif*, the sole acceptable, legitimate, and self-evident perspective on the Nazi past tolerated no rival versions of the past" (2011, 190). Associations of war veterans became important actors in Austria's memory culture as the case of the Ulrichsberg Gathering demonstrates.

Like the Dresden commemoration, the Ulrichsberg Gathering has been linked with large gatherings of the extreme right in Europe. It offers an example of veterans' groups and the far-right Austrian Freedom Party (FPÖ) cooperating to use an established commemorative site and rituals to normalize Austria's participation in World War II by representing its SS veterans as just like other soldiers in history. The Gathering has provided a stage for extremists to join veterans in commemoration, boosting the legitimacy of the far-right, presenting a platform for extremist leaders like the late FPÖ leader, Jörg Haider, to espouse nostalgia and even revisionism.

The evolution of the Ulrichsberg Gathering

Ulrichsberg has a long history as a gathering place; it became a memorial site to fallen soldiers in the 1920s following World War I and the end of the Habsburg monarchy (Loschberger 2013). Initially a Christian site centered on a church, it was appropriated by nationalists, primarily from Carinthia, the state in which the Ulrichsberg is located. Later the site became a gathering place for nationalists from all over Austria and Europe. During the Allied occupation from 1945 to 1955, the Ulrichsberg was inactive as a site of commemoration, but once the Allies left Austria, nationalist sentiments and activities were free to emerge. The FPÖ was founded in 1956, and in 1958, the Ulrichsberg again became a site of commemoration. Instead of commemorating "defense fighters," annual meetings there began to honor military "returnees" from both world wars (Loschberger 2013, 13). Carinthia was led for many years by Jörg Haider, a regular FPÖ speaker at the Ulrichberg Gatherings. His remarks often came under fire for being apologetic toward Nazism.

The Ulrichsberg Gathering received government support and was often attended by other regional and local officials. Official endorsements and visits largely ended in recent years, owing to the image of the Ulrichberg Gathering as a radical right-wing event. During the postwar period, the Gathering occurred each October on the Ulrichsberg, a hill, where the ruins of a church with memorial plaques and a large metal cross are located. In the 1980s, as many as ten thousand people attended. Please see Figure 2.3. As Loschberger's analysis of the commemoration finds:

> Interpretations of what constitute the Ulrichsberg meetings range from a peaceful display of cultural tradition decrying the universal horrors of war, to a pilgrimage of right-wing extremists and neo-fascists honouring the fighters of a war they wish they had won. The public perception of the Ulrichsberg gatherings has evolved in a parallel trajectory with Austrian memory politics in its gradual transition from denial and victim thesis . . . to official admissions of guilt and political polarization.
>
> (2013, 8)

Many of those veterans who "returned" from fighting in World War II were members of the Waffen-SS.

Figure 2.3 The Ulrichsberg Gathering in 2006
Source: © Phoenix/APA PictureDesk.

According to Loschberger:

> The inviting tone of the UBG's [Ulrichsberg Society, an organizing body]
> motto, "The Ulrichsberg is calling you!" (*Der Ulrichsberg ruft!*), attracted
> underground veterans' organizations of SS volunteers from countries like
> Croatia, Latvia, Holland, Belgium, Norway, Denmark, and Spain who made
> pilgrimage to southern Austria to add their honorary plaques, lay wreaths,
> make contacts with like-minded individuals and pay annual homage to their
> fallen comrades in a safe environment.
>
> (2013, 15)

Like the German commemoration of the Dresden bombing, this memorial
event was appropriated by groups and parties on the far-right seeking to use
it as a vehicle for legitimation. The chapter that follows will demonstrate how,
commemorations of fallen Waffen-SS in Eastern European countries have also
emerged, serving similar functions of legitimation and white-washing. The
far-right uses the Ulrichsberg Gathering to manipulate memory of the war
by casting the Austrian Wehrmacht and various nations' SS soldiers as innocent and brave. The Gathering's narrative infers that Wehrmacht soldiers were

merely following tradition and nothing more, certainly nothing sinister, nor ideological. Their self-image as innocent, as "the better Germans," continues the older postwar trope of Austria as a small, peace-loving nation that became Nazi Germany's first victim.

The story told at the UlrIchsberg Gathering ignores the Austrian role in the Holocaust. A common rhetorical approach frames war veterans not as perpetrators but as the opposite; they were not only victimized by wartime violence but also by present-day neglect by the official memory culture and government funding priorities. Frustration over this perceived slight focuses on the policies of mainstream parties, which the memory challengers view as damaging to veterans and to the country. While the AfD in Germany could not memorialize Wehrmacht soldiers as model citizens, the lack of a similar cultural taboo in Austria lends the far-right there a cause and a constituency. In 1995 Haider expressed gratitude to Wehrmacht veterans at the Ulrichsberg: "in these difficult times, where there are still honest people with character and who until today remain true to their convictions despite strong contrary winds. [...] We give money to terrorists, to violent newspapers, to work-shy rabble, and we have no money for respectable people."[18] Haider's memory talk ignored the role the Austrian Wehrmacht soldiers played in perpetrating crimes on behalf of the Third Reich. He also drew on obfuscation with a "what-about" tactic, pitting government support for veterans against alleged government support of terrorists, violent newspapers, and work-shy—a term reminiscent of Nazi ideology—rabble, by which he likely meant to criticize migration, freedom of speech, and welfare policies.

In terms of both rhetoric and ritual, the Ulrichsberg saga casts veterans and the regime for which they fought as anti-communist defenders of Europe. In 1994, Gathering attendees erected a Stone of Europe "to symbolize the brotherhood of the European peoples in a peaceful, democratic continent, free of communism," a mantra deployed by other conservative, nationalist, and far-right groups in Europe. As Loschberger reports, "Insiders knew, however, that the *Europastein* was meant primarily as coded homage to the cooperation between international SS volunteer veterans' organizations, rather than any real support for greater European integration" (2013, 16). Even for outside observers, the mention of "communism" as a common enemy or stain on European nations is noteworthy. Clearly, the Ulrichsberg Gathering pits any number of ideologies and regime types, whether fascisms of the

---

[18] Cited in Ruth Wodak, Anton Pelinka, The Haider Phenomenon in Austria (Transaction 2002) 211.

past or present-day democracies, against communism. The rhetoric involving "defenders of Europe" against communism or any other "outside influence" creates a dichotomy between us and them, insiders and outsiders and is a thinly veiled anti-leftist and anti-Muslim message.

Reactions to the Ulrichsberg Gathering

As in Dresden, anti-fascist groups have protested the Gathering, utilizing information booths to educate the public about the fascist past and contemporary threats to minority rights and humanitarianism. There have also been counter-demonstrations. In 2009, the president of the Ulrichsberg Society was caught buying and selling Nazi memorabilia, resulting in the loss of logistic support from the Defense Ministry, though the Carinthian government continues its support. Evidence of extremists' association with the meeting sufficed to have it put under observation by the Austrian Federal Office for Protection of the Constitution and Anti-terrorism. In contrast to Germany, though, the cultural and institutional constraints on this type of memory challenge are much weaker.

The Ulrichsberg Gathering of former Wehrmacht and SS soldiers, and their families, has survived changes in Austria's memory culture. It remains a site for far-right groups to tell a particular story about Austrian soldiers in World War II. That story serves to pit the veterans, the true patriots, and European defenders against communists, against politicians and political parties that increasingly identify with a more contrite memory regime. The FPÖ and its leaders, especially Jörg Haider, sympathized with the Gathering and used it to broadcast its revisionist views about the Nazi period and people affiliated with the various National Socialist institutions. Rather than dabble in outright Holocaust denial, the party avoids the topic of the Holocaust entirely, at least in public statements linked to the Ulrichberg Gathering. Given its nostalgia for military traditions, a glorious past, and in its celebration of a conservative, nationalist, and pan-Germanist present, the commemoration at the Ulrichsberg runs contrary to the belated, if now dominant Holocaust-centered memory in Austria. It also runs somewhat contrary to Austria's status as a neutral country above the fray of Cold War-era ideological conflicts.

While it has not succeeded in eliminating the Holocaust-centered memory in Austria, the persistence of the Ulrichsberg Gathering says something about lingering disenchantment with the dominant narrative and a desire to whitewash the past rather than learn from it. It is also noteworthy that the

FPÖ remains a significant political force in Austria. In 2016, it put forward a candidate, Norbert Hofer, for the country's (largely ceremonial) presidency, coming within thirty thousand votes of winning over Alexander Van der Bellen of the Greens. After the Austrian constitutional court annulled the election results due to irregularities in the counting of the ballots in some districts, the election was held again several months later, with Van der Bellen prevailing over Hofer with almost 54 percent of the vote.[19] The FPÖ's vote potential has fluctuated but remained consequential, while mainstream parties have offered relatively muted opposition to its rhetoric and policy prescriptions (Weilandt 2016). In such an environment, it is not surprising that a commemoration like the Ulrichsberg Gathering persists and has become a topic for debating the Austrian past. Austrian society remains divided over how to remember the wartime past and how to treat the Ulrichsberg Gathering and those who attend it. In 2021, for example, the head of the Carinthian State Office for the Protection of the Constitution, Stephan Tauschitz of the center-right ÖVP, was removed from his position when it was revealed that he had attended and given speeches at Ulrichsberg in 2008 and 2010. At the 2010 Gathering, Tauschitz implored the audience "not to judge the dead" (Puls24, February 28, 2023). Most striking, perhaps, was his new posting one year later at the Austrian Interior Ministry.

Liberation Day in Italy

Italy was the birthplace of fascism, where it lasted twenty years. A key ally of Nazi Germany and Japan, Italy eventually introduced racial laws, deported 7,300 Jews to their deaths, and participated in atrocities in the Balkans and in Africa. As in World War I, Italy switched sides in World War II, ending the war on the side of the victors. National memory of World War II centered around a myth of widespread resistance to fascism and externalized all guilt for wartime suffering and the Holocaust to Germany. The notion that Italians were "*brave gente*," good folks, was widely adopted and rarely challenged. This memory narrative that Italians had struggled valiantly against fascism—and especially against "evil Germans" and their Nazism—and whose Jews had high survival rates, thanks to their own humanitarianism, amounted to a form of popular

---

[19] Although the FPÖ lost seats in most recent parliamentary election in 2019, it was the third largest party in the legislature, with fifty-one seats, one seat less than the center-left SPÖ. In a February 2023 state parliamentary election in Lower Austria, the federal state that surrounds the city-state of Vienna, the FPÖ came in second place with 24.2 percent of the vote, up 9.4 percentage points.

and official amnesia. Italy and Germany were often remembered as opposites, not as onetime allies and fellow fascists. According to Focardi:

> On the one hand are the fanatical and racist German people, and on the other are the peaceful and goodnatured Italian people who did not accept the totalitarian regime imposed by Il Duce . . . On the one hand is the dark portrait of the German soldier as a disciplined and bloodthirsty fighter, a relentless and sadistic oppressor of the defenseless, and on the other hand is the image of the Italian soldier deeply opposed to the war and reticent to carry out acts of violence and oppression, always ready to express solidarity with and bring aid to populations, including those in the territories occupied by the Fascist regime.
>
> (Focardi 2014, 9)

After 1945, there was no occupation and partition of Italy and no equivalent of the Nuremberg Trials. Italy was ordered to turn war criminals over to the Allies for trial in London, but the Italian authorities refused to comply, arguing they would hold trials themselves. Although a few Italian military leaders were eventually tried by the British and American-led tribunals in Italy, the relative lack of justice for Italy's wartime political and military crimes nurtured a silence about the roots and consequences of fascism and undergirded a self-image of *brave gente*.

Italy had been a deeply divided country during the war and after. Its surrender to the Allies on September 8, 1943, followed by the flight of the Italian king and government from Rome and the invasion of the country by the Allies and the Germans, led to civil war. Mussolini led the Italian Social Republic, or Salò Republic, in effect a German puppet state. (The "young" and "idealistic" Italians who remained loyal to fascism and Mussolini are known as "the boys of Salò.") Opposing the German puppet state were the Italian partisans, who, with help from Allied troops, prevailed over the fascists in April of 1945, setting up committees of liberation in northern Italian cities.

The first postwar government, led by Alcide De Gaspari, declared April 25, 1945, a day of commemoration in 1946. The date marked a key moment in the defeat of the fascists, the "proclamation of insurrection" by the newly installed National Committee for the Liberation of Upper Italy. It was chosen over other dates, such as May 8, 1945, when Germany surrendered, "because April 25 recognized more explicitly the contribution of the Resistance to the defeat of Nazi-Fascism" (Carli 2015, 254). Carli notes that there was no mention of how the commemorations should be marked, leaving it to localities and the

National Association of Italian Partisans to decide. The commemoration met with some ambivalence about how it should be observed, given the division of Italians during and to some extent after the 1943–1945 civil war. Rebecca Clifford's study of war remembrance in Italy cites regional differences over marking the day: in the capital Rome, the commemoration was "sober, and official," featuring Catholic masses for the dead, while the commemorations were more joyous in the north (Clifford 2013, 99). Occasionally, politicians used the holiday to make speeches, sometimes entering into the fray of memory debates. With greatest attention extended to significant anniversaries, this holiday did not attract significant public engagement in particular rituals or reflection until the major upheaval in Italian politics in the 1990s.

Prior to the 1990s and the collapse of communism in Eastern Europe, mainstream Italian political parties clung to the myth that most Italians had been resistors. This had two effects: a refusal to give the Communist Party of Italy (CPI) the credit it deserved for having served as the backbone of the antifascist resistance; and discomfort on the far-right, especially the neo-fascist Italian Social Movement (MSI), whose national identity narrative centered on the wartime resistance to fascism. The MSI and others on the right cast communists, past and present, as far worse than fascists. Since the Italian party system was dominated by centrist parties, the far-right's representations of the past held little importance for Italian memory.

A space for mnemonic debate in Italy opened up after two shocks, one external and one internal: the collapse of communism in Eastern Europe, followed closely by the *tangentopoli* corruption investigation. These shocks resulted in the implosion of the main centrist parties, helped produce new electoral rules, transformed the party system, and "triggered a fierce confrontation that was based on an unprecedented use of history for political purposes" (Focardi 2017). The new party system featured two poles or alliances, on the right and left. Among the forces in the right-wing alliance were media magnate Silvio Berlusconi's new party, Forza Italia, which campaigned on protecting Italy from communists, and the renamed neo-fascists, the National Alliance (AN). The AN was part of right-wing coalition governments led by Berlusconi following the elections in 1994 and 2001. The leader of the AN, Gianfranco Fini, became deputy prime minister in 2001, then foreign minister in 2004.

The Right's Memory Manipulations

In this new party landscape, with this new governing coalition of rightist parties, "One of the main factors behind the struggle for memory in the country was the need of the centre-right to legitimize Gianfranco Fini's MSI-AN as a force to sit in government" (Focardi 2017, n.p.). The Berlusconi-Fini coalition sought to supplant the memory narrative of anti-fascism with one of "anti-totalitarianism," which placed fascism and anti-fascism on the same moral plane (Clifford 2013, 143). The creation of an equivalence between communism and fascism served to blackwash the wartime communist resistance and, by ideological association, the present-day left, while it whitewashed the fascist past and, by ideological association, the new and renamed right-wing parties. With its anti-anti-fascism orientation, the Italian right seized the moral high-ground from the left by insisting that, "Anti-fascism was a force that actively hoped for the defeat of its own nation" and had showed "its feebleness at the 1946 Paris peace conference, when . . . the nation was humiliated, forced to pay reparations, (and) throw away the best parts of its armed services and the empire" (Ellwood 2005, 390). The rightist memory narrative also contains a critique of postwar Italian democracy: it claims that the democratic constitution of 1948 sold out "the true anti-Communists" because it legitimated the PCI, abandoned sovereignty by choosing Atlanticism, and gave too little power to the executive and too much to the legislature (Ellwood 2005, 391–3).

There have been plenty of examples of such whitewashing of the past, including Fini's reference to Mussolini as "the greatest statesman of the century" and Berlusconi's description of Italian fascism as a "benign dictatorship."[20] The AN lobbied to give veterans who fought for the Republic of Salò (and with the Germans) the same honors, pensions, and rehabilitation for their "good faith" as veterans of the resistance (Ellwood 2005, 391). A similar tactic was used by US President Trump, who famously claimed there were "very fine people on both sides" of the 2017 Charlottesville protest, meaning white supremacists and racial justice protesters alike. In the next chapter, we will see a similar set of mnemonic moves among nationalist-populist actors seeking to defame former communists and side-line post-communist parties of the center and left.

Efforts to distance Italian fascism from German fascism and from anti-Semitism also entail a kind of whitewashing. As Berlusconi said in 2013 (on Holocaust Memorial Day, ironically):

It is difficult now to put yourself in the shoes of people who were making decisions at that time [in 1938]. Obviously, the government of that time, out of fear that German power might lead to complete victory, preferred to ally

---

[20] Fini's quote from a 1994 interview in an Italian newspaper and Berlusconi's from a 2003 interview in *The Spectator*, both cited in Focardi 2017, n.p.

itself with Hitler's Germany rather than opposing it. As part of this alliance, there were impositions, including combating and exterminating Jews. The racial laws were the worst fault of Mussolini as a leader, who in so many other ways did well.

(quoted in Lichtner 2015, 26)

Berlusconi did not, of course, mention Mussolini's shifting positions on race and anti-Semitism before 1938, nor the atrocities Italians carried out in its colonies. As Licthner notes, Berlusconi's praise of Mussolini received much media attention, while the distortions about "impositions" and whether racial laws were Mussolini's "worst fault" remained unchallenged (27).

Another tactic utilized by conservative-nationalist right memory challengers—Forza Italia, the AN, and occasionally the Lega—sought to neutralize the left by using the rhetoric of national unity, reconciliation, and the "pacification" of old enemies. This memory move, which Clifford (147) described as "forgetting for the benefit of national unity," seeks to normalize fascism. It uses patriotism as a balm in the service of mnemonic harmony over mnemonic pluralism and critical reflection. D. W. Ellwood highlights a further purpose for the rhetoric of reconciliation: "revisionism served as an important political glue for parts of the Berlusconi coalition itself, a heterogeneous group springing from radically different roots" (Ellwood 2005, 390). Behind the rhetoric about letting bygones be bygones, though, is an effort to associate anti-fascists and leftist with dangers to stability.

Efforts to alter the calendar of war remembrance

For the Right, the civil war and the liberation of April 25, 1945, were tragic and traumatic. Writing about "memory wars" in Italy in the post-Cold War period, Filippo Focardi observed, "Anti-Fascism and the memory of the Resistance were depicted as politically obsolete and even dangerous ideals for Italy's 'new Republic,' a country in need of a somewhat 'patriotic' renewal" (Focardi 2017, n.p.). The Right's memory narrative emphasized the honor, "good faith," and "ethical patriotism" of the "boys of Salò" who supported Mussolini until the bitter end (Focardi 2017). Berlusconi's government tried to "reconcile" the memory of Italian fascism through legislation equating the fighters of Salò Republic with the Partisan resistance. Another legislative proposal submitted by the right would have abolished the national holiday on April 25, replacing it with a commemoration of anti-totalitarianism on April 18, the date when the

Christian Democrats defeated the Communist and Socialist parties in the 1948 elections. The legislation implied that the Communists and Socialists of the early postwar years, and the contemporary left parties, were threats on par with right-wing totalitarianism, so their defeat deserved a national commemoration. Neither law passed, but the prime minister and his government imprinted the political and public debates, further exacerbating the memory divide. More recently, proposals to replace April 25 with March 17, the anniversary of Italian unification, have come from Giorgia Meloni, the leader of the Brothers of Italy (Fratelli d'Italia) party, which emerged in 2012 as a successor of the AN. Motivated by discomfort with the dissonance between their image of Italy and its dark past, the Right wielded a variety of tools to challenge the narrative around Liberation Day, including ignoring it and shifting attention to themes of heroism and unity. Meloni, who joined the youth movement of the neofascist MSI when she was fifteen, became postwar Italy's most far-right prime minister following elections in 2022, demonstrating how socially acceptable this reconfiguration has become. It will be interesting to see whether the neofascist-led government revisits the proposal to downgrade or do away with Liberation Day and if it takes further measures to sanitize the fascist past.

In another approach, the Right has sought to construct a narrative of victimization focused on the *foibe*, the sinkholes where between three and five thousand Italians captured and killed by Tito's Partisans were buried during the last years of the war.[21] The *foibe* has become an important symbol of communist violence and Italian martyrdom on the Right as well as an excuse for anti-Slavic sentiment. In 2004, the national parliament passed a law creating a Day of Remembrance on February 10—two weeks after International Holocaust Remembrance Day—for the victims of the *foibe* and the exile of Italians from their homes in Istria and Dalmatia. Please see Figure 2.4.

Appropriating terms from the Holocaust, the Right has described the *foibe* as an "act of genocide" and as the "Italian Shoah" (Focardi). In 2018, the film *Rosso Istria* (Red Land) about the *foibe* was promoted on social media to millions of followers of then Interior Minister Salvini of the far-right Lega. According to Salvini, who is currently the deputy prime minister in the Meloni-led government, "For decades, left-wing politicians and intellectuals have done everything to hide this truth . . . Go and watch it and pass the word

---

[21] For more on the memory politics surrounding the *foibe*, see Pamela Ballinger, "Exhumed Histories: Trieste and the Politics of (Exclusive) Victimhood," *Journal of Southern Europe and the Balkans*, Vol. 6, No. 2 (August 2004): 145–59 and Marco Bernardi, "Toponymy as Method: Official Italian Rhetoric, History and the Foibe," *Journal of Historical Sociology*, Vol. 32 (2019): 478–91.

Figure 2.4 Participants in the memorial to the "martyrs of the *foibe*"—the preferred wartime commemoration among the Italian Right

Source: NurPhoto SRL / Alamy Stock Photo.

along, so that those who were killed simply for being Italian may at least be honoured by our memory."[22]

Historian Eric Gobetti, author of *E allora le foibe*? ("But what about the *foibe*?") (2021), said of the right "the *foibe* is an issue central to their political strategy, because it rekindles nationalism and recasts fascism as a victim of supposed aggression."[23] Observing how commonly used the term "martyrs of the *foibe*" has become, historian Marco Bernardi explained, "The association of the term 'martyrs' to the victims of the *foibe* is the outcome of a political project: it testifies to the success of a specific political message that aimed to support a self-acquitting, self-pitying, and chauvinistic interpretation of the past" (2019, 489). It will be interesting to see if this relatively new commemoration of Italian victims of communism will offer further occasion for far-right parties and groups to broaden and deepen their preferred memory narrative about the war, as has happened with the Ulrichsberg Gathering in Austria and, later chapters show, in several Eastern European countries. Although only in government a few months, the right-wing coalition of the Brothers of Italy and the Lega marked Remembrance Day in 2023 with particular vigor, using social media to amplify their nationalist messages. Salvini wrote fifteen posts about the *foibe* on Twitter, Instagram, and Facebook, compared to five posts about Holocaust remembrance the month before. For Meloni, the numbers were nineteen posts and two posts, respectively (Siviero 2022).

Giorgio Ghiglione suggests that the *foibe* killings have become a feature of a civil religion in Italy, "elevating the massacre to almost the same level as the extermination of European Jews for part of the Italian public" (2021). Lamenting that the *foibe* still lack the kind of recognition accorded the Holocaust, conservative politician Enrico Michetti opined, "Maybe it's because [the *foibe* vicitms] did not own banks or belong to a lobby" (Ghiglione 2021, n.p.). While victimhood claims are not usually so explicitly anti-Semitic, they do implicitly suggest an equivalence that is a form of Holocaust distortion and a powerful tool of memory challengers.

Commemorations of the "martyrs" of the *foibe* have become part of the "crowd-sourcing" of alternative memory online and through social media. Scholars like Trillò and Shifman (2021) refer to this activity as "memetic commemoration"—as in shared memes—and the construction of an "alternative calendar" of events and people to memorialize. Their study of memetic content online included posts from the Forza Nuova party, Casa Pound Italia movement, the youth movements Azione Studentesca and Blocco Studentesco, the far-right news outlet *Il primo nazionale*, and a "pseudo-intellectual figure close to the far-right." Among the most frequent posts about alternative commemorations was the *foibe* massacre, ranking second after the anniversary of Italian unification in 1861 (2021, 2491).

Responses to the Right's Revisionism

In response to the election that brought Berlusconi to power in 1994, tens of thousands of Italians protested on Liberation Day, giving new importance to the commemoration. Presidents Ciampi (1999–2006) and Napolitano (2006–2015) "revived and defended the memory of the Resistance by protecting and defending against the revisionist campaign" (Focardi 2019, n.p.). Ciampi, who had earlier led a technocratic government and, as such, was deemed above party politics, began his presidency by insisting that memory work (*Il lavoro della memoria*) was important and should be nurtured. He also stressed reconciliation without amnesia, implying the right's reconciliation approach furthered amnesia (Thomassen and Forlenza 2011, 708). In a speech on April 25, 2002, Ciampi reasserted the notion that all Italians could claim the heritage of resistance:

> There was active Resistance of those who took up arms, partisans, soldiers, military who followed the impulse of their own consciousness; there was the silent Resistance of the people, of citizens who helped, assisted the wounded, the refugees, the fighters, exposing themselves to substantial risks. There was the painful Resistance of the prisoners of the concentration camps, of those who refused to collaborate.
>
> (quoted in Thomassen and Forlenza 2011, 716)

While Ciampi's remarks opposed the right's anti-anti-fascism, it did not signal a shift to a more reflective type of memory work. Napolitano's pushback against the memory challengers of the right took a different approach. He suggested trying to "transform the *foibe* from a nationalist memory into a memory of European reconciliation between, Italy, Slovenia, and Croatia, based on the mutual recognition of the wrongs that the parties have historically inflicted on each other and on a fruitful future collaboration inside the European Union" (Focardi 2019, n.p.). Were something like this to occur, it would be an example of an antagonistic mode of remembrance developing into a more cosmopolitan one.

In contrast to commemoration of the Dresden bombing, the April 25 commemoration of Italy's liberation from fascism did not become an occasion for annual rituals, important speeches, or a subsequent dramatic memory challenge from the far-right. Its role in the Italian memory of the war was, like the postwar memory itself, rather subdued. This might explain why Holocaust denial was not made illegal until 2016.[24] The postwar memory narrative about a broad societal resistance to fascism in Italy was challenged, however, when the far-right MSI/AN broke out of the Cold War freezer and found new life in the transformed party landscape of the 1990s. Since then, right-wing parties have split and merged, joined and quit electoral alliances, formed multiple governments and, in the process, tried to create a cultural and mnemonic

---

[24] The law, which also outlaws denial of the existence of genocide or crimes against humanity, updated an earlier law criminalizing propaganda or incitement to violence on racial, ethnic, or religious grounds. See Haaretz June 6, 2016, https://www.haaretz.com/world-news/europe/holocaust-denial-law-adopted-in-italy-1.5393802

shift.[25] Their efforts to whitewash the fascist past and blackwash the communists have borne fruit. While April 25 remains a commemorative holiday, the right has tried to downgrade its importance to Italian memory and to supplant it with other days of remembrance. Current political party system instability and the electoral fortunes of the far-right suggest that memory challenges are likely to resurface, particularly in the economic context of the pandemic, mass migration, and growing euroskepticism.

The Commemoration of the Vél d'Hiv Roundup in France

In contrast to the other three commemorations discussed earlier, this one was introduced as a national commemoration much later, in 1993. Since then, it has become both a central memorial site and an important commemoration, prompting greater debate about how to remember Vichy and the role of the French in the Holocaust. The emergence of a more truthful, reflective official memory of the Vél d'Hiv, however, has not been without its own memory challengers. Far-right presidential hopefuls Marine LePen and Eric Zemmour have publically questioned the meaning of the commemoration and have promoted revisionist narratives.

Unlike Austria, France was not annexed and brought into the Third Reich; nor was it ruled by home-grown fascists who became allies of Nazi Germany, unlike Italy. Instead, France was defeated by Germany in the spring of 1940. The French Third Republic was superseded by the Vichy government, led by Marshal Phillipe Pétain; the northern and southeastern parts of France were occupied by Germany and Italian forces for four years and two years, respectively. During that time, the provisional French government in London was led by Charles de Gaulle. The Allies liberated France in 1944, after which the French were free to interpret their wartime role as they wished without outside interference. National memory of the war, profoundly shaped by de Gaulle, centered on two ideas: the myth of national resistance to fascism and the notion that Vichy was not France but an aberration. As a result, the French neither examined their homegrown racism and anti-Semitism, nor their collaboration with Nazi Germany. After the French Resistance carried out its purge of collaborators, starting in the last year of the war, there was no

---

[25] A number of histories, commercial books, and public broadcast programs about fascists have appeared since the resurgence of the far-right, including the twenty-part RAI radio series in 1997 about veterans of Mussolini's forces called "The Voice of the Defeated."

political or public reckoning with the wartime crimes as there had been in Germany. For five decades, the official memory perpetuated de Gaulle's narrative whereby the French bore no guilt, shame, or responsibility for what happened to Jews or other minorities in France; all guilt for crimes against humanity lay with the Germans. The French collective memory portrayed the nation as inherently anti-fascist and virtuous by nature of French republican values. In fact, the official narrative cast France as a victim of the Nazis, not as their accomplice.

The Rafle du Vél d'Hiv, one of several roundups to clear France of Jews, flies in the face of the French national memory. This particular roundup, named for the Vélodrome d'Hiver/Vél d'Hiv, the Winter Velodrome, occurred in Paris on July 16–17, 1942. There more than thirteen thousand Jews were held in unsanitary conditions and with little water or food. The victims of this roundup were mainly immigrants from Eastern Europe, many of whom had already fled anti-Semitic persecutions in Nazi-occupied lands. Among these thirteen thousand or more Jews who were arrested, detained, and deported, 4,051 were children. Over the course of the Occupation, seventy-six thousand Jews were deported from France; 2,600 of these deportees survived, fifty of whom were victims of the Vél d'Hiv roundup. None of the deported returned to France after 1945 (Lees 2012).

It was the Vichy regime, not the German occupation forces, that first introduced anti-Semitic measures in France. Two statutes, in October 1940 and June 1941, placed quotas on the number of Jews permitted to work in the liberal professions and completely forbade Jews from holding public office. The Rafle du Vél d'Hiv was the culmination of Vichy's anti-Semitic policies, carried out by French police with the backing of the German occupiers. Prime Minister Pierre Laval and the chief of Paris police René Bousquet had engaged in a series of negotiations with the German authorities prior to the roundups, reaching an agreement to exempt French Jews from arrest and expulsion. The planning and execution of the operation was very much a French concern, with the final decisions to go ahead with the roundups taken by the Vichy council of ministers. After seven days of detention in the Vél d'Hiv, the families were transported to camps in the Loiret region, where conditions were just as deplorable. They were then deported to Auschwitz.

Evolution of the Commemoration

In 1946, an anti-racist association installed a memorial plaque at the site of the Vél d'Hiv (now an office building) where private commemorations took place (Carrier 2005, 71). In 1982, then mayor of Paris Jacques Chirac visited the commemoration, marking the onset of national attention to the site and the anniversary.

President François Mitterrand, who himself had worked for the Vichy government before joining the Resistance, maintained the Vichy-was-not-France myth. Despite this, in early 1993, Mitterrand officially introduced a day of remembrance of the Vél d'Hiv. Since then, either the president or the prime minister has attended this solemn commemoration each July 16, falling just two days after the national day of rejoicing, Bastille Day. The official name given to the Vél d'Hiv commemoration was the "National Day of Remembrance of the Victims of Racist and Anti-Semitic Crimes of the So-Called 'Government of the French State' and in Homage to the Righteous among Nations from France." The day was intended to commemorate Jewish victims of the Holocaust; since 1954, the last Sunday of April had been used to remember all victims of National Socialism.[26] The qualifier in the name of the Vél d'Hiv commemoration, the "Crimes of the So-Called 'Government of the French State,'" signaled a continuation of the notion that Vichy was not genuinely French; Vichy is commonly referred to as the "French State" to distinguish it from the "French Republic." Following the Gaullist interpretation, the French State/Vichy had interrupted the continuity of the Republic, separating the Third French Republic from the Fourth. The implication was that the current French government, state, and society bore no direct responsibility for the actions of Vichy; thus there was no obligation to face endogenous racism and anti-Semitism, no need to explore why and how republican values had been weakened and discarded, and no need to link the unflattering decisions or behaviors of French leaders, police, and citizens to the present and future. In other words, the commemoration did not invite reflection or contrition. It set the record straight in the most exculpatory way. Despite lobbying by and petitions from civil society organizations, in particular the Committee Vél d'Hiv 42, Mitterrand refused to publicly (or privately) acknowledge responsibility for the crimes committed under the Vichy regime (Carrier 2005).

In 1986, Chirac, the next prime minister, unveiled a stele marking the location of the stadium and attributing responsibility for the roundup to Vichy state police under the orders of German occupiers. At the same time, a street near the site was renamed Place des Martyrs Juifs. The fiftieth anniversary

---

[26] Council of Europe https://www.coe.int/en/web/roma-genocide/virtual-library/-/asset_publisher/M35KN9VVoZTe/content/finland-remembrance-day?inheritRedirect=false#:~:text=The%20day%20commemorates%20the%20rounding,Mitterrand%20on%203%20February%201993, accessed March 22, 2021.

of the event on July 16, 1992, was the occasion of the first official ceremony held at the site. Its participants included President Mitterrand, leaders of the National Assembly, government ministers, the chief of police, and church leaders. Please see Figure 2.5.

For the next several years, the Vél d'Hiv commemoration served as the focus of debate regarding continuity between Vichy and the Republic and whether or not the Republic should assume responsibility for the roundup and participation in the Holocaust. On July 17, 1994, while Mitterrand was still president, the monument to the roundup's victims was dedicated in a park near the site of the Vél d'Hiv, which had been destroyed by fire in 1959 and subsequently demolished. The monument inscription reads: "The French Republic in homage to victims of racist and anti-Semitic persecutions and of crimes against humanity committed under the authority of the so-called 'Government of the State of France.'" The answer, then, to the question regarding continuity and responsibility remained a clear *non*. During his presidency, Mitterrand would continue to lay a wreath each year at the grave of Philippe Pétain, making it clear he did not wish to usher in a period of closer scrutiny of Vichy and its role in the Holocaust and other crimes. While he was president, the French Parliament nonetheless passed the Gayssot Act of 1990, making it illegal to question the existence of crimes against humanity.

Figure 2.5 Mitterrand at the Vél d'Hiv Memorial
Source: REUTERS / Alamy Stock Photo.

After just two months as President, Jacques Chirac, Mitterrand's successor, parted with tradition, shattering the narrative of French innocence in his speech of July 16, 1995. Unlike his predecessors, who had refused to recognize France's role in the Holocaust for fifty years, Chirac declared: "France, the homeland of the Enlightenment and of the rights of man, a land of welcome and asylum, on that day committed the irreparable." As to the French role in the roundup, he held, "Breaking its word, it handed those who were under its protection over to their executioners." He made it clear that France owed the victims "an everlasting debt."[27] Fifty-three years after the event, Chirac's speech marked the beginning of a new official narrative about the Vél d'Hiv and thus Vichy. Carrier described the speech as not only a lament against the injury inflicted on Jews by the Vichy regime but also as a warning for the present. Chirac spoke "against the persistence of racism, anti-Semitism, fear and 'exclusion,' combined with an appeal to memory and 'vigilance' in order to counteract enduring 'obscure forces,' a lightly veiled reference to the Front National" (Carrier 2005, 94). Consistent with the emergent European Holocaust memory, Chirac's "appeal to memory" sought to connect the past with the present and future, emphasizing the need to resist illiberalism and to respect human dignity.

The Far-Right Rejects the New Holocaust-Centered Narrative

Discussions surrounding the commemoration of Vél d'Hiv cannot be separated from the struggle of French mainstream parties to isolate the radical-right party of Jean-Marie LePen, the Front National (FN). LePen objected to this new memory narrative, suggesting Chirac was settling an "electoral debt" toward the Jewish community; he reportedly claimed the president had "soiled our nation and its memory."[28] Like other far-right memory challengers, LePen publicly questioned the patriotism of the president and the government for efforts to construct a more reflective memory culture in France.

On July 22, 2012, Chirac's successor, François Hollande, gave a speech at the Vél d'Hiv memorial to commemorate the seventieth anniversary of the

---

[27] Chirac quoted in The Jewish Telegraphic Agency, September 26, 2019, https://www.jta.org/2019/09/26/opinion/how-the-late-french-president-jacques-chirac-started-frances-reckoning-with-the-holocaust

[28] Carrier cites a 1995 publication by Stephanie Trano (Carrier 2005, 104).

roundup. His speech was striking for its insistence on a truthful reckoning with the French past:

> We owe the Jewish martyrs of the Vélodrome d'Hiver the truth about what happened seventy years ago. The truth is that French police—on the basis of the lists they had themselves drawn up—undertook to arrest the thousands of innocent people trapped on July 16, 1942. And that the French gendarmerie escorted them to the internment camps. The truth is that no Gestapo soldiers—not a single one—were mobilized at any stage of the operation. The truth is that this crime was committed in France, by France.[29]

For years, many French citizens, not just the far-right, openly denied that France had anything to atone for in relation to its wartime behavior. Jean-Marie LePen denied that the Holocaust had even happened. When his daughter Marine took over leadership of the FN 2011, part of her effort to "de-demonize" the party was to reject outright Holocaust denialism and overt anti-Semitism. Her National Rally, the name of the party since 2018, espouses traditional French republican ideals such as secularism and liberty, while also protesting what LePen sees as a "tyranny of penitence." According to this perspective, Hugh Mcdonnell writes, "French society is plagued by self-castigation for historical injustices which have no bearing in reality outside the minds of domineering leftists" (Mcdonnell 2017, n.p.).

On July 22, 2012, Hollande recognized the importance of continually pushing back on memory challengers who seek to distort the truth and deflect guilt and responsibility for crimes against humanity:

> The challenge is to fight tirelessly against all forms of falsification of history: not only the insult of Holocaust denial, but also the temptation of relativism. Indeed, to pass on the history of the Shoah is to teach how uniquely appalling it was. By its nature, its scale, its methods, and the terrifying precision of its execution, that crime remains an abyss unique in human history.

Succeeding Hollande, President Emmanuel Macron was only in office a few months when he delivered a powerful speech at the memorial on July 17, 2017, the seventy-fifth anniversary of the roundup. The commemoration was attended by Holocaust survivors and the Israeli Prime Minister Benjamin Netanyahu. Macron began, "I am with you today on this dark and solemn

---

[29] Hollande's speech was reprinted in the *New York Review of Books* as "The 'Crime Committed in France, by France'" on August 18, 2012.

occasion to perpetuate the guiding thread initiated in 1995 by Jacques Chirac."
His next words addressed Holocaust memory-challengers in France:

> Just recently, what we considered to be established by the authorities of the
> French Republic across the party lines, proven by all historians and con-
> firmed by the national conscience, was contested by French leaders prepared
> to trample on the truth. Responding to these counterfeiters is to do them
> too much honor, but to leave them unanswered would be worse, making us
> accomplices.

He insisted, "I condemn all the tricks and subtleties of those who claim today
that Vichy was not France," a direct refutation of Marine LePen. He held further, "I condemn those who practice relativism, explaining that exonerating
France from responsibility for the Vél d'Hiv round-up would be a good thing."
As with previous speeches of French leaders at this commemoration, Macron's
message reflected much about the current political and cultural context. For
Macron, a recent resurgence of anti-Semitism in France was very much on his
mind. Acts of violence against French Jews challenged the French to be aware
of the country's history of anti-Semitism and other forms of racism and to be
vigilant in fighting against them. He reminded listeners:

> Because Vichy and its doctrine unleashed the vices that were already a stain
> on the Third Republic: racism and anti-Semitism . . . Yet neither racism nor
> anti-Semitism were born with the Vichy regime. They were there, alive and
> present under the Third Republic. The Dreyfus affair showed their virulence.
> The 1930s gave them new momentum through the emergence of intellectuals,
> parties and newspapers that made them their doctrine.

He reminded France of these facts, "because every nation runs the risk of sleep-
walking and accepting the unacceptable by habit, apathy." As Macron made
clear, the past and those "habits" have not passed; they persist and they have
been amplified by new media:

> Worldwide conspiracy theories, delusions about global finance, insidious
> iconography, identity crises bringing out the most toxic of clichés are all
> spreading at great speed and are reaching gullible or porous minds. Racism
> and anti-Semitism have unprecedented means of propaganda at their dis-
> posal to carry out their insidious work. Social networks are the great pur-
> veyors of such propaganda and we are yet to understand the scope of their
> influence.

Macron appears to address the role of extreme-right leaders and groups when he said:

> In today's France, the corruption of minds and moral and intellectual weakness that racism and anti-Semitism represent are still present and notably so. They take new shapes, new faces and choose more surreptitious wording.[30]

The activist and Nazi hunter Serge Klarsfeld hailed Macron's 2017 address at the commemoration as "a precedent-setting speech that went deeper, on a pedagogic level, than addresses that preceded it by French presidents."[31]

It was not long before Marine LePen revived a form of soft denialism, focusing specifically on the Vichy-not-France myth. Less than two weeks before the first round of the 2017 presidential election, LePen said on French television:

> I don't think that France is responsible for the Vél d'Hiv. I think that in general . . . if there were those responsible, it was those who were in power at the time. This is not France. France has been mired in people's minds for years. In reality, our children are taught that they have every reason to criticize her, to see only the darkest historical aspects. I want them to be proud to be French again.[32]

Like other memory challengers in Europe, LePen is critical of a reflexive memory culture and seeks to replace an open and critical examination of the French past with a partial, deliberately positive narrative.

A handful of historians and journalists have likewise contributed to challenging the dominant interpretation of Vichy as willing participant in the Holocaust. Indeed, two of the most prominent memory challengers are themselves Jewish. Jacques Sémelin, a history professor at the Sciences Po, has written that 75 percent of French Jews survived the Holocaust because of French citizens' efforts to protect them. In that, Sémelin clearly revives the Vichy-as-protector thesis that was debunked in the 1970s by historian Robert Paxton in works such as *Vichy France: Old Guard and New Order, 1940–1944*. The journalist and author Eric Zemmour, born in France to Algerian-Jewish

---

[30] The preceding passages from President Macron's speech, found at the Elysee Palace website https://www.elysee.fr/front/pdf/elysee-module-2020-fr.pdf.

[31] Quoted in Cnaan Liphshiz, "6 reasons Why Macron's Speech about the Holocaust Matters," *The Forward*, July 17, 2017, https://forward.com/news/377208/6-reasons-why-macron-s-speech-about-the-holocaust-in-france-was-groundbreak/

[32] "France not responsible for 1942 mass round-up of Jews, says LePen," I24news, April 9, 2017, https://www.i24news.tv/en/news/international/europe/142295-170409-france-not-responsible-for-1942-mass-round-up-of-jews-says-le-pen, acccessed April 5, 2021.

parents, has argued in several books and public appearances that Philippe Petain has been treated unfairly by historians and the French political establishment, that he did not treat French Jews badly. Zemmour has insisted that Vichy protected French Jews by negotiating with the Nazis to keep them in France, while deporting only non-French Jews, mainly from Eastern Europe. As already noted, the Vichy regime did actively cooperate with the deportation of Jews and even passed anti-Jewish legislation before it was demanded by the Nazis. Zemmour has further questioned the innocence of Alfred Dreyfus and characterized the 1945 D-Day landing as an American operation of liberation and colonization. He and Sémelin represent a strain of the French New Right in the tradition of Charles Maurras's far-right nationalism.

President Macron's passionate embrace of a Holocaust-centered memory of the war almost guarantees that the far-right will continue its memory challenge, particularly at election time. Macron, LePen, and Zemmour faced off in the 2022 presidential election. At some points in the months prior to April 2022, polls put Zemmour ahead of LePen, though he only won 4 percent of the vote in the first electoral round. Once again, Macron and LePen advanced to the second round of voting, which Macron won, though by a smaller margin than in 2017: 18 percentage points (59 percent to 41 percent), as opposed to 32 percentage points (66 percent to 34 percent) in 2017.

The fact that public debate about France's wartime role persists suggests that facing other dark chapters, namely French colonialism and its legacies, will likely meet with resistance. Efforts to connect the wartime and colonial pasts or to link those pasts to contemporary questions about French identity and culture are also likely to meet with various forms of obfuscation and denialism, perhaps sparking further racism and anti-Semitism, which, Macron pointed out, were not born in Vichy.

Challenging Dominant Narratives through Diversion

As a region, postwar Western Europe developed institutions like the European Union and the Council of Europe to encourage reconciliation between nations and peoples and mediate past harms. World War II and the Holocaust became negative memories at the center of a quasi-official European culture of remembrance that imparted norms about "never forgetting" the past, so as not to repeat its mistakes; it pursued vigilance in the protection of human dignity, basic human rights, and tolerance for difference. These developments took several decades. As the late historian of Europe Tony Judt observed, the countries allied with or occupied by Nazi Germany constructed narratives about their own roles in the war in a similar, two-step fashion: first by claiming the mantle of resistance to fascism and Nazism, and secondly by externalizing guilt to the Germans (2005). In Austria, Italy, and France, this pattern led to a delayed reckoning with their own roles in the Holocaust and other wartime atrocities. National myths about victimhood or about heroic resistance to fascism were eventually debunked or downgraded, leading to a general consensus involving European Holocaust memory, at least at the official level. The situation in Germany was different for reasons described earlier: Germany constructed a memory of contrition that, while not perfect, has served as an example to many other countries, including the United States (Neiman 2019).

The development of a European memory culture committed to "never forgetting" is not immune to debate. Indeed, a lively debate inside Germany in recent years has shown that a dominant memory narrative of contrition can, itself, become hegemonic, rigid, and unreflective. An "orthodox" memory narrative that insists on the uniqueness and incomparability of the Holocaust to the exclusion of the memories of other groups can open spaces for memory challengers. On the right in Germany, memory challengers insist on recognition for the suffering of Germans during and after the war, while on the left, memory actors point out the insensitivity of the "German catechism," a term proposed by Dirk Moses in 2021 to describe a practice that ignores other victims of the German state, past and present.[33] For critical scholars, victims of the past that are often ignored by Germany's official memory culture include, for example, the Herero and Nama people of Namibia who were massacred (for the Herero almost entirely) by German colonists early in the twentieth century. Present victims of the state, critics argue, are many migrant communities, particularly those who have come from outside of Europe and are Muslim, who remain marginalized in German (and European) society, politics, and the economy.

This chapter has called attention to the facts that far-right apologists for fascism never entirely disappeared in Europe, and their resurgence raises new concerns about their potential electoral and policy impact. The cases

---

[33] See Dirk Moses, "The German Catechism" at https://geschichtedergegenwart.ch/the-german-catechism/. Moses' essay sparked a new debate in Germany and beyond about the comparability of the Holocaust that some have called the Historians' Debate 2.0. It sought a "decolonization," a "global turn" in genocide and Holocaust studied, whereby the Holocaust of Jews may be examined alongside colonial violence and white supremacy. See also the New Fascism Syllabus curated by Jennifer Evans at http://newfascismsyllabus.com/.

examined here show how far-right actors have instrumentalized the wartime past to oppose the memory culture of contrition—*not* in order to make it more inclusive of victims of colonialism in the past or racism today but to re-nationalize wartime memory. These memory challengers have sought to delegitimize any linkage between their national wartime records and their governments' rhetorical and policy commitments in the present. Using role reversal, appropriation, and other discursive strategies to whitewash the fascist or collaborationist past, memory challengers in the four Western European cases considered here were motivated by discomfort with a dominant narrative that had become more reflective, critical, and contrite. Frustration with the values associated with a more cosmopolitan wartime narrative, such as tolerance for difference and respect for human rights of all, often found expression in their attempts to re-nationalize commemorations and turn them into occasions to unite against outsiders. Attempts to equate threats to the nation in the past with those in the present, for example, regarding immigration policy or the threat of terrorism, were meant to impugn the current government and its memory culture as misguided and harmful.

In each of the four cases examined here, commemorations offered high-profile arenas for pushing back against European Holocaust-centered memory. In Germany and Austria, far-right parties and groups used commemorations to renationalize wartime memory by distancing collective memory from the perpetration of crimes, shifting it either to a memory of victimization or one of heroism. Regarding the Dresden bombing commemorations, memory challengers like the NPD, AfD, or right-wing fraternities deflected guilt, ignoring the larger context of the war in order to cast the Germans themselves as innocent victims of evil acts undertaken by the Allies. In Austria, the FPÖ and veterans' groups sought to normalize the wartime service of soldiers under the Third Reich and Axis and link it to protecting Europe from its enemies. In Italy and France, commemorations of wartime events have served as battlegrounds for far-right political party leaders seeking to whitewash the fascist or collaborationist past and deflect responsibility for wartime atrocities. Memory challengers in Italy have operated inside the national government, while those in France have mobilized outside government but continue to come perilously close to winning the country's highest political office. In Italy, questions of wartime guilt are diverted to occasions for commemorating victimhood; in France, they are redirected from France and the French to a regime that was either an aberration or a shield from greater danger.

Far-right memory challengers in the four Western European countries continue to use a variety of approaches to deflect from guilt and responsibility, including:

- Emotional appeals to national pride that are largely rhetorical, although in Germany and Austria, they were also performative, involving marches and other rituals;
- Obfuscation, by downplaying perpetrator role of own country, and in Dresden, "what about-ism";
- Construction of equivalence, putting fascists and communists on equally negative footing, with the ultimate goal of marginalizing the left and diluting or delegitimizing anti-fascism;
- Revisionism, by whitewashing the fascist past and externalizing guilt, and in the case of the Dresden memory challengers, distorting the numbers of victims and other circumstances;
- Inversion, especially in Italy and Austria, treating fascists as freedom fighters against the communist threat, just as worthy of praise as leftist Resistance fighters.

While outright denialism was not a common feature in all four cases, memory challengers nonetheless share the argument that it was high time to turn away from a culture of contrition. Though memory challenges in each case respond to particular national and partisan contexts, the right-wing challengers in all cases described here expressed a preference for an alternative memory narrative that:

- uses emotions grounded in patriotism. Patriotism was generally used as a smokescreen for deflecting responsibility for past harm;
- claims the mantle of the popular resistance (elites-vs-people) and projects themselves as the protector of European (white, Christian) heritage (insiders-vs-outsiders);
- and aims to neutralize the image of fascists, collaborators, or soldiers as having fought "for Europe" or against communists, rather than for a hyper-nationalist, racist, and murderous regime. In doing so, it normalizes them.

The Dresden, Ulrichsberg, Day of Liberation, and Vél d'Hiv commemorations show that memory challengers primarily aim to influence domestic audiences with their discourse and rituals. They urge their countrymen and women to resist narratives of guilt and responsibility for events that happened three-quarters of a century ago, to unburden themselves, and either to feel sorry for the soldiers who served fascist leaders, or to view them as heroes for holding back communism from Western Europe. Beyond targeting domestic audiences, some far-right memory challengers have instrumentalized Holocaust memory in their relations with other countries, such as Israel, as a way of marginalizing other minorities like Muslims in their own countries.

Far-right parties have enjoyed electoral successes just about everywhere in Europe and at every level of government, including in the EU Parliament. The web of extremist groups has become transnational, amplified by social media and, as later chapters show, supported by Putin's Russia. These groups exert influence on public debates and popular understandings of events and their meanings. As the cases here have illustrated, the far-right often couches its challenges in terms of free speech, patriotism, or the "reconciliation" of divisions. This study suggests there is a potential to weaken the cosmopolitan, human rights-focused Holocaust memory in order to ignore the past or whitewash it. The proliferation of far-right parties and movements has strengthened that momentum. In Italy, where right-wing parties already held power and currently dominate politics, there is a real threat that they will move further away from European cosmopolitan memory. However, in each country examined here, political leaders from mainstream parties have often come out strongly against manipulations of wartime memory. Just as importantly, civil society groups have countered the memory challengers, reclaiming commemorations for the purpose of "never forgetting," as was the case in Germany and Austria. Other constraints include Holocaust denial laws and prohibitions of hate speech, independent media, decades of Holocaust education in schools, and longtime identification with the liberal democratic norms of the European Union. The cases examined in this chapter suggest that the longer these constraints are in place, and the more reinforcement they receive by actors at the local, national, and transnational levels, the more difficult it will be for a narrow, revisionist memory to displace the cosmopolitan memory of World War II. In the next chapter, we examine cases where engagement with cosmopolitan memory has been less extensive, and the institutional and cultural constraints against revisionism less well established.

3

Restoration of Fallen Soldiers to the Pantheon of National Heroes

Commemorations in Eastern Europe

The Introduction (chapter 1) noted ways in which the collapse of communism and the breakup of the USSR and Yugoslavia opened space for mnemonic debate in Eastern Europe. As part of efforts to reinterpret the history of the twentieth century and to construct a national memory narrative of World War II that is more compatible with their self-image, some political actors in post-communist countries have whitewashed the fascist past while also blackwashing the more recent experience with communism. In the process, wartime roles and events have been distorted, highlighting heroism and sacrifice, along with emphasizing victimhood and mourning for lost members of the national community. They simultaneously downplay or even erase dark spots in the national past, specifically the participation in wartime atrocities and collaboration with Nazi Germany. Another aspect of such mnemonic moves has been to re-nationalize remembrance of wartime tragedies and triumphs.

On one hand, there is a tendency to overlook or minimize the suffering of minorities, such as Jews or Roma, in favor of remembering the suffering of the nation per se during and, especially, after the war. Far-right memory challengers resist a Holocaust-centered (West-)Europeanization of memory by asserting a re-nationalized interpretation of World War II as a glorious, but ultimately unsuccessful, fight against communism. Their rhetoric and rituals are devoid of Holocaust remembrance or recognition of the role that homegrown anti-Semitism played in the murder of their Jewish compatriots.

On the other hand, Central and Eastern European memory reconstruction overwhelmingly focuses on the Red Army, the Soviet Union, communist ideology, and leftist governments as the primary threats to national sovereignty and identity. As such, the collaborators and perpetrators of war crimes are recast as patriots, martyrs, and victims, first of communist tyranny and then of the communist regime's version of the past. A range of policies, often involving state-funded institutes for historical memory or government-sponsored

World War II Memory and Contested Commemorations in Europe and Russia. Jennifer A. Yoder, Oxford University Press.
© Jennifer A. Yoder (2024). DOI: 10.1093/oso/9780198894162.003.0003

investigative commissions, have resulted in the rewriting of textbooks and official histories; the passage of memory laws criminalizing disagreement with
official history; the renaming of streets and other geographic locations; and
the removal of communist-era monuments. This is accompanied by the construction of new memorials and the revival of old, or even the creation of
new, national myths and symbols. The disowning of the communist past and
the search for alternative, national histories and memory acquired additional
legitimacy and urgency in reaction to Putin's Russia: the bear looms once again
as a threat—increasingly an existential one—to the national sovereignty of
Eastern Europeans.

In this chapter, I examine how and why fascist forces and Nazi collaborators, such as the Ustaše in Croatia and the Waffen-SS in the Baltics and
Ukraine, became the focus of efforts to reinterpret the past, in order to construct an exculpatory, anti-communist memory narrative. I also consider
examples of anti-communist forces, such as Poland's so-called "cursed soldiers" or Hungarian resistors during the siege of Budapest, who have recently
been mythologized in the service of national-conservative agendas. Among the
memory challengers who insist on commemorating these particular "fallen"
and "cursed" soldiers are veterans' organizations, far-right associations and
political parties and even governing parties that increasingly adopt illiberal
discourses and policies.

The examples from Latvia, Ukraine, Croatia, Hungary, and Poland discussed in this chapter illustrate revisionist strategies that both whitewash the
history of Nazi collaboration born of homegrown fascism and blackwash
the history of communism. These memory challenges operate in a different
environment than their counterparts in West Europe, where the dominant
Holocaust-centered memory culture and official commemorations became
targets of right-wing mnemonic instrumentalization. Although memory cultures are still in flux in Eastern Europe, actors there are engaged in efforts to
move away from Soviet and communist era narratives and to accommodate
the national past in the European mnemonic landscape.

Memory manipulations of World War II examined in this chapter have
both domestic and foreign policy objectives. Domestically, memory challengers aim to relieve the discomfort of "dissonant memories" (Subotic 2018)
about the war, foregrounding a national identity renewal that is positive rather
than one marred by anti-Semitism, racism, or collaboration with the Nazis.
Blackwashing former communists not only allows memory challengers to
deprive communists of roles as victors and liberators from fascism, recasting them as enemies of the national community and of freedom. It also

allows memory challengers to impugn contemporary leftists as inheritors of that sinister legacy. By whitewashing the fascists and collaborators of the past, far-right memory challengers posit themselves as heirs of a heroic, anti-communist legacy. In short, their goals are to blind and bind, to obscure the ugly or embarrassing past and to reinterpret it in a way that both strengthens national and in-group identity, in addition to legitimating their own claim to represent it.

The retelling of the past is meant to inspire and unify the national community in the face of old and new enemies. The point is not simply to reject Soviet memory narratives and the commemorative symbols and rituals associated with this period by reclaiming national sovereignty over collective memory; it also seeks to oppose Russia's contemporary neo-imperialist ambitions. In the case of Latvia, which is home to a sizeable ethnic Russian population, the renationalization of memory can have both domestic and foreign policy consequences: war commemorations have turned into arenas of intense memory debate between Latvian nationalists and Russians, both inside and outside of Latvia (Sander 2022).

The renationalization of wartime memory also clearly runs counter to the cosmopolitan mode of remembrance characteristic of European institutions and Western European countries. Before turning to the five cases of memory challengers in relation to Eastern European commemorations, I briefly describe the wartime figures at the center of memory debates in the region as they have evolved since 1990.

Honoring Fascist Forces against Communism

The rehabilitation of wartime collaborators and the commemorations of fallen fascist soldiers is part of an effort by conservative nationalists in post-communist societies to construct narratives of national heroism, strength, and independence. During the Cold War, official national memories rarely included positive representations of soldiers who served Nazi Germany, the Axis, or other anti-communist forces. To the contrary, democracies in Western Europe commemorated anti-fascist resistors and victims of fascism, while in Eastern Europe, commemorative practices influenced by the Soviet Union focused on the heroism and sacrifices of the Red Army, or in the case of Yugoslavia, the Partisans. When remembrances of fallen soldiers on the losing side of the war occurred, they were private, within families or groups of veterans.

By destigmatizing and including collaborationist leaders and soldiers among the "glorious dead" to be remembered collectively, memory challengers turn the tables on their opponents; they delegitimize those who remember collaborationists as villains, namely the communist regimes of the past, as well as the domestic political parties associated with the left today. They are especially concerned with Russia under Putin, who puts his country at the center of World War II as the great savior and who denigrates any renationalization of wartime narratives in former Soviet republics or satellite countries. Memory challengers also seek to downgrade the dominant, Holocaust-centered memory of Western Europe, since it encourages reflection on attitudes and behaviors that permitted mass atrocity rooted in ethnic and racial hatred, casting many nationalist "heroes" in a negative light.

Among the most prominent collaborators undergoing rehabilitation in post-communist countries are Stepan Bandera in Ukraine, Miklos Horthy in Hungary, and Jozef Tiso in Slovakia. Bandera led the ultra-nationalist party Organization of Ukrainian Nationalists (OUN) as well as the Ukrainian Insurgent Army (UPA), which participated in massacres of Jews and Poles during the war.[1] Bandera's birthday is commemorated each year on January 1 with a torchlit parade in the capital Kiev. In 2014, the year of the Euro-Maidan uprising, the Bandera commemoration drew fifteen thousand people. Bandera's face was featured on many posters held by opponents of the Russia-friendly Yanukovych government. Horthy, who led Hungary from 1920 to 1944, was one of Hitler's closest allies and oversaw the implementation of anti-Jewish laws and the deportation of hundreds of thousands of Hungarian Jews to death camps. A monument of Horthy was erected in 2013 in Budapest, and in 2020, far-right groups organized a torchlit march on March 1 to commemorate the 100th year anniversary of Horthy's assumption of power. In Slovakia, the country's wartime clerical dictator and Hitler ally Tiso has been rehabilitated by many on the right, with some even calling for his beatification.[2]

---

[1] For more on Bandera and his place in contemporary Ukrainian memory debates, see David R. Marples, "The Resurrection of a Ukrainian National Hero," *Europe-Asia Studies*, Vol. 58, No. 4 (2006): 555–66.

[2] At the helm of the Hlinka Slovak People's Party, with its paramilitary Hlinka guards, Tiso led a state that was virulently anti-Semitic and fascist. The postcommunist Slovak governments officially supported his rehabilitation until the elections of 1998, which brought a less nationalist government to power. Since then, far-right parties and groups continue to press for the revival of the memory of Tiso. Although there is no Slovak wartime commemoration considered in this study, readers interested in Slovak memory may consult Jeffrey Blutinger, "An Inconvenient Past: Post-Communist Holocaust Memorialization" (2010) as well as Nadya Nedelsky, "'The Struggle for the Memory of the Nation': Post-Communist Slovakia and its World War II Past" (2016).

In several countries where there have been efforts to re-nationalize wartime memory, commemorations of military units that collaborated with the Nazis have appeared. Often veterans' associations, the families of veterans, or groups of so-called "patriots" are founding and organizing these commemorations, which are then joined by nationalist movements, far-right groups and political parties. As nationalist, racist, and anti-Semitic trends have intensified across Europe in recent years, memory challengers have been emboldened to come out of the shadows and appeal to the general public. They are often accorded legitimacy through the support of right-wing leaders, such as the Ukrainian Presidents Viktor Yushchenko (2005–2010) and Petro Poroshchenko (2014–2019) or the Hungarian Prime Minister Viktor Orban (1998–2002, 2010 to the present). Revisionist efforts at rehabilitation and commemoration have drawn strong criticism from domestic actors on the center and left of the political spectrum, from Russian minorities in the Baltic states, from Russian leaders in Moscow, from neighboring countries, as well as from EU officials.

The next sections will examine revisionist memory associated with the commemorations of three groups of World War II combatants in Eastern Europe: Waffen-SS soldiers in Latvia and Ukraine; pro-German Croatians and Hungarian forces; and anti-communist Polish partisans who continued fighting even after the war ended.

Whitewashing the Waffen-SS

The Waffen-SS, or "Armed SS," was the military wing of the Nazi Party's paramilitary Schutzstaffel (SS), or Protection Squadron. Created in 1933 at SS commander, or Reichsführer, Heinrich Himmler's urging, the Waffen-SS was originally comprised exclusively of people considered to be of "Germanic origin," including Danes, Norwegians, Dutch, and Flemish men. In 1940, the rules were relaxed to allow for the recruitment of volunteers and conscripts in occupied Hungary and Ukraine and non-occupied Latvia. Polish soldiers were not permitted to join, because the racialized ideology and laws categorized them as inferior (*Untermenschen*).

The Waffen-SS participated in atrocities across numerous campaigns. It counted among the organizations tried for war crimes and was deemed a criminal organization by the International Military Tribunal at Nuremberg in 1946. After the verdict, veterans in postwar Germany and Austria organized to defend their eligibility for pensions, as well as to commemorate their battles and sacrifices (Hurd and Werther 2016b, 424). The Mutual Aid

Association of Former Waffen-SS (HIAG/Hilfsgemeinschaft auf Gegenseit-igkeit der Angehörigen der ehemaligen Waffen-SS), the main lobbying organi-zation in West Germany since the 1950s, espoused an exculpatory, revisionist narrative of the organization's wartime role. A right-wing press in Germany began publishing a newsletter, *der Freiwillige* (The Volunteer), to articulate veterans' interests and to connect Waffen-SS veterans in Germany with those living abroad. During the Cold War, it had been impossible to cultivate con-nections with Waffen-SS veterans in communist Eastern Europe. In Western Europe, some Waffen-SS members were imprisoned, although most veterans were reintegrated into West German and Austrian societies, including into the armed forces (Large 1987).

Some of the veterans' organizations in the West continued to defend a narrative similar to that applied by Heinrich Himmler: the war had been a trans-European (Himmler would have added "Germanic") struggle against communism. These organizations cast the war as a fight for freedom, focus-ing on the sacrifice and honor of fallen soldiers, not on the crimes against humanity they had committed in the name of racist ideology and a totalitarian regime. Waffen-SS veterans' associations maintained that accounts of partic-ipation in atrocities were "untrue, vastly exaggerated and/or irrelevant: they were not involved" (Hurd and Werther 2016b, 429). They also relied on "yes, but" arguments, claiming that the actions of the Red Army had been "infinitely worse" (429) This discourse sought to erase the role of racist ideology in the Waffen-SS, suggesting that Hitler was forgotten, and that "Europe's enemy had always (only) been the Soviet Union" (430).

I turn now to examples of commemorations of the Waffen-SS in Latvia and Ukraine, tracing their origins and their activity since the end of com-munist rule in 1990–1991. I examine the organizers and adherents of such commemorations, as well as public reactions and political elite responses to them. These Waffen-SS commemorations demonstrate how seemingly isolated remembrances of fallen soldiers can be instrumentalized by memory chal-lengers who seek to whitewash the memory of fascism and blackwash that of communism.

Remembrance Day of Latvian Legionnaires

War commemorations and monuments have long been sites of particularly intense contestation of memory in the Baltic states. Their centrality to mem-ory struggles stems from the tumultuous experiences of Soviet occupation in

1940 and subsequent incorporation into the USSR, followed by the Nazi occupation of 1941 and citizen collaboration with the Nazi forces, then their 1944 reincorporation into the USSR. The postwar re-Sovietization of the Baltics affected not only their political and economic systems but also their demographic make-up. Following the independence of the Baltic states secured in the early 1990s, the reassertion of national identity and collective memory have been important projects, with concrete implications for the Russians living there, as well as for their relations with the powerful neighbor to the east.

Two decades after its struggle for independence in the aftermath of World War I, Latvia's fate as a sovereign country was thwarted once again by great powers; the 1939 Molotov-Ribbentrop Pact between the Stalin and Hitler allowed the Soviet Union to occupy Latvia and the other two Baltic states. Following that Soviet occupation, which ended when the USSR was invaded by Germany in 1941, Germany occupied Latvia for three years. This resulted in the murder of over seventy thousand Latvian Jews, and the conscription of many Latvian men required to aid Nazi Germany in fighting against the Soviets. In 1944, the Soviet Union retook Latvia from the Germans and began a process of "russification" that brought 1.5 million Russians to Latvia to assist with Sovietization. Russians assumed many positions of power and influence in the Latvian Soviet Socialist Republic, while Latvian history, language, and culture were suppressed.

Tensions escalated between the ethnic Latvians and ethnic Russian minorities after Latvia once again became independent in 1991. With a new citizenship law passed in the mid-1990s, many Russians in Latvia became non-citizens. Russian language instruction in public schools has also become contentious. Predictably, these tensions between ethnic Latvians and Russians spilled over into interpretations of the wartime past and its aftermath, as part of the construction of identity in post-Soviet states, a process that often plays out in public spaces and in public rituals. Commemorations of soldiers who fought on the side of Nazi Germany against the Red Army offer a window into the role of memory in the reconstruction of Baltic national identity. Corresponding with wartime commemorations in Western Europe, nationalists in Latvia have sought to shape the discourse and rituals of remembrance of soldiers who fought alongside Nazi Germany. In addition to whitewashing their association with the Hitler regime, the commemoration of the Latvian units of the Waffen-SS aims to blackwash the communist past and to assert independence from the Soviet and (later) Russian narrative of the war. One could view the commemoration as a constitutive element of an anti-colonial, anti-imperial narrative, one that sits uncomfortably alongside the Holocaust-centered memory encouraged by the European Union and its Western European members.

The Latvian Legion as model patriots

As a result of the manpower shortages of the German army, in 1943 Hitler asked Himmler to order the creation of the Latvian Legion, a formation of the Waffen-SS. Between 15 and 20 percent of the approximately eighty-seven thousand men who served in the Latvian Legion were volunteers. The rest were conscripted by the German military. Because the overwhelming majority had been conscripted, the Latvian Legion was not classified as a criminal organization at Nuremberg. Gareth Pritchard and Desislava Gancheva note, however, that many of the men in the Legion had been members of nationalist militias that began massacring Jews even before they were affiliated with the Waffen-SS (2014, n.p.). The battalion unit Arajs Kommando, which later became part of the Legion, carried out war crimes early on, including the murder of twenty-six thousand Jews.[3] That fact, and their association with the Nazi cause, meant that the Legionnaires could not be celebrated as war heroes after 1945. In fact, the USSR considered Legion members as fascist traitors; they were officially forgotten by the communist regime. Despite their defeat and processes of re-Sovietization after 1945, some Legionnaires, the so-called "Forest Brothers," continued fighting the Soviets inside Latvia well beyond the war's end.

In the aftermath of the war, a Latvian exile organization called Daugavas Vanagi (Hawks of the Daugava, after a river that flows through Latvia) started to commemorate the Legionnaires for their patriotism, ignoring the Legion's affiliation with Nazi Germany as well as evidence that members had participated in the Holocaust. According to researchers at the anti-communist Latvian Occupation Museum, March 16, 1944, was chosen as the date for this commemoration, because it marked the beginning of a two-day period—the first and only time that both divisions of the Latvian Legion (the 15th and 19th) had fought together against the Red Army.[4] It was also the only battle of the war that was led solely by Latvian commanders. Daugavas Vanagi sought to perpetuate a heroic myth that, despite their willingness to fight under Nazi Germany, Legionnaires "were fighting for a free Latvia and their fight against

[3] This figure for the number of Jewish victims of the Arajs Kommando from David Pugliese reporting in the *Ottawa Citizen* on March 20, 2019. Pugliese reported that the Latvian SS Division were among the last hold-outs of pro-German forces that defended Berlin in the last days of the war.

[4] Occupation Museum, "The Latvian Legion and March 16" http://okupacijasmuzejs.lv/en/news/the-latvian-legion-and-16-march-520/, accessed March 11, 2021.

the Red Army was morally justified on the grounds of the repressions that the Soviet rule carried out in Latvia during the occupation from 1940 until 1941."[5] Other observers suggest that the commemoration was a way to "fill the lack of heroes that resulted from the fact that Latvia did not show armed resistance to the Soviet occupation in 1940" (V. Zelče 2011, cited in Braslava 2017, 33). Either way, this kind of whitewashing arose from their discomfort with the past and the search for an exculpatory narrative that would also project strength and heroism in the face of external enemies.

In 1989, families of the fallen soldiers residing in Latvia, when it was still part of the Soviet Union, began marking the day with an annual procession. Several years after Latvia became independent from the Soviet Union, in 1998, the commemoration was officially recognized by the Latvian parliament, the Saema, as the "Remembrance Day for Latvian Soldiers" rather than one for the more controversial "Legions." In the face of international pressure, the commemoration was, by 2000, no longer considered an official commemoration day. Unofficial commemorations continue, however, featuring a parade of veterans and younger supporters honoring the Legion. Please see Figure 3.1.

Figure 3.1 Veterans marching in Riga in 2009
Source: REUTERS/Ints Kalnins.

---

[5] Māra Braslava, "Ethnic Cleavage in Politics and Mnemonic Tensions: An Analysis of World War II Commemorative Practices in Latvia," Masters Thesis, University of Tartu (2017) 33.

The march typically follows a memorial service at the Riga Cathedral and ends at the Freedom Monument, where veterans lay a wreath, make speeches, and sing hymns. The attendants also lay flowers at a nearby cemetery where Legionnaires are buried. Video footage of the annual march shows aged veterans clad in military uniforms and armbands, flanked by nationalist supporters; they carry Latvian flags and banners, and hold posters of Hitler and Stalin with a big X through them. The message is that the two leaders and their regimes were twin evils, while the Latvian Legion itself was innocent. The commemoration drew a crowd of 2,000 people in 2010, 2,500 in 2012, and merely a few hundred participants in 2018. In 2019, about a thousand people marched in the annual parade, some wearing "swastikas and other Nazi insignias" (Pugliese 2019). Despite the onset of the covid-19 pandemic in 2020, some people reportedly gathered to commemorate the Legion, however, there was no commemoration due to the pandemic the next year.[6] In general, since 1991, coming to terms with the past in Latvia has focused on replacing the Soviet official narrative about the war with a renationalized version, which includes the victimization of Latvians by the Soviet Union. The history of homegrown anti-Semitism or the role of Latvians in the persecution and murder of Jews in the Holocaust has largely been ignored.

In recent years the commemoration has not been endorsed by the government, nor is it condemned by it. According to online information posted in 2012 by Karina Petersone, Director of the Investment and Development Agency of Latvia—titled "Why March 16?"—the unofficial commemoration is of "the war dead, as one might expect, by church memorial services and flower laying." It is not an official day of remembrance

> because the state of Latvia was occupied during the war and could not exercise its power, moreover, it did not have an army of its own, the former officers of the Latvian army were in their majority massacred and punished by the USSR occupation forces in 1940.

The government's own website states that the commemoration has "no ideological basis. No Nazi uniforms, symbols or slogans . . . (and) is a sensitive subject which still raises emotions because the men commemorated

---

[6] International media has been fascinated by this gathering of supporters of the Legion. Observers have included Efraim Zuroff of the Simon Wiesenthal Center and researchers from the Defending History project, led by Dovid Katz, which posted an online petition to stop to stop the March 16 marches. See the petition at https://www.petitions.net/stop_the_16_march_marches_and_latvians_revising_history, accessed April 1, 2022.

did fight on the side of the Nazi Germany" (https://www.latvia.eu/blog/why-march-16).

Mainstream political parties and officials have not embraced the commemoration, preferring to commemorate the Legionnaires along with other Latvian soldiers on November 11 (Braslava 2017, 34). The far-right National Alliance Party, the main proponent of the notion of Legionnaires as freedom fighters, has sought unsuccessfully to restore the official designation to the commemoration. Officials tend to avoid the commemoration; however, in 2014 a government minister from the National Alliance defied then Prime Minister Laimdota Staujuma's suggestion that government officials ought not attend the commemoration, resulting in the minister's dismissal.

Having participated in governing coalitions since 2010, the National Alliance (NA) uses an equivalence/two totalitarianisms approach to justify the actions of Latvian Legionnaires as resistors of the Soviets and communism. One of NA's members in the Latvian government, Einars Cilinskis, asserts, "[t]he meaning of March 16 procession is not only to clearly condemn two totalitarian regimes of the past that have brought enormous destruction to Latvia and the world, but also to address the rebirth of fascism today" (Braslava 2017, 36). Here it is important to clarify that Cilinskis refers not to the rebirth of fascist parties in Europe, but rather in Russia, reflected in its aggression toward Ukraine. He explains exactly how the commemoration has been politicized: "March 16 for sure will not be merely a date on which we commemorate those who fell for Latvia. It will be a protest against the aggressor Russia" (36).

Another tactic the NA members use is to paint themselves as the only true Latvians, as the defenders of the Latvian nation and its independence. The NA even casts itself as the defender of Europe. As Braslava's study of the March 16 commemoration suggests, memory warriors linked to the NA claim to be the only ones willing to tell the truth about the Latvian Legion; in doing so, they are struggling against those who would make compromises and concessions that betray the nation. They allegedly engage in this mnemonic struggle because "forgetting" wartime heroes opens the door for Russian aggression ("fascism"), which could lead to a repetition of history (Braslava 2017, 41).

In Novikova's reading of the cult of the fallen soldier, the Legion's commemoration is part of a quest for national assertiveness and a heroic national history. Further, it represents "ideal masculinity for the revived nation and is contrasted with the tradition of the feminised victim and martyr of the former Soviet occupation" (Novikova 2011, 592). The nationalist memory politics uses the Legion as a symbol of the heroic defense "of European civilization against the onslaught of communists and Russian vandals," which gained traction in the context of the 2014 annexation of Crimea and invasion of eastern Ukraine by Russia (592).

Reactions to the commemoration of the Latvian Legions

Inside Latvia, scholars like Dovid Katz and groups concerned about Jewish life there have spoken out against the commemoration and, especially, the timid responses from Latvian officials. Katz edits a blog called "Defending History" and has written extensively about Latvia's and other post-communist states' embrace of the Double Genocide theory, which blatantly ignores the role of indigenous fascism and anti-Semitism as well as collaboration with the Nazis in the Holocaust.[7]

In 1999, the Simon Wiesenthal Center in Jerusalem voiced criticism of the commemoration:

> Although these units were not involved in crimes against humanity, many of their soldiers had previously served in the Latvian security police and had actively participated in the mass murder of civilians, primarily Jews ... The stubborn insistence of Latvia's SS Legion veterans to conduct a public march to glorify their role as combatants on behalf of the Third Reich is a clear indi-cation that many Latvians have still not internalized the lessons of WWII ... far too many Latvians feel free to identify with those who fought alongside the perpetrators of the Holocaust rather than with its victims.[8]

In 2012, the Council of Europe's Commission against Racism and Intolerance (ECRI) issued a report criticizing the commemoration and recommending that "the Latvian authorities condemn all attempts to commemorate persons who fought in the Waffen SS and collaborated with the Nazis. ECRI further recommends that the authorities ban any gathering or march legitimizing in any way Nazism."[9] In 2019, the Canadian government, which leads a NATO battlegroup in Latvia, likewise condemned the annual parade. A spokeswoman for Global Affairs Canada declared that "Canada is strongly opposed to the glo-rification of Nazism and all forms of racism, racial discrimination, xenophobia,

---

[7] The Defending History website can be found at https://defendinghistory.com/.

[8] Cited in Bjarke W. Bøtcher, "The Debate on the Latvian SS Volunteer Legion," *Baltic Defense Review*, vol. 2000, No. 3, https://www.baltdefcol.org/files/docs/bdreview/10bdr100.pdf.

[9] Council of Europe, ECRI Report on Latvia, February 2012, https://rm.coe.int/fifth-report-on-latvia/1680934a9f.

intolerance and extremism . . . that is why we condemn the parade to commemorate the Latvian SS Brigade held in Latvia on March 16th" (Pugliese). Despite protests from Jewish and Russian groups, organizations like the Simon Wiesenthal Center, the European Parliament, and the United Nations, the commemoration is still observed by many.

Ethnic Russians, who constitute one-quarter of Latvia's population, have expressed concern about the nationalistic and revisionist dimensions of the Latvian Legion commemoration. For some time, Russian media have voiced grave concerns, over presenting the commemoration "as evidence of Riga's nationalist leanings" (Pugliese 2019). Russia sees the event as a refutation of its most sacred day of remembrance, May 9, which marks the end of World War II and celebrates the heroism and sacrifice of the Red Army (see chapter 5). In Latvia, such criticisms are likely to be characterized as Russian disinformation.

Although the honoring of Latvian Legionnaires attracts relatively small numbers, its persistence suggests tolerance of its core challenge to both the Soviet-era and Holocaust-centered narratives, implying that World War II was not a battle against Nazi Germany and its allies but rather a national independence struggle primarily against the USSR. The Legion members, clearly a part of Nazi Germany's Waffen-SS, are recast as national resistors against communism and colonialism, rendering them as heroes. This stance—opposition to communism and the USSR—finds greater acceptance in the face of a resurgence of aggressive Russian foreign policy, including hybrid warfare and neo-imperialism designs on former Soviet republics. This renationalization of wartime memory, further complicates the sensitive politics of language and citizenship inside Latvia, as well as between Latvia and Russia.

Ukraine and the Waffen-SS: Freedom Fighters or War Criminals?

In yet another former Soviet republic, Ukraine, two more commemorations have honored former soldiers that fought on behalf of homegrown fascists, alongside Nazi Germany. The first involves a gathering that some have called the Embroidery March, named for the traditional *Vyshyvanka*, an embroidered folk shirt. It normally occurs in the western Ukrainian city of Lviv on April 28, the founding anniversary of the 14th Waffen Grenadier Division of the SS in 1943, also called the Waffen-SS Galician (*Halychyna*) or the 1st

Galician. The second centers on a commemoration observed in Ukraine by German and other West European Waffen-SS veterans from the multinational "Germanic" Viking Division. Constrained by Germany's culture of contrition and unable to commemorate their lost comrades at home in Germany, memory challengers found a more receptive host in this post-communist, post-Soviet state.

Whether honoring fallen Ukrainian Waffen-SS members or Waffen-SS soldiers from other countries, these commemorations share an origin in veterans' organizations with Latvia, particularly those who became part of the post-World War II diaspora; they have been further legitimized by growing interest in the commemorations by right-wing groups, political parties, and leaders. Like their Latvian counterparts, commemorations of Ukrainian Waffen-SS members advance a narrative that whitewashes the role of homegrown fascists and Nazi collaborators, positing them as having defended Europe from communism. Whether these Ukrainian Waffen-SS soldiers were war criminals or freedom fighters has been debated by political actors inside as well as outside of Ukraine, sparking competing narratives about these soldiers and the meanings of World War II.

We turn first to the Ukrainian commemoration of the Waffen-SS Galician; comprising Ukrainian volunteers, it eventually numbered about eighteen thousand troops. This Division was founded in 1943 when significant losses at Stalingrad caused Nazi Germany to look for more fighters and to rethink its ban on integrating Slavic *Untermenschen* into its forces. Like the Latvian Legion, the Waffen-SS Galician as an organization was not found guilty of war crimes at Nuremberg or in subsequent investigations. While the Division itself was not initially found to have participated in crimes against humanity, many of its ranks had committed such crimes, particularly against Jews, prior to joining the Waffen-SS.

During the Cold War, competing narratives about the Division arose. In the Soviet Union, the soldiers were cast as fascist thugs, while outside the East Bloc, they were viewed more sympathetically as anti-Bolshevik freedom fighters. This was especially true in Canada and the United Kingdom, to which many POWs from the unit had emigrated (Khromeychuk 2012; Marples 2007). More recent scholarship has benefited from archival evidence not available during the Cold War; evidence suggests that the Division was involved in the massacre of about five hundred civilians, mostly women and children, at Huta Pieniacka on February 28, 1944. It likely took part in other atrocities both in eastern Galicia and in Slovakia, where the Division assisted the crushing the

Slovak National Uprising against the Germans and their puppet regime led by Tiso. As Per Anders Rudling asserts, "The division faithfully served Adolf Hitler, the unit's journal dispersed anti-Semitic propaganda until the very last days of the war" (2012, 360).

Ukrainians today are also divided over the memory of the Division: were the soldiers traitors, opportunists, and war criminals, or were they seeking only to defend the motherland (Khromeychuk 2012, 443)? The memory divide is largely geographical and ethnic in nature: Russian-speakers in the east prefer to characterize it as a celebration of the Red Army over Nazi invaders; Ukrainians in the west have embraced an anti-communist narrative. The commemoration of the Division as heroes has only been observed in the western part of Ukraine, that is, in Lviv, where in 2018 marchers displayed both Nazi symbols and the Nazi salute (*Times of Israel*, April 30, 2018). In 2021, for the first time, about three hundred people gathered in Kyiv for observance of the April 28 anniversary of the Galician's founding.

Seen elsewhere in post-communist Europe, the anti-communist narrative in this commemoration either equates communism and fascism, or openly presents the fascists as freedom fighters fit to be honored. The ultranationalist political party Svoboda has promoted a narrative of freedom fighters/resisters of communism who deserve reverence. Opposing them are Communists, Socialists, and other left-wing parties in Ukraine, such as the Party of the Regions under former prime minster Yanukovych. In places where the Waffen-SS Galicia is honored, rallies feature families in traditional Ukrainian dress, such as the *Vyshyvanka* shirt, along with others who wear Nazi SS uniforms and carry flags with Nazi or far-right symbols. Observing the commemoration in July 2013, journalist Maria Danilova offered this explanation: "In much of the post-Soviet Union, people generally do not receive strong education regarding Holocaust horrors. Such ignorance plays a strong role in events . . . that glorify Nazi imagery—and most participants do not belong to the hard right. The tendency to overlook Nazi crimes, however, does breed tolerance of the few neo-Nazi elements among them, and can also lead to vulnerability to the xenophobic rhetoric of parties such as Svoboda" (Danilova 2013). In other words, without the cultural constraints resulting from decades of Holocaust education and engagement with Europe's cosmopolitan memory, memory manipulators find little resistance. In the context of war waged by Russia against Ukraine in 2022, the "freedom fighters" trope is particularly appealing and even motivational. As discussed in later chapters, Putin has made "wiping out Nazis" a primary excuse for the invasion of Ukraine.

The Viking Division

A second significant commemoration takes place in eastern Ukraine in Uspenka, very close to the border with Russia. It centers on a graveyard where, during the last few years of the war, fallen soldiers of the Viking Division, who were German, Austrian, Belgian, Finnish, and Dutch—in other words, "Aryan," were buried. The cemetery was later destroyed by the Red Army and a field of potatoes was planted there. Just two years after the collapse of the USSR and the achievement of Ukrainian independence, three dozen elderly veterans and relatives of fallen Waffen-SS men gathered at the site to honor their comrades and to sing the official anthem of the SS, the *Treuelied*. By 2010, the potato field "had been transformed into an opulent memorial park" (Hurd and Werther 2016a, 331). It is a site where marches and ceremonies of veterans of the Viking Division do not draw the attention of authorities or the criticism of anti-fascist protestors, as they would in Western Europe or in most Eastern European members of the European Union. The veterans who traveled to Uspenka to commemorate their fallen comrades "were greeted as former brothers-in-arms, as Europeans against Bolshevism" (Hurd and Werther 2016b, 434). Whereas objections by authorities and civil society have led to declining attendance at the Ulrichsburg Gathering in Austria over time, post-communist societies seem to offer new possibilities for commemorating fallen soldiers of the Waffen-SS.

Consider the narrative supplied by these veterans and their supporters:

> The Waffen-SS had been no collection of brutes; it was a military elite, volunteering where others were drafted, fighting with terrific heroism . . . [it] had had nothing to do with war atrocities . . . had been completely apolitical; neither Nazi ideology nor racism, but love of country and of Europe, had fired (as they contended) these young men's breasts. The foreign recruits to the Waffen-SS, in particular, had fought to save both their own countries *and* all of Europe. All the Waffen-SS had, in fact, had but one goal in mind: to save Europe from the deadly Red Army of Bolshevism.[10]

Veterans and their supporters who perpetuate a "defenders of Europe, freedom fighters" memory have met no resistance in Uspenka. Indeed, veterans from the West and nationalists in the East have found common cause there: whitewashing their roles in the war as heroes and defenders of Europe. They

---

[10] Hurd and Wether 2016a, summarizing veterans' publications and discourse, p. 338.

also have developed a common appreciation for the ability to come out of the shadows—of the West European Holocaust-centered memory of World War II and of the former East Bloc's anti-fascism—in order to honor soldiers who, in their assessment, did not fight on the wrong side of the war; instead, they were vindicated by the collapse of communism.

It is rather ironic that the site of this Waffen-SS commemoration does not lie in western Ukraine, where Ukrainian nationalism is strongest, but rather in eastern Ukraine, where larger numbers of ethnic Russians might be expected to adhere to the Soviet/Russian grand narrative. The veterans from the West who traveled to Uspenka claimed to be agents of reconciliation in relation to former enemies and victims. Certainly, the invasion of Ukraine by Russia in February 2022 and the war that followed has put a stop to the "reconciliation" activities of the Waffen-SS veterans there. Russian propaganda before and during the war has focused on the presence of "Nazis" in Ukraine today. This narrative originated during Soviet times but it has been resurrected and amplified by Vladimir Putin, about which more is said in the next two chapters.

Neither of the two commemorations of Waffen-SS soldiers in Ukraine have been institutionalized by way of official sites or national days of remembrance, but they both represent the potential for transnational networks of history obfuscators, nationalists, and neo-Nazis to promulgate a revisionist narrative about the past.[11] That narrative whitewashes the past in service of a contemporary nationalist political agenda and an exclusivist vision for the nation and for Europe. It further serves to legitimate the memory challengers' own roles as patriots and defenders against communists/leftists/outsiders. These commemorations are part of a broader memory politics in a geographically and politically divided Ukraine, as well as between the governments of Ukraine and Russia.

As in Latvia, far-right groups, and especially their youth, have enthusiastically joined the commemorations, leading the veterans to "acknowledge this welcome addition of new blood" (Hurd and Werther 2016b, 442). Such rituals inspire and resonate with some local youth, who are nationalists, transnationally networked, and enjoy the spectacle of uniforms, flags, and celebrations of wartime battles. Please see Figure 3.2.

According to Hurd and Werther, "One can understand their adopting the Waffen-SS 'European' narrative of World War II; it provides them with historical legitimacy and an ultra-masculine ideal" (2016a, 351). Putting a positive

---

[11] Hurd and Werther note that transnational publications and websites unite "collectors, historical revisionists, war-buffs, would-be Nazis, and modern racist activists in narratives, pictures, and symbols" (2016a, 351).

Figure 3.2 Commemoration of the Waffen-SS in Ukraine
Source: AP Photo/Efrem Lukatsky.

spin on a questionable past has enabled some Ukrainians to feel pride and, perhaps, a sense of unity in a context of persistent instability and division. A similar dynamic is at work in Croatia and in Hungary, where commemorations of fascist forces from the war bring together a wide range of far-right actors.

Since many of the surviving members of the Galician Division emigrated to the West after 1945, it is not surprising that the memory contestation regarding the Division has also taken place outside of Ukraine. Some veterans became prominent public figures in the diaspora, including academics at Canadian and West German universities.[12] In 1985, the Canadian Government established a formal Commission of Inquiry on War Criminals in Canada, known as the Deschênes Commission. In the course of its work, the Deschênes Commission investigated the activities of the Galician Division more closely. Inside Canada, the commission's work heightened tensions between Jewish groups

---

[12] For example, Per Anders Rudling reports that, in 2011, the Canadian Institute of Ukrainian Studies at the University of Alberta "funded primarily by donations from diaspora donors, instituted three new endowments in the names of leading Waffen-SS veterans." See his article "'They Defended Ukraine': The 14. Waffen-Grenadier-Division der SS (Galizische Nr. 1) Revisited." *The Journal of Slavic Military Studies*, Vol. 25, No. 3: 329–68.

and Ukrainian groups, with the latter complaining that the commission's assertion that over seven hundred war criminals still lived inside Canada were grossly inflated. More recently, in 2018, more than fifty members of the US Congress signed a letter condemning the glorification of the Galician Division and the Ukrainian Insurgent Army (UPA).[13] The Israeli foreign minister and many Ukrainian Jews have moreover protested the commemoration of the Galician Division.[14]

Had it not been for the war in Ukraine, these external actors might have continued to influence some opinions inside Ukraine, but this is probably no longer the case. The Russian war against Ukraine increased the sense that the Galician Division symbolizes patriotic resistance to threats to Ukrainian national sovereignty.

Croatian Memory Challengers at Bleiburg

The collapse of communism was not the only cataclysmic event to spark a reassessment of World War II and its aftermath in post-communist Eastern Europe; added to this was the disintegration of three multinational states. While the USSR and Czechoslovakia dissolved without significant violence, the Yugoslav state fell apart as a result of a series of civil wars. Vjeran Pavlakovic observes that, "In many ways, the Yugoslav wars of the 1990s were a continuation of the unresolved conflicts from World War Two, and certainly the discourse of the warring sides were saturated with references to Partisans, Ustaše, and Cetniks" (2010, 2).

The three groups Pavlaković referenced played important roles during the war, particularly after the occupation of the Kingdom of Yugoslavia in 1941 by German, Italian, Hungarian, Bulgarian, and Albanian forces. The Partisans were a pan-Yugoslav anti-occupation resistance organized by the Communist Party of Yugoslavia and led by Josip Tito. The Četniks were a guerrilla organization that had aligned themselves with Serbian nationalists and Yugoslav royalists, while the Ustaše, or Croatian Revolutionary Movement, was a staunchly Catholic, nationalist organization that sought an independent Croatian state. After the Axis invasion and occupation of Yugoslavia, the Ustaše proclaimed an Independent State of Croatia (Nezavisna Drzava Hrvatska/NDH) which was, in fact, a puppet of Nazi Germany. The Ustaše

---

[13] Pugliese 2019.
[14] See Cnaan Liphshiz's reporting in *The Times of Israel*, "Hundreds in Ukraine Attend Marches Celebrating Nazi SS Soldiers," May 4, 2021.

terrorized and murdered hundreds of thousands of Serbs, Jews, and Roma, all of whom it deemed racially inferior. Many of those murders occurred at the Jasenovac concentration and extermination camp run by the Ustaše. One of the central memory struggles in Croatia since the 1990s has been the role of the fascist Ustaše: were they Nazi collaborators who directed their own genocidal campaign against Serbs, Jews, and Roma, or were they anti-communist resistors and victims of Partisan revenge?

While Yugoslavia existed from 1945 to 1990, the memory of World War II remained frozen and de-ethnicized, focusing steadfastly on the heroism of the Tito-led Partisans (Gödl 2007, 44). As Yugoslavia imploded over the course of three phases of civil war in the 1990s, wartime memories were re-ethnicized and instrumentalized to emphasize old slights and to support the narrative of national renewal and independence. Newly independent, Croatia's first leader Franjo Tudjman officially supported a "reconciliation" of memory between anti-fascist Partisans and pro-fascist Ustaše, but in practice, official memory favored a more "useable" reinterpretation of the Ustaše (Pavlaković 2009, 126). Tudjman instrumentalized the memory of Croat suffering at the hands of the Partisans and Serb nationalist Četniks. Serbian leader Slobodan Milosovic did the same with the memory of Serb victims of Ustaše-led killings at Jasenovac. In that atmosphere, a commemoration of Croatian forces, including many Ustaše who were killed at a place called Bleiburg, emerged from the shadows and gained importance on the nationalist right in Croatia.

Like other commemorations discussed thus far, this one focuses on events that occurred during the last days of the war, centering on questions of who did what to whom and in what numbers. There are several commemorations of wartime events in Croatia, but Bleiburg is the only one that takes place outside of the country, in Austria, and for reasons explained below, it is organized by a private organization registered in Austria rather than in Croatia. Another striking feature of the Bleiburg commemoration has been its large size, averaging between nine and ten thousand participants, peaking at fifteen thousand in 1995 on the fiftieth anniversary of the Bleiburg events.

The origins of the Bleiburg myth

Bleiburg is a small Austrian town near the Slovenian border where in May of 1945 the retreating forces of the Ustaše and NDH forces, along with Montenegrin, Serbian, and Slovene Nazi collaborators, surrendered to the British, hoping to escape retribution by their communist foes. The British, however, refused to accept their surrender and extradited them to areas controlled by their allies, the Partisans. While the Partisans executed some on the spot, other Ustaše leaders, military forces, and accompanying civilians endured a march back to Yugoslavia, called by Croatian nationalists the "Way of the Cross death marches," remembered thereafter as martyrs for the Croatian state (Pavlaković 2009, 4). During the final battles of the war, the Partisans executed these Croatian forces in Slovenia and elsewhere across Yugoslavia. Bleiburg, Austria became the site for mobilizing the memory of the killings, however, since a memorialization of fascists' deaths at the hands of communists was unthinkable in communist Yugoslavia. During the Cold War, that chapter of wartime killing was suppressed by the Tito regime. Pal Kolstø makes an important point about Yugoslav official silence:

> [T]he Titoist regime suppressed information about the Bleiburg massacre and denied the Croats the possibility to come to terms with this trauma. Mythologies thrive in a culture of silence and suppression ... In this situation, it was Bleiburg survivors and other Ustasa sympathizers abroad who kept the memory of Bleiburg and they were able to present their version of the event unchecked. When it finally became possible to talk about the Bleiburg killings openly in Croatia after 1990, the basic premises for the commemoration were already in place.
>
> (2010, 1154)

It was Croatian émigrés who began organizing in the early postwar years, gathering as close to site of their comrades' deaths as they could—in neighboring Austria. The first commemoration ceremony occurred at Bleiburg on November 1, 1952, All Saints Day. That year Croatian World War II veterans formed the Bleiburg Honorary Guard (PBV) for the purpose of organizing the annual commemoration. The PBV met twice a year, on All Saints Day and on the closest Sunday to May 15. Only the May 15 event became a major commemoration. Despite pressure from British and Yugoslav authorities, Austrian officials did not prevent the commemoration from occurring (Kolstø 2010, 1159). In the mid-1960s, the PBV purchased some land on Bleiburg Field, renovated the graves of Croat soldiers, and eventually erected a monument with the inscription, "In Honor and Glory of the Fallen Croatian Army, May 1945" (Pavlaković and Pauković 2019, 14). In 2004, the inscription was changed to "In Memory of Innocent Victims of the Bleiburg Tragedy May 1945," reflecting the shift in the official memory to a victim-centered one.

Now broadcast on Croatian television each year, the commemoration has developed into a "cross between a religious service and a secular, political demonstration" (Kolstø 2010, 1159). Activities begin at a church and cemetery outside of the Bleiburg Field where a Catholic priest leads a procession to the site of the surrender. Originally, the Croatian graves at the cemetery were decorated with Ustaše helmets, though they were later removed. The gathering features the singing of the Croatian national anthem and observation of a minute of silence for the victims, followed by a Catholic requiem mass, on a stage especially built for the delivery of speeches and a mass. The speeches at Bleiburg are frequently tinged with nationalism, and re-presentation of the NDH forces as freedom fighters. The earlier lip service to "reconciliation" is largely gone. In 2018, the president of the Croatian Parliament (the Sabor) tried to resurrect that earlier message when he ended his official remarks with the words, "we all must contribute to further successful democratic development of our one and only Croatia," to which there was no applause, only some booing from the audience (Hopkins 2018). Along the side of the commemoration stage, venders sell food, drinks, and souvenirs with Ustaše symbols and references to the NDH (Pavlaković and Pauković 2019, 15). Participants often wear military uniforms, shirts featuring a U (for Ustaše) with a grenade inside it; they moreover carry flags with the checkerboard coat of arms of the NDH, banned by Austrian officials since 2020 (Vladislavljevic 2020).

Croatians from inside Croatia began attending the commemoration—and the media began reporting on it—in 1990, marking the forty-fifth anniversary of the Bleiburg surrender. The commemoration began to acquire more official recognition when it gained the attention of the Croatian Democratic Union party (HDZ), founded in 1989 by Franjo Tudjman. A former Partisan and historian, Tudjman claimed to find value in the commemoration as a vehicle for "reconciling" various nationalities, although he did not attend the commemorations himself. Perhaps sensing the commemoration's potential as a flashpoint, "he decided that it was wiser to control it rather than allow his political opponents to use it against him" (Pavlaković 2010, 19). Despite official rhetoric, the Bleiburg commemoration remained a right-wing event. The Sabor assumed organizational control in 1995, in time for the fiftieth anniversary of the Bleiburg surrender.

The political nature of the commemoration is clearly reflected in its official name and its changing status. The conservative Croatian Democratic Union (HDZ)-led Sabor named May 15 (or the closest Sunday to it) the "Day of Remembrance of Croatian Victims in the Struggle for Freedom and Independence." Following a shift in power in 2012 to a center-left coalition led by the

Social Democratic Party of Croatia (SPD), state sponsorship of the event was withdrawn. When subsequent elections in 2015 bought a new "Patriotic Coalition" consisting of the HDZ and several right-wing parties, state sponsorship was re-instated.

The growing cast of memory challengers

The initial memory actors creating the Bleiburg myth and organizing the annual commemoration were veterans found in the Croatian diaspora, particularly those who had survived the battles at the end of the war and the comrades and families of those who had been killed. The Bleiburg Honorary Guard served as the organizational arm of those memory actors. Since the Yugoslav wars of the 1990s, renewed attention to the Bleiburg myth and the commemoration has come from Croatian nationalists, who have forged a connection between the struggles of the 1940s and those of the 1990s. This obsession with the events of May 1945 serves to further divide Croatia along the ideological left-right spectrum and also evinces ethno-national dimensions. Memory challengers at Bleiburg use the past to legitimize a right-wing nationalist culture and identity for independent and democratic Croatia.

As already noted, since Tudjman assumed leadership of the party and the country, the HDZ has walked a fine line between embracing revisionist narratives of the fascist past and giving lip service to reconciling divided memories. Some party members have cautioned against providing overt support for fascist symbols or rhetoric though, in general, the party's ambivalence about the Bleiburg commemoration is itself noteworthy. Other right-wing parties from the 1990s, like the Croatian Party of Rights (HSP), proudly defended the honor of the Ustaše and have supported a restoration of the Ustaše slogan, "For the homeland—ready!" for the Croatian army (Czerwinski 2016). Participants from the United Croatian Rightists call for the removal of references to anti-fascism from the Croatian constitution (Hopkins 2018).

Right-wing Catholic clergy have also supported the Bleiburg myth and have lent legitimacy to the commemoration by holding a Catholic mass each year. The Bleiburg myth itself carries religious overtones: the people killed there are characterized not just as victims but as martyrs who died for Croatian independence. Bleiburg has been labeled the Croatian Calvary, and the path the marchers in May 1945 took from Austria to Yugoslavia has been called the "stations of the cross" (Kolstø 2010, 1155). In a May 2008 sermon, one bishop declared Bleiburg "the first station of the cross. At the first station Pilate condemned Jesus to death," just as the sons of Croatia were condemned to death at Bleiburg (1170). Finally, the people who gather at the site each year are called "pilgrims," and Bleiburg Field is called a "holy place." In 1995, the speaker of the Croatian Sabor called Bleiburg "the Holocaust of Croatian Martyrs, who sacrificed their lives for the idea of Croatian statehood" (1171). The role of Catholic clergy has sparked outrage among other Catholics in Europe, including the Catholic Diocese in nearby Gurk-Klagenfurt, Austria. When the 2020 commemoration at Bleiburg was cancelled due to Austrian pandemic restrictions, the event was shifted to Sarajevo where Cardinal Vinko Puljic, the Roman Catholic Archbishop of Vrhbosna, held a mass. Thousands of people protested in Sarajevo. When asked about the protests against his attendance, the Cardinal told a Catholic radio show, "the Church has always respected innocent victims" (DW May 16, 2020).

Also notable is Bleiburg's location in the southern state of Carinthia, where the late FPÖ leader Jörg Haider had served as governor. For much of the postwar period, staunchly conservative Carinthian political and church leaders had tolerated the Bleiburg commemoration. That has changed in recent years once the FPÖ began to lose its grip on regional politics; it is no longer in the national governing coalition. Subotic noted that the attention the Bleiburg commemoration has brought to Austria has been unwelcome and uncomfortable, given Austria's own challenges in dealing with its fascist past. A coalition of various groups in Austria has repeatedly tried to have the commemoration banned (Strickland 2018). Others have monitored the activities and posted photographs and videos of attendees making the Hitler salute or wearing or carrying fascist symbols. Because the commemoration serves several functions, conservative groups and parties continue to attend and support it, even at the risk of damaging relations with neighboring Austria and with the European Union.

Memory challengers' aims and approaches

The aims of the right-wing organizers and attendees at the Bleiburg commemoration include deflecting from the collaboration with Nazis and the atrocities committed by Croatian nationalists during the war and creating a sense of Croatian national pride and identity. Historical revisionism regarding the fascist past has two benefits for Croatian nationalists: First, it removes the stigma of association with racism and fascism, ideologies that run contrary to the postwar European mainstream and particularly the European Union, which

Croatia joined in 2013. Whitewashing the Ustaše and the NDH as patriotic resistance fighters, not only erases the ugliness of the 1940s, it also makes it possible to see present-day nationalists, and those who fought for Croatian independence in the 1990s, as descendants of a long tradition of Croatian patriots.

Secondly, Bleiburg has been used to blackwash the Partisans and Yugoslav communism as the brutal oppressors of Croatian culture and identity. According to this interpretation, the Croats were not perpetrators but rather the victims of Serb Četniks and pan-Yugoslav communists. As Subotic observed, "An important piece of Croatia's new identity construction post-1991 was a complete rejection of the communist past and conflation of this past with Serbian hegemony" (2018, 304). Whitewashing the fascist crimes of the past and blackwashing communists are strategies used to strengthen the legitimacy of the right-wing in Croatia's political system by connecting their vision of Croatia to "the pre-communist, mythically 'nationally pure' character of its statehood" (Subotic 2018, 305).

There are several ways in which memory challengers use the Bleiburg commemoration to distract from Croatians' perpetrator role and to claim Croatian national victimhood. In the 1990s, there was a discernable shift in rhetoric from "fallen soldiers" to "civilian victims," including those subject to communist oppression over four decades. Bleiburg has been perceived by memory revisionists as an exclusively Croatian site of memory, and its casualties as innocent and civilian victims. The number and identity of those killed has nonetheless been inflated and debated, with estimates on the left ranging in the tens of thousands, to those on the right who claim hundreds of thousands. Historians believe that among the two-hundred thousand soldiers who tried to enter Austria to surrender to the British, about seventy thousand were killed by Partisans, of whom about fifty thousand were Croatian (Kolstø 2019, 1157). Nonetheless, Bleiburg has been perceived as an exclusively Croatian memory site, symbolizing their "greatest tragedy," a "deliberate genocide against Croats," and a "Croatian Holocaust" (Pavlaković 2010, 131).

Analogy is a common approach utilized by memory challengers at Bleiburg. The Bleiburg commemoration is infused with religious overtones, describing "martyrs for Croatian independence" and "the Croatian Calvary." It is considered a place of pilgrimage and Bleiburg Field a "holy place." These memory challengers frequently appropriate the term "Holocaust" to memorialize Croatian fascists. Further examples of obfuscation include the focus on Croatian suffering while conveniently forgetting that the captured and killed included Montenegrins, Serbs, Slovenes, Cossacks, and Germans. Another example

centers on the inversion of the role of Ustaše agents as victims rather than perpetrators, avoiding the truth that the Ustaše consisted of collaborators with the
Nazis, homegrown fascists and racists. Croat nationalists likewise forget that
the NDH passed its own racial laws and carried out state-sponsored murders.
Bleiburg has a Serbian counterpart, Jasenovac, serving as the Ustaše concentration and extermination camp where thousands of Serbs, Jews, Roma, and
anti-fascist Croats were killed. As Pavlaković has argued, the myth of Bleiburg
separates events of surrender and massacre in May 1945 from the four years
of warfare that preceded it (2009, 8).

Finally, relativism and insider-outsider framing are additional tools in the
Bleiburg memory challengers' toolkit. When these right-wing memory challengers invoke the Jasenovac camp, they do so to construct a comparison that
hides more than it reveals. It offers an example of what aboutism—"sure Jasenovac, but what about Bleiburg?" The two sites of memory are often compared.
Todor Kuljić points out reasons why such a comparison is problematic:

> Jasenovac is an example of violence and Bleiburg an example of counter-
> violence; the former an act of fascist and the latter an act of anti-fascist crime.
> There are also various motives for killing: in the former case, they were bio-
> logical and racist, and in the latter case, it was the actual or alleged dangerous
> conduct rather than anything related to race or biology.
>
> (in Luthar 2017, 111)

As a strategy, Kuljić argues that this kind of comparison of crimes serves
to trivialize and distract: "The crimes of one's own group are almost subcon-
sciously minimized or relativized by accentuating the crimes of others: Dresden vs. Auschwitz, German refugees from the East vs. the German genocide,
Hitler vs. Stalin, Bleiburg vs. Jasenovac" (113).

Ultimately, the intentions and actions of right-wing memory challengers
in Croatia reveal a great deal about the fragility of post-communist Croatian identity. Transcending the shame of fascism and ignoring painful truths
about complicity, silence, and victimhood has allowed people to reimagine
themselves as well as overcome dissonant memories. Casting the national
community as a victim and resistance force against communists and Serbs in
the 1940s as well as the 1990s helps to create a sense of continuity with the
past, along with a sense of shared fate. It is a way of drawing a clear historical
distinction between insiders and outsiders.

Compounding the discomfort of a deeply divided society in the early 1990s
was the role of external actors. The International Criminal Tribunal for the

former Yugoslavia (ICTY) shed a negative light on war crimes committed by Croatian militias in the 1990s, thus inflaming the conservative-nationalist victim narrative of Croatia's memory challengers. The European Union soon followed with expectations that Croatia hand over suspected war criminals to the ICTY, enact many reforms and, especially, adhere to human rights practices and norms. Some may have resented these actors simply because they were outsiders making demands on Croatia. Even more significant, both of these actors exacerbated the existing ontological insecurity surrounding the events of World War II and Holocaust—events that had long been repressed or distorted—giving them a contemporary relevance. By insisting that Croatia examine its past, external actors created more discomfort, particularly for nationalist-conservatives, who had tried to link the 1940s and 1990s in the service of patriotism, rather than to introspection. That the Bleiburg commemoration persisted throughout the ICTY proceedings and the EU accession processes suggests its powerful role in strengthening Croatian identity and projecting Croatian independence.

Reactions to the Bleiburg commemoration

Inside Croatia there have been few cultural and institutional constraints to counter the distortions outlined above, although some protestors have mobilized. The most significant reactions have come from the international community, particularly from Austria (where the commemoration occurs) and from the Council of Europe. In the weeks before the 2018 Bleiburg commemoration, three Austrian members of the European Parliament held a press conference with representatives of the Documentation Archive of Austrian Resistance, the Austrian Mauthausen Committee, and Austria's Jewish community to condemn the event. One Austrian official called the commemoration "Europe's largest fascist meeting," while another labeled it "an outrageous provocation" for the Jewish community.[15] That year five Croatians were arrested at the commemoration, then convicted by Austrian authorities for displaying Nazi salutes and shouting Ustaše chants.[16] In 2020, the Council of Europe released a statement about the commemoration, declaring it would "fly in the face of the ideals and principles of antifascism on

---

[15] Sven Milekic, "Austrian MEPs Call Croatian Memorial 'Platform for Extremists,'" *Balkan Insight*, April 24, 2018, https://balkaninsight.com/2018/04/24/austrian-meps-protest-europe-s-largest-fascist-meeting-04-24-2018/.

[16] Sven Milekic, "Croatians Convicted of Doing Nazi Salutes in Austria," *Balkan Insight*, July 5, 2018.

which European countries have been built after WWII, and deal a severe blow to the efforts towards reconciliation in the region."[17] In 2021, a group of experts advised the Austrian Interior Ministry to ban the gathering at Bleiburg.[18]

A member of the European Union since 2013, Croatia remained impervious to international criticism. In 2018, the Council of Europe's Commission against Racism and Intolerance published a report on Croatia, finding that, "Racist and intolerant hate speech in public discourse is escalating; the main targets are Serbs, LGBT persons and Roma. There is a growing rise of nationalism, particularly among the youth, which primarily takes the form of praising the fascist Ustaša regime ... The responses of the Croatian authorities to these incidents cannot be considered fully adequate" (ECRI Report on Croatia 2018, 9). Similarly, in 2020 Freedom House reported that, "Jewish communities and other groups have expressed increasing concern about Holocaust denial and displays by right-wing nationalists of symbols and slogans associated with the fascist Ustaša regime that governed Croatia during World War II. Revisionist accounts of the Ustaša period continued to be promoted by far-right groups and newspapers in 2021" (Freedom House 2022). While the Bleiburg commemoration of the Ustaše and the NDH "martyrs" has not centered on the Austria site due to pandemic restrictions and the subsequent ban, it has shifted to a new military memorial graveyard at the central Mirogoj cemetery in the capital Zagreb (Grgurinovic 2021).

The Siege of Budapest—The Hungarian Day of Honor

Like the Bleiburg gathering and the Remembrance Day of the Latvian Legionnaires, this commemoration marks a single event, the February 11, 1945, Festung Budapest, or siege of Budapest, comprising a failed attempt by German and Hungarian forces to resist a takeover of the city by the Red Army. February 11 was a key date in the battle, reportedly "plucked . . . out of the history books as a day of Nazi mourning" by Istvan Györkös in 1997 (Szijaro and Schwartzburg 2020). A neo-Nazi and self-proclaimed "Hungarist," a reference to the interwar fascist ideology, Györkös founded a paramilitary group in 1989 called the Hungarian National Front; the latter is known to have ties to

---

[17] Commissioner for Human Rights, Council of Europe, May 15, 2020.
[18] Matea Grgurinovic, "Austrian Interior Ministry Advised to Ban Croats' WWII Bleiburg Event," *Balkan Insight*, November 24, 2021.

transnational networks of extremists and encouraged by Russia.[19] He led the organization until 2016, when he was arrested and subsequently found guilty of murdering a policeman, for which he is serving a life sentence.

Unlike other commemorations examined thus far, this one is overtly fascist, having been created by and for neo-Nazis. It is not an official day of remembrance, but it is tolerated by the government of Viktor Orban, whose memory politics emphatically embrace a conservative-nationalist (increasingly authoritarian and illiberal) and revisionist narrative that focuses on enemies and dabbles in conspiracy theories. I include the so-called Hungarian Day of Honor among the commemorations of fallen World War II soldiers, because it has become an annual event that seeks to hyper-nationalize memory of the war and its aftermath. When the commemoration of the siege of Budapest began in 1997, it attracted only a few dozen neo-Nazis. By 2009, the event was attracting about two thousand marchers, having become an annual gathering of neo-Nazi groups from all over Europe.[20] One of the organizers in recent years is Legio Hungaria, a far-right group founded in 2018 known to have attacked a Jewish community center in Budapest in 2019. Other participating groups include the Hungarian Hammerskins,[21] Blood and Honor Hungary,[22] and the Party for National Revolution (Hurd and Werther 2016a, 342).

Still an unofficial day of remembrance, the event it commemorates and the hyper-nationalist tenor of the annual gathering are not out of step with the Orban government's memory politics since 2010. Orban and his Fidesz Party typically conflate the totalitarian regimes of the Nazis and the Soviet-style communists (e.g., reflected in the Terror Museum in Budapest), emphasizing Hungarian national victimhood as well as heroism in the face of threats from outsiders. In the past, the threats were attributed to occupation and from foreign cultural influences. Today, they come from globalization, transnational institutions, progressive norms, and migrants and refugees. Historians and journalists close to the Orban government help to construct a memory narrative in the service of national unity and Orban's brand of illiberalism. The official narration invoking Hungarian collective memory focuses relatively

---

[19] "Intent on Unsettling EU Russia Taps Foot Soldiers from the Fringe," *New York Times* (December 24, 2016), https://www.nytimes.com/2016/12/24/world/europe/intent-on-unsettling-eu-russia-taps-foot-soldiers-from-the-fringe.html.

[20] Reuters report February 14, 2009, https://www.reuters.com/article/idINIndia-38018720090214

[21] Little is known about this group, though Hammerskin groups of white supremacists exist in the United States and are known to travel abroad to attend neo-Nazi gatherings.

[22] This neo-Nazi group was founded in the United Kingdom and has affiliates in several European countries. Its name comes from *"Blut und Ehre,"* the motto of the Hitler Youth.

little on World War II; instead, it is obsessed with the Trianon Treaty of 1920 that reduced the Hungarian territory by two-thirds and its population by 60 percent after World War I and, to a lesser extent, the 1956 Hungarian Revolution. In the case of Trianon, the official memory blames outsiders, namely Western powers, for failing to respect the integrity of the Hungarian nation; in the case of 1956, it emphasizes the West's failure to answer Hungary's cry for help in the face of Soviet oppression. These fixations hold important implications for World War II remembrance. Eva Kovács contends that "Trianon is inseparably linked to the history of Hungarian nationalism, anti-Semitism and the Shoah. If the current trauma of Trianon retains its hegemonic position in Hungarian social memory . . . it will block, as we actually see in Hungarian politics of memory, the reckoning with the past" (2016, 531). Orban brazenly displayed his revisionist memory politics by wearing a scarf showing a map of "Greater Hungary" to a football match in November 2022.

Focusing on national honor and strength, especially heroic anti-communism, the Orban government has embraced a nostalgia for Admiral Miklos Horthy's interwar rule (Berend 2006). According to Benazzo, "Being considered the last fully sovereign Hungarian regime before the communist take-over, it became a reference for Fidesz" (2017, 204). Orban and his party have whitewashed Horthy and other interwar Hungarian elites, minimizing their role in the persecution of Hungarian Jews and their active collaboration with Nazi officials, and even "arguing that they were victims of the German occupation . . . and most assuredly not their allies" (Benazzo 2017, 204). A slew of anti-Semitic attacks in the Hungarian media have portrayed Jews as responsible for communism in Hungary and as a persistent threat to the Hungarian nation (Berend 2006, 172–5).

Orban's disdain for political liberalism, what Michael Shafir has called his "radical conservatism" (2006, 270), coupled with his open embrace of Putin's style of Russian illiberalism have further distanced Orban from the European cosmopolitan Holocaust memory. It has also inclined Orban to temper the focus of his memory politics on the crimes of the Soviet Union and, by extension, Hungarian communism—something that seems less important in the face of a collapsing left in Hungary. The delicate skirting around the complexities of twentieth-century conflicts and alliances has one constant: Hungarian nationalism. In this context, the cultural constraints on right-wing and even neo-Nazi commemorations have been significantly relaxed. The government need not officially mark the commemoration of the Siege of Budapest in order to bestow it with legitimacy.

Rituals and rhetoric of the "Day of Honor"

The seventy-fifth anniversary of the Siege of Budapest was commemorated in 2020 by several hundred far-right attendees. Many participants dressed in black, others in German military uniforms, and carried banners of their various neo-Nazi organizations. They gathered in a park which had been the site of a bloody battle in 1945. The site was also where the Arrow Cross death squads had killed elderly Jews from a nearby home for the aged on January 12, 1945. One of the speeches quoted lines from Hitler (without attribution). Another claimed, "We have the same enemies today, like we did 75 years ago . . . The enemy isn't named Muller or Mayer. No, our enemy is named Rothschild or Goldman and Sachs."[23]

Later at the 2020 commemoration, several neo-Nazi bands held a concert, while a "memorial hike" was organized by an association publicly funded by the Orban government's Ministry of Human Resources, whose leaders own a media company that produced a documentary "glorifying Hungary's role in World War II" (Szijaro and Schwartzburg 2020).[24] Intended to replicate the path that SS and Hungarian soldiers had taken in February 1945, the hike was attended by over three thousand people. Among them were people dressed in military and SS uniforms and who displayed extremist symbols, including swastikas. These rituals not only feature symbols and discourse meant to create solidarity among members of neo-Nazi groups; the concert and hike are intended to attract a wider audience and engage them in rituals meant to create comfort and affinity with symbols of white supremacy.

Like other memory challengers discussed here, these groups see themselves as continuing the mission of their wartime fascist heroes. They carry banners proclaiming "Heroes of Europe," presumably about the German and Hungarian "defenders" of Budapest but likely also referring to themselves. They see Hungarian and Europeans as threatened by outsiders. As Pax Hungaria member Janos Endre Domokos stated at the 2009 commemoration, "Europe's old inhabitants, losing their traditions, have been reduced to existing here on the margins."[25] The narrative behind the Siege of Budapest commemoration glorifies the fascist past but also constructs a clear division between insiders—ethnic Hungarians and white, Christian Europeans—and outsiders.

---

[23] Michael Colborne, "Neo-Nazis from across Europe Rally in Budapest," *Al-Jazeera* (February 8, 2020), https://www.aljazeera.com/news/2020/2/8/neo-nazis-from-across-europe-rally-in-budapest

[24] See also https://hungarianspectrum.org/tag/legio-hungaria/.

[25] Reported by Reuters, February 14, 2009, https://www.reuters.com/article/idINIndia-38018720090214.

Interestingly, the commemoration does not weaponize anti-communism. The whitewashing of the fascist, collaborationist past is not harnessed as a companion to blackwashing but rather as a way to distinguish between Hungarian nationalist interpretations of the war and the European cosmopolitan memory. Wartime memory is renationalized to legitimate an illiberal understanding of identity and belonging in Hungary today.

Reactions to far-right mobilization

The Budapest commemoration seems to elicit less media attention than others described thus far, most likely owing to Orban's curbing of independent media in Hungary and the normalization of extreme nationalist rhetoric in the country's public sphere. Several anti-fascist groups routinely seek to have the commemoration banned; anti-fascist protestors moreover turn out every year to oppose the neo-Nazis and their revisionist narrative. Budapest police tolerated the gathering of extremists until 2022, when the commemoration was banned, citing police concerns about violence between those marking the event and those protesting it.[26] Despite the ban, the commemoration resumed on February 11, 2023, with opposing demonstrations organized by Legio Hungaria and other far-right groups and groups of counterdemonstrators. Each side attracted hundreds of participants, including some who came in from outside of Hungary. Demonstrators clashed in several parts of the city, with both sides as well as bystanders reporting injuries (*The Budapest Times*, February 13, 2023).

National Cursed Soldiers Remembrance Day in Poland

The final commemoration in Eastern Europe included here entails a clear-cut case of blackwashing the communist past by whitewashing, indeed, reifying anti-communist resistors who had engaged in war crimes. In this case, the primary is the ruling Law and Justice party (PiS), a right-wing populist and nationalist-conservative descendant of the Solidarity trade union. Kristen Ghodsee describes efforts "to paint the communist era as unequivocally evil, to ignore or belittle inconvenient historical facts that might explain

---

[26] Nermina Kuloglija, "Hungary Bans Annual Neo-Nazi Gathering in Budapest," *Balkan Insight*, February 2, 2022.

(or at the very least complicate) the actions of the communist governments that came to power after WWII."[27] The National Cursed Soldiers[28] Remembrance Day of March 1st constitutes a prime example of a glorification of "anti-communist heroes" that has become central to PiS's memory politics. This commemoration celebrates Polish soldiers who waged underground resistance to the Soviet occupation after the war. Some of those partisans had committed war crimes against civilians during the war, however, many of whom were Jewish, Ukrainian, Belarussian, and Slovakian minorities.

The context in which this commemoration developed reflects a growing polarization of politics in Poland with roots in the transition from communism itself. On one end are the moderate successors of the Solidarity movement, such as the Civic Platform, as well as the former communist party, now known as Social Democrats. This segment of Polish political elites and voters are more accepting of the European Holocaust-centered narrative of World War II and of pluralistic and critical discussions about the past. On the other side is PiS as well as smaller, more extreme right parties. PiS, in particular, pushes back against the memory of contrition in favor of one that emphasizes Polish suffering, martyrdom, and righteous resistance to outsiders. The party also dabbles freely in conspiracy theories, particularly since the 2010 airplane crash in Smolensk that killed numerous members of the Polish political class, including PiS co-founder and national President (2005–2010) Lech Kaczyński. Since then, PiS has harnessed Polish memory to strengthen its own legitimacy and to marginalize opponents. The official memory culture, discourages truthful examination of the past; one can only portray Poles as victims or heroes, never as perpetrators.

The term "cursed" or "doomed" soldiers (*żołnierze wyklęci*) was coined in the first decade after communism collapsed in 1989; it referred to partisan units, or "forest brothers," who fought the Red Army during the war and continued to fight against the communist authorities until 1947. Some Poles sympathetically referred to the units as "cursed," because the postwar communist regime stigmatized them. March 1 marks the date in 1951 when communist authorities executed the last seven leaders of the partisan group. Despite the current government's branding of the "cursed soldiers" as innocent heroes, that characterization has long been disputed. Before 1989, Polish communist authorities claimed that these partisan fighters had engaged in the

---

[27] Kristen Ghodsee, "Blackwashing History," *Anthropology News*, 2013.
[28] Also known as "accursed," "doomed," and "indomitable."

killing of an estimated ten thousand Polish civilians, twelve thousand Polish security forces, and a thousand Soviet soldiers, though the exact numbers and identities are unknown (Kończal 2020, 69). In the convoluted memory politics emerging after the collapse of communism in Eastern Europe, the enemy of the communists was remade as a hero of the anti-communists. The result has been a whitewashing of wartime atrocities committed by the partisans in an effort to blackwash the communist period, in this case the postwar regime's interpretation of the partisans and their activities.

While these fighters were not necessarily fascists or part of the Waffen-SS, their emergence as a national cause célèbre followed a similar pattern as that witnessed in Croatia, Latvia, and Ukraine. As long as Poland was ruled by communists, the partisans were remembered as bandits and reactionaries (Darasz 2018, 138). Polish émigrés, often themselves former partisans, had already begun to challenge the official communist narrative in the 1970s, as did some dissidents inside Poland. After 1989, the partisans became a focus, almost an obsession, of historians and civil society actors, such as the We Remember organization; the latter involves itself in commemorative activities, such as the restoration of tombstones and the creation of plaques and monuments to the post-war partisans (Kończal 2020, 72). With the help of the Institute of National Remembrance (IPN), a state research institute founded in 1998 to investigate crimes of Nazism and communism and now a conservative appendage of the PiS government, the We Remember organization transformed "the cursed" into a symbol of national honor.[29] As Gregorz Wasowski, chairman of We Remember, insists on his website, "The term 'Doomed Soldiers' is also an indictment against the media elites of the III Republic of Poland: an indictment for their conscientious omission, and elimination of this dramatic and heroic chapter of our history—an indictment for amputating history, written in blood and suffering by those who fought and died for [Poland's] freedom."[30] This kind of patriotic hyperbole is typical of Polish right-wing organizations.[31] Next to this quotation taken from the We Remember website is an undated photograph of Adam Michnik, editor of *Gazeta Wyborcza*, shaking hands with Czesław Kiszczak of the Polish Secret Police.

---

[29] The IPN is one of a handful of memory institutes that emerged in post-communist countries to research and, in some cases, prosecute crimes committed under periods of totalitarian oppression. The IPN sees its mission as helping to "popularize" modern Polish history. See the IPN website https://ipn.gov.pl/en. See also Valentin Behr's "How Historians Got Involved in Memory Politics: Patterns of the Historiography of the Polish People's Republic before and after 1989," *East European Politics and Societies*, Vol. 36, No. 3 (2022): 970–91.

[30] http://www.doomedsoldiers.com/doomed-soldiers-memorial-day.html

[31] See the essays in Jo Harper (ed.) *Poland's Memory Wars: Essays on Illiberalism* (CEU Press 2018).

The message is clear: leftist intellectuals and the communist regime's secret police were unpatriotic collaborators.

Associated rituals

The soldiers were included in the IPN's major publication, the *Atlas of the Independence Underground in Poland* (2007), "considered to be one of the main triggers of a broad social interest in the post-war partisan struggle" (Kończal 2020, 73). Interest in the commemoration has certainly been broad, propelled by legitimating rituals like a Catholic mass and, often, a roll call of the fallen. Local authorities and military officials typically attend, while historians from the IPN have shared life histories of the soldiers. As president between 2005 and his death in 2010, Lech Kaczyński regularly attended the commemoration. In 2011, following the Smolensk plane crash, the Polish parliament passed a law—with the support of all political parties in parliament—honoring the "heroes of the anti-communist underground who fought, armed or otherwise, for the independence of the Polish State, its right to self-determination, and the fulfillment of the democratic values of Polish society" (74).

At the direction of the IPN, 2013 was officially deemed The Year of the Cursed Soldier. In 2015, the government arranged for the exhumation of the remains of thirty-five soldiers and their burial in the newly built Pantheon-Mausoleum of the Cursed-Indomitable Soldiers in Warsaw's Powazki Military Cemetery. A large crowd turned out for the 2016 re-burial of the remains of one of the most famous fighters, Major Zygmunt Szendzielarz, who had been a member of the ultranational National Radical Camp (ONR in Polish). Szendzielarz was posthumously promoted to colonel, and his medals were carried on a red pillow by a member of the Polish military. This visible manifestation of PiS's memory politics was attended by Polish President Duda, Defense Minister Antoni Macierewicz, and many other military and political officials.[32] The Polish President's words are worth quoting at length:

> Venerable Family of Colonel, Venerable veterans—last surviving Indomitable Soldiers, Dear Marshals, Dear Prime Ministers, Mr. Minister, Dear Ladies and Gentlemen Ministers, Dear Ladies and Gentlemen MPs, Senators, Your Excellency, Reverend Bishop General, Venerable priests, all gathered here Dear Compatriots, 65 years to restore dignity. But not to restore the dignity

---

[32] See a photo gallery of the event at https://archiwum2019-en.mon.gov.pl/multimedia/photo/the-funeral-of-colonel-zygmunt-szendzielarz-nom-de-guerre-lupaszka-h2016-04-25/.

of Major Zygmunt Szendzielarz "Łupaszka," who became Colonel today. The Colonel always had this dignity, never lost it, and through his heroic death and suffering for the homeland, will have this dignity forever. So he and his fallen comrades. Today, after 65 years, by finding the mortal remains of Colonel, by remembering the heroism of the Indomitable Soldiers, by this state funeral, we restore the dignity of Poland. The dignity, trampled by those who once tortured and murdered then Major Zygmunt Szendzielarz "Łupaszka," the dignity, which those blurring the memory had thrown into nameless pits together with the Indomitable Soldiers. Today, this dignity comes back with the proud Republic, proud Poland, which bends her head low and pays tribute to her great son, a hero, indomitable to the end. And that's why I wanted to thank from this place the family of Colonel, families of all fallen Indomitable Soldiers, but also scouts, riflemen, sports fans and all young people who have been for years worshiping the memory of Indomitable Soldiers. I wanted to thank the families for always preserving dignity and always remembering about your loved ones. For always worshiping what was important: the truth, memory of heroism, indomitability, through the attitude of your loved ones, despite all the difficulties and persecution for several years by the communist authorities. For all this, for keeping the memory I wanted to immensely thank you.

(Polonia Institute, "The Funeral of
Colonel Szendzielarz, 'Łupaszka,'" May 16, 2016)

The clear implication of Duda's remarks is that Poland's post-communist governments after 1990 failed to recover the nation's dignity. This commemoration has been weaponized by PiS and its allies against former communists, as well as to marginalize opposition groups and parties.

The PiS government set about "styl[ing] itself as the only defender of the legacy left behind by 'cursed soldiers'" (Kończal 2020, 80). It did so in several ways: by transforming the burials of partisan remains into spectacles of nationalist celebration, by creating a museum honoring the cursed soldiers, and by naming a reserve military unit after them. More than any of the other commemorations discussed in this study, this one has been commodified, with the phrase cursed soldiers appearing on patriotic clothing and mugs. This was especially apparent in 2017 when the date fell on Ash Wednesday, moving—and extending—the commemoration of the cursed soldier. That year the celebration lasted for weeks between February and early April, including hundreds of events, with the main venue in Warsaw at the Powazki Military Cemetery. The National Bank even issued a ten-złoty coin with the "Fearless Soldiers—they did right" slogan (Kończal 2020). Popular history publications, including comic strips aimed at youth, propagated the right-wing memory narrative.

The role of the government and the IPN in constructing a memory narrative around the cursed soldiers, along with the commodification of the commemoration, suggests that the strategy of these memory challengers is not backward-looking: it is not merely about "correcting the record" or trying to integrate a previously ostracized group of citizens. Rather, it is about the bending the past to conform to the new nationalist narrative of the Polish government. The National Cursed Soldiers Remembrance Day is a key part of PiS's campaign to oppose a memory narrative of shame, responsibility, and contrition, especially the so-called "pedagogy of shame" it associates with the examination of the Holocaust and the unflattering recognition of endogenous anti-Semitism. The explosive debates over Jan Gross's *Neighbors: The Destruction of the Jewish Community in Jedwabne, Poland* (2001) and *Fear: Anti-Semitism in Poland after Auschwitz* (2006) exemplified the conservative-nationalist backlash to pluralistic and complex memory.[33] Beyond opposing a Holocaust-centered memory of the war, PiS seeks to replace it with a right-wing narrative that is heroic and unified.[34]

Hoping to inspire feelings of patriotism and pride, the PiS's obsession with commemorating the cursed soldiers perpetuates an exclusionary, insider/outsider politics of memory. In its effort to "finish the unfinished revolution of 1989," involving a negotiated transition that included communists, national-conservatives seek to blackwash the entire communist period, and thus to paint contemporary rivals on the left as tainted by the postwar past. By constructing a commemorative culture focused on resistance to communism, PiS casts itself as the savior of Poland. While commemorations of Waffen-SS in other post-communist countries serve much the same purpose, that is, to

---

[33] Although Princeton historian Jan Gross's 2001 account of the murder of Jews by their Polish neighbors in Jedwabne in 1941 basically did not uncover previously unknown facts, it served as an uncomfortable reminder that Poles were not only wartime victims but also bystanders and even perpetrators of the murder of Jews; that their widespread indifference to the fate of their Jewish countrymen and women was based on homegrown anti-Semitism; and that Poles had for decades after the war either turned away from the facts or blamed Germans for the murders of the 1,600 Jews of Jedwabne. The latter Michael Shafir has called "deflective negationism." See his chapter "Denying the Shoah in Post-Communist Eastern Europe," in Robert S. Wistrich, ed. *Holocaust Denial: The Politics of Perfidy* (Berlin: de Gruyter, 2012) 27–66. For an excellent reflection on Poles' reactions to the Jedwabne debate as well as a "reconstruction" of the crimes to address criticisms *Neighbors'* evidence, see Anna Bikont, *The Crime and the Silence: Confronting the Massacre of Jews in Wartime Jedwabne* (New York: Farrar, Strauss and Giroux, 2015).

[34] See Piotr Zuk, "Nation, National Remembrance, and Education—Polish Schools as Factories of Nationalism and Prejudice," *Nationalities Papers*, Vol. 46, No. 6 (2018): 1046–62.

honor resistance to communism, the Polish government has appropriated the fallen soldiers/resistors as a central element of its exclusionary memory politics. In doing so, it gives legitimacy to the communism–fascism equivalency and advances an anti-totalitarian paradigm that ignores historical context as it grows ever more authoritarian and illiberal itself. Aggressively resisting communism lies at the center of PiS's commemorative culture, which "raises a number of questions related to the collective needs, fears, and desires of Polish society" (Kończal 2020, 85). It especially triggers questions about the need to claim victimhood at the hands of communists, about the fear of being implicated in war crimes, and about its desire to identify with martyrs. In short, this choreographed and commodified commemoration belies more insecurity than confidence about Poland's wartime past.

Reactions, or lack thereof, to PiS's memory politics

The commemoration of these once-controversial soldiers has become normalized in Poland and, it seems, in the eyes of the international community; as with Hungary and Fidesz many have come to expect nationalist memory talk from the leaders of PiS. One indication of the normalization of March 1 was the 2022 celebration, during which American soldiers stationed in Poland joined the so-called Wolf's Trail race run, a central feature of the nationwide commemorations of cursed soldiers. The race amounts to 1,963 meters in length, a distance that symbolizes the year of the death of the last cursed soldier, Józef Franczak, whose *nom de guerre* was Lalek. Organizers claim that, in 2022, over a thousand commemorative events occurred in Poland and in other parts of the world.[35]

As in Hungary, Poland has experienced a significant re-nationalization and politicization of wartime memory that has benefited from several years of conservative-nationalist party rule. Aided by the pervasive role of the IPN, Polish families and children are immersed in narratives and rituals that simplify a complex wartime history in favor of homegrown heroes and martyrs. In contrast to many of the commemorations examined here, the remembrance of the "cursed soldiers" has become a high-profile, nationwide event. "Cursed" no longer, the anti-communist fighters are firmly established in the nation's pantheon of heroes.

---

[35] Ben Koshcalka, "US Paratroopers Join 10th edition of 'Cursed Soldiers' Run in Poland," March 7, 2022, post https://notesfrompoland.com/2022/03/07/us-paratroopers-join-10th-edition-of-cursed-soldiers-run-in-poland/.

The Utility of National Heroes in Eastern Europe

Among these post-communist commemorations of fallen World War II soldiers, we saw a similar pattern of memory challenges emerging. First émigrés
and, especially, émigré organizations comprised of veterans are seeking to
construct a narrative about their own and their fallen comrades' wartime
military service as heroic and patriotic for their opposition to the Soviets
and to communism. These groups often raised funds and organized care
for graves, erected memorials, and held annual meetings and commemorations for fallen comrades. The end of the Cold War has removed obstacles to
broadening and institutionalizing their efforts. With the Soviet-driven anti-
fascist ideology no longer determining the official memory, and with barriers
to travel to Eastern European countries lifted, the émigré groups have been
free to cooperate with veterans and their families inside post-communist
countries. As veterans began to organize annual commemorations of fallen
anti-communist fighters, far-right parties and affiliated groups saw opportunities to influence the memory of the war in service of contemporary political
goals: conservative-nationalism and anti-communism/anti-leftism.

The countries examined in this chapter were profoundly affected by Nazi
and (except Croatia in the former Yugoslavia) Soviet occupations; most
served as sites of some of the most traumatic events of World War II. It
is therefore not surprising that discussions about who-did-what-to-whom
and why are often targets of memory challengers. Victim and perpetrator
are not merely categories of fact, they are mantles claimed by individuals and groups to salve or wound, to reassure or cast doubt, to excuse or
punish, and to unify or divide. Any notion of collaboration with homegrown or German fascists arising out of conviction or survival is, either
way, uncomfortable. The complexities of wartime trauma in this part of
Europe were not adequately confronted and examined under communism
after 1945, nor were they explored when the Cold War freezer thawed out;
after a wave of examination by some historians, post-communist political
actors on the right shifted to national self-pity, or self-aggrandizement. The
emotional appeal of a re-nationalized memory of war lay in the desire to
forget humiliating, painful memories in order to find strength in a narrative of unity, bravery, and, often, victimhood. The innocence and "virility"
of the nation, along with the sense of belonging to something larger than
oneself helped to blind and bind people in uncertain circumstances, starting with the transition to capitalism and exacerbated by the financial crisis
of 2008–2009.

The cultural and institutional constraints on memory challengers in post-communist Eastern Europe are less well-established than in Western Europe. For one, the post-communist countries have had a shorter, less organic experience with cultivating Holocaust memory, making that less of a constraint than in the cases discussed in chapter 2. Also, the internal checks on memory challengers are likely weaker in post-communist countries, given their liberalization decades later and, more recently, given the hostile political environment faced by civil society groups and critical media across the region, especially in Hungary and Poland. In Croatia and Poland, the Catholic Church was far from a constraint on memory challengers; instead it participated in the renationalization of wartime memory by emphasizing national resistance and martyrdom rather than the universal lessons of the Holocaust and repentance for silence or, worse, complicity. Finally, the constraining influence of the European Union on memory challengers weakens once a country becomes a member, as it has in the cases of Poland and Hungary. Once inside the Union, even the threat of censure or denial of funds seems to have little impact on the behaviors of nationalist leaders and governments.

More so than in Western European, the cases of memory challenges at commemorations in post-communist countries entailed rituals to bind participants through marches, wearing of symbols or special clothing, giving speeches, and engaging in special activities, like hikes or races. Numerous other strategies have also been deployed to blind, in ways similar to memory challengers in Western Europe:

- Obfuscation, by whitewashing the country's past support for fascism, or its soldiers' collaboration with the forces allied with Nazi Germany, and presenting it as healthy patriotism;
- Inversion by casting perpetrators of war crimes as defenders of the nation and of Europe;
- Emphasis on their own national victimization over that of other nations or minority groups.

Eastern European memory challengers differ from their Western European counterparts, however, in regard to their laser focus on the crimes of communism:

- Their construction of an equivalence between fascism and communism, in the form of the Double Genocide or Two Totalitarians discourse, places communism at the forefront and portrays it as the more pernicious form of despotism for its affront to national sovereignty, culture, and identity.

• Revisionism, casting their nation or the soldiers that defended it as actively repelling the communist takeover, while ignoring the fact that there were homegrown communists or that many people supported or complied with the communists.

Insisting on unequivocal blackwashing of communism as the historical and common enemy of Europeans, Eastern European memory challengers oppose the old Western and Soviet narratives of the war as a fight against fascism. They also downplay or ignore the primary dimension of Western European memory, the Holocaust of Jews, as well as their country's homegrown anti-Semitism and racism.

Another strategy preferred by Eastern European memory challengers is to link the heroic past resistance of communism to the present. Like far-right memory actors in Western Europe, the challengers at various commemorations described in this chapter link communism of the twentieth century with what they see as Europe's twenty-first century civilizational confrontation with outsiders, primarily Muslims but also with Jews (albeit usually in less explicit terms). While the enemy had been the USSR, now it is cosmopolitan values of the European Union that pull migrants into the region and introduce "gender ideology." Whereas the master narrative of the Soviet Union had restricted culture and memory in Eastern Europe, it is now the Holocaust-centered memory of the West that confounds them. So, too, does the possibility of embracing a pluralistic, complex memory that decenters the nation-state. Certainly, for former republics of the USSR, like Latvia and Ukraine, Russia remains an existential threat and an important figure in the politics of memory.

The commemorations described here, along with the strategies used by memory challengers to bind and blind their target audiences, clearly sought to upgrade the status of the nation and to sweep away the Cold War era-imposed Soviet version of wartime actors, events, and consequences. The emotional appeals, discursive strategies and rituals contained familiar mnemonic moves of obfuscation, comparison, construction of dichotomies, and revisionism, but were they used for the same purpose? Were they engaged primarily to construct a national story independent of the one foisted on them after 1945? Or did they seek to push away the Holocaust-centered, cosmopolitan memory imported from the West? Whatever their intentions, their words and actions suggest that right-wing forces are prepared to do both of these. Their flagrant use of symbols of wartime fascism, the hero-worship of suspected or confirmed war criminals, and their complete disregard for homegrown racism, anti-Semitism, and/or the suffering of other groups and communities during World War II, challenged the dominant narratives of the other two meso-regions. The intended outcome of the memory challenges at wartime commemorations—defining the national community in narrow, exclusive terms with an emphasis on victimization—may offer a kind of catharsis to participants, but the catharsis is partial at best. Much is left unexamined, and in the silences and deflections lie the dangers of repetition of the past.

In chapter 4, we turn to a day of remembrance that entangles two mnemonic regions and examine how Eastern Europeans react to Russia's mnemonic moves.

4

August 23, 1939

From a Non-Event to a Russian Weapon against Poland (and the West)

This chapter considers the construction of memory and, later, memory eruptions, surrounding August 23, 1939, the date of the signing of the Molotov-Ribbentrop Pact between Hitler's Germany and Stalin's Soviet Union. Whereas chapters 2 and 3 explored a number of wartime commemorations in two mnemonic meso-regions of Europe, the focus here is on a single date in history; the aim is to investigate the ways it has been interpreted in different meso-regions and with what consequences. While the commemorations examined in chapters 2 and 3 were more or less self-contained, with little or no interaction between them, the August 23rd commemoration creates a feedback loop: rhetoric and rituals in one mnemonic region cause a reaction in another.

Roger Moorhouse, author of *The Devil's Alliance: Hitler's Pact with Stalin, 1939–1941* (2014), wrote an essay close to the 2022 anniversary of the pact in which he noted that the agreement "barely features in the Western narrative; passed over often in a single paragraph, dismissed as an outlier, a dubious anomaly, or a footnote to the wider history" (2022, 1). Rafał Rogulski, director of the European Network Remembrance and Solidarity, explains the lack of attention by Western Europeans to the Molotov-Ribbentrop Pact in another way: "Western European countries do not have a common experience of both totalitarian regimes. Most of them did not suffer in any way from communism . . . What is more, in some countries in the post-war period various communist circles were quite active and they still function to a limited extent today" (2022, 2). Deliberately forgotten by the Soviets and their satellites during the Cold War, this event began to command attention in all three meso-regions of memory soon after the fall of the Iron Curtain, however it only became contentious in two: Eastern Europe (including the three Baltic countries) and Russia.

The Baltic countries first revived the memory of August 23 in the early 1990s; it has become central not only to their commemorative calendars but

World War II Memory and Contested Commemorations in Europe and Russia. Jennifer A. Yoder, Oxford University Press.
© Jennifer A. Yoder (2024). DOI: 10.1093/oso/9780198894162.003.0004

also to the broader post-communist Eastern European memory of the war. In the first decade of the new millennium, the new post-communist members of the European Union lobbied to place August 23 at the center of the European memory of the war, to which the Western European member states responded positively. In reaction to developments in Eastern European memory, Russian President Vladimir Putin posed a serious challenge to the memory of August 23. His reinterpretation of the Molotov-Ribbentrop Pact used deflection, disinformation, and distortion of the facts to construct a particular historical narrative inside Russia, provoking anger and fear outside of the country.

Before turning to the divided memory of the pact and the mnemonic struggle in which it became entangled soon after Eastern countries became part of the European Union, I turn briefly to the pact and its impacts.

German-Soviet Cooperation, Soviet Forgetting

The Molotov-Ribbentrop Pact was a non-aggression agreement between the Soviet Union and Germany. Negotiated in Moscow by their respective countries' foreign ministers, Joachim von Ribbentrop and Vyacheslav Molotov, the pact stated that there would be no military action between the two powers for ten years.[1] If one party were to go to war with a third country, the other party promised to remain neutral in the conflict. The agreement gave Germany the confidence to invade Poland without fear of Soviet reprisal. Soon after Germany's invasion of Poland on September 1, 1939, the USSR also invaded Poland, on September 17, 1939, effectively splitting Poland between them. The pact moreover contained a secret protocol pertaining to Soviet and German spheres of influence in Eastern Europe, which allowed the Soviet Union to gain control of Estonia, Latvia, and Finland. A second secret protocol, signed in September 1939, designated most of Lithuania to the Soviet sphere. These Soviet–Germany deals also affected Romania's territorial integrity. In addition to leading to war and erasing the sovereignty of several countries, the pact effectively handed large numbers of Eastern Europe's Jews over to the Nazis. None of the countries or peoples in question had a choice in the matter.

---

[1] Hitler originally proposed 100 years without military action between the two countries, but Stalin insisted that ten was sufficient.

The USSR and Germany cooperated for the first two years of the war, signing treaties and maintaining commercial ties. On September 28, 1939, the two countries signed the German-Soviet Border and Friendship Treaty: "across two expansive economic treaties, they traded secrets, blueprints, technology and raw materials, oiling the wheels of each other's war machines. Stalin was no passive or unwilling neutral in this period, he was Hitler's most significant ally" (Moorhouse 2022, 2). Germany broke the pact on June 22, 1941, when it invaded the USSR. It is that date, June 22, 1941, that the Soviets considered (as do Russia and Belarus now) as the start of their involvement in the war, not August 23, 1939, or September 17, 1939. The Soviet Union denied any role in the violence and destruction in Eastern Europe prior to June 1941.

Although interpreted by Russian historians today as a necessary act of self-defense that allowed Stalin to build up the Soviet military in preparation for a likely future war with Germany, after 1945, the non-aggression pact faded from the official Soviet remembrance of wartime events. The secret protocols were not made public until the Nuremberg Trials and following the discovery of microfilm records of the pact in Marburg, Germany. Despite the discovery, however, the Soviets denied the existence of the secret protocols, claiming the Baltic countries became part of the USSR as a result of endogenous uprisings by workers and peasants rather than through exogenous force. Following the US State Department's publication of the text of the Secret Protocols, Stalin reacted by releasing (and partially writing himself) a book called, *Falsifiers of History* in which he claimed the Secret Protocol was a capitalist fake and the West was to blame for failing to stop Hitler in the first place (Moorhouse 2022, 3). An official history from 1970 called *A Short History of the Communist Party of the Soviet Union* explained the annexation of the three Baltic countries this way: "In 1940, when the threat of German invasion loomed over Lithuania, Latvia, and Estonia, and their reactionary governments were preparing to make a deal with Hitler, the peoples of these countries overthrew their rulers, restored Soviet power and joined the USSR" (Wertsch 2008, 61). As James Wertsch said of the Soviet narrative, it "suggests that the period of independence in Estonia, Latvia, and Lithuania in the 1920s and 1930s was somehow unnatural" (Wertsch 2008, 62). The non-aggression pact with Germany was effectively erased in the Soviet memory of the Great Patriotic War—until 1989. That year, the Congress of People's Deputies of the Soviet Union condemned the pact, calling it "legally deficient and invalid." What had changed? Under Mikhail Gorbachev, the policy of *glasnost* permitted the opening of archives and encouraged objective historical analysis.

Divided Memory

Western European war memory focused little on the event until recently, when Eastern European partners pushed the event onto European agendas. Eastern Europeans view August 23, 1939, as one of the first and most significant steps of their abandonment by the West, followed by Yalta in 1945, Hungary in 1956, and Czechoslovakia in 1968. For Poland and the Baltic states, in particular, the pact marked the beginning of the war and of their victimization. For Russia, the event's meaning has shifted: from a non-event during Soviet times, to an event for critical reflection under Gorbachev (and Boris Yeltsin), to an event reinterpreted and weaponized by Vladimir Putin against real and perceived enemies in Europe.

The Eastern European Perspective: A Memory Revived

It is fitting to begin with the Eastern European perspective, since the Molotov-Ribbentrop Pact directly affected tens of millions of people there and because Eastern European memories were denied a place in the construction of wartime narratives during the Cold War. Like other commemorations discussed here, this one was initiated by people in exile or otherwise living outside of the countries where the events in question occurred. Eastern Europeans in Canada first commemorated August 23 in 1985. Associations representing refugees from specific countries, such as the Estonian Central Council in Canada, cooperated to form an International Black Ribbon Day Committee; black ribbons are a universal symbol of mourning. In 1986 the first commemorations of Black Ribbon Day were held in twenty-one Western cities, including Ottawa, London, Perth, Washington, DC, and Los Angeles. Spreading to the Baltic countries in 1987, the day of remembrance became associated with the growing anti-communist, pro-independence protest movements there. On the pact's fiftieth anniversary on August 23, 1989, two million people in the Baltic states joined hands in a human chain that spanned six-hundred kilometers. The mass peaceful protest and show of Baltic solidarity became known as the "Baltic Way." Please see Figure 4.1.

Initially, Black Ribbon Day commemorated victims of Soviet oppression; it now includes victims of Nazism and is officially called the European Day of Remembrance for Victims of Stalinism and Nazism. Unlike other commemorations examined here, this one achieved recognition through the mobilization of international actors who advocated for the institutionalization of the day of

Figure 4.1 The "Baltic Way" Human Chain
Source: © Aivars Liepins.

remembrance. Starting in 2006, the Parliamentary Assembly of the Council of Europe (PACE) issued a resolution condemning the "crimes of totalitarian communist regimes." Pushed by the Baltics but opposed by Russian representatives, the resolution failed to gain enough votes in the assembly to pass. Meanwhile, new post-communist members of the European Union also mobilized to affect European memory discourses and practices. Marlene Laruelle has called these efforts "using European institutions to promote 'Communist Nuremberg.'"[2] While not a legal process, these efforts constituted a trial in the court of public opinion. Bolstered by the credibility of having successfully and peacefully removed communist regimes, and often flanked by some of the best-known dissidents of the velvet revolution, post-communist countries sought to upload their own memories of the war, particularly their victimization during and after the war, symbolically and rhetorically integrating Europe's mnemonic landscape.

The next step was to enhance the status of totalitarian left-wing regimes to the level of significance of totalitarian right-wing regimes in the "European conscience." One of the most significant developments in this process

[2] See Marlene Laruelle, *Is Russia Fascist? Unravelling Propaganda East and West* (Cornell University Press 2021) 70.

centered on a conference on European Conscience and Communism convened on June 2–3, 2008, in Prague. Hosted by the Committee on Education, Science, Culture, Human Rights and Petitions of the Czech Senate, the conference brought together many former dissidents, historians, and political representatives from post-communist and Western European countries. The conference panels included presentations about the crimes of "world communism," crimes involving communism from Czech and European perspectives, coming to terms with communism, institutes of national memory, and the establishment of an Institute of European Conscience.[3] The conference culminated in the Prague Declaration, which identified nineteen actions to promote a Europe-wide understanding of communism as a totalitarian regime to be taught, studied, evaluated, and remembered as a criminal and human rights-violating system on par with Nazism. In addition, it appealed to Europeans to place the victims of communism on par with the victims of Nazism; point five of the Prague Declaration recommended "ensuring the principle of equal treatment and non-discrimination of victims of all the totalitarian regimes"; point eight asked that there be "acceptance of pan-European responsibility for crimes committed by Communism." One concrete action to come out of the conference was the European Parliament's official recognition of August 23 as the European Day of Remembrance for Victims of Stalinism and Nazism. It is not clear whether the European Parliament was aware that UNESCO had already declared August 23 International Slave Remembrance Day in 1998, marking the slaves' uprising in Santo Domingo, Haiti in 1791.

In April 2009 the European Parliament passed a resolution on European Conscience and Totalitarianism that reaffirmed its supporting for efforts to shed light on the crimes of communism, and specifically called for the establishment of a Platform of European Memory and Conscience to increase awareness about crimes of totalitarianism through education. The resolution was co-sponsored by eastern members of the European Parliament's center-right European People's Party (EPP) party group as well as those from the liberal, nationalist, and Green party groups. In July 2009 the OCSE Parliamentary Assembly adopted its own resolution condemning totalitarianism and opposing the glorification of the Nazi and/or Stalinist past.

With these actions, the post-communist countries succeeded in symbolically and rhetorically placing August 23 on the same level of mnemonic importance as January 27, Holocaust Remembrance Day. Heidemarie Uhl

---

[3] See the conference proceedings at https://www.ustrcr.cz/data/pdf/konference/sbornik-svedomi-en.pdf, accessed June 2, 2021.

points to several reasons why this mnemonic development was problematic. First, the events remembered "derive from different points of historical reference." Yehuda Bauer concurs:

> The two regimes were both totalitarian, and yet quite different. The greater threat to all of humanity was Nazi Germany, and it was the Soviet Army that liberated Eastern Europe, was the central force that defeated Nazi Germany, and thus saved Europe and the world from the Nazi nightmare. In fact, unintentionally, the Soviets saved the Baltic nations, the Poles, the Ukrainians, the Czechs, and others, from an intended extension of Nazi genocide to these nationalities. This was not intended to lead to total physical annihilation, as with the Jews, but to a disappearance of these groups "as such." The EU statement, implying a straightforward parallel between Nazi Germany and the Soviet Union, therefore presents an a-historic and distorted picture (. . .) World War II was started by Nazi Germany, not the Soviet Union, and the responsibility of the 35 million dead in Europe, 29 million of them non-Jews, is that of Nazi Germany, not Stalin. To commemorate victims equally is a distortion (. . .) One certainly should remember the victims of the Soviet regime, and there is every justification for designating special memorials and events to do so. But to put the two regimes on the same level and commemorating the different crimes on the same occasion is totally unacceptable.
>
> (Bauer cited in Troebst 2012a, 13)

Uhl moreover suggests the events remembered by August 23 and January 27 are "indicative of the divergent interpretations of what the function of memory is able to achieve in a given society," which in the case of the Holocaust Remembrance Day is to ponder "a given society's culpability in past acts and the moral and ethical consequences for the present." In the case of August 23 this means "presenting the given society as a victim of foreign powers, and 'externalizing' any participation in the regime and its crimes" (Uhl 2009, 68).

Through obfuscation and by drawing a false equivalence, this mnemonic move contained echoes of the *Historikerstreit* in Germany twenty years earlier. This time, however, former dissidents and political representatives, not conservative historians, led the effort to change the dominant memory narrative of the war.

The false equivalence strategy, sometimes referred to as "Double Genocide" theory, figures prominently in the memory talk of many political officials and institutions in post-communist Europe. A prime example going back to 2004 was Lithuanian Prime Minister Sandra Kaniete, who sparked controversy by opening the Leipzig Book Fair by declaring, "both totalitarian regimes—National Socialism and Communism—were equally criminal."[4] With these words Kaniete blackwashed the entire communist experience, crudely drawing on the equivalence that is problematic for its reductionism and trivialization of events, their causes, and their legacies. Emphasizing the Molotov-Ribbentrop Pact does, arguably, devalue the Nazi invasion of Poland on September 1, 1939, as the start of the war. The conflation of the two regimes and two ideologies as "totalitarian" further gives the impression, as Troebst warns, that:

> The war and genocide are the result of a conflict in which the totalitarian states on one side were confronted with the democratic states on the other. Nothing could be less true. The Nazi decision to invade Poland was certain from 1933, whereas until the Munich Agreement of 1938 the Soviets were in serious negotiations with the Western powers and Poland. Poland too was an authoritarian state which until the beginning of 1939 fostered friendly relations with the "Third Reich" and in November 1938 had a military part to play in the division of the democratic Czechoslovakia. The attempt to create a culture of anti-totalitarian remembrance therefore accepts an alarming decontextualisation and homogenization, the consequences of which are immeasurable. Anybody wishing to learn from history for the future development of a common European future must not pay this price.
>
> (n.d., 14)

Dovid Katz has persistently raised the alarm about Double Genocide discourse because it equates both the crimes and also the victims of Nazism and communism. This is a type of Holocaust obfuscation that paves the way for expanding the concept of genocide to include a vast array of Soviet deeds. It also makes it easier to turn local perpetrators of the Holocaust into national/anti-communist heroes.[5] As Katz and others have repeatedly pointed out, while undoubtedly traumatic and horrific, oppression and violence under Soviet-style communism in Eastern Europe is not equal to the genocide of a group of Europeans—Jews—perpetrated by the Nazis and their collaborators. When political elites give legitimacy to mnemonic moves like the Double

---

[4] Her March 24, 2000 speech is cited by Heidemarie Uhl, "Conflicting Cultures of Memory in Europe: New Borders between East and West," *Israel Journal of Foreign Affairs*, Vol. 3, No. 3 (2009): fn 36.

[5] Dovid Katz, "The Seventy Years Declaration and the Simple Truth," *The Algemeiner*, February 3, 2012, https://www.algemeiner.com/2012/02/03/the-seventy-years-declaration-and-the-simple-truth/.

Genocide idea, it fosters a cultural acceptance of oversimplified interpretations. The consequences of such a memory politics fuel the legitimation of a partial and exculpatory memory and the erosion of barriers to extremist rhetoric and behavior.

The memory of the Molotov-Ribbentrop Pact has certainly been revived in the three Baltic countries, particularly in their occupation museums, located in Vilnius, Riga, and Tallinn, respectively. The pact's date is generally associated in those countries with the Baltic Way and with independence from the Soviet Union. While there is a high level of awareness of the impact of that date in 1939, there is also a positive memory, invoking the peaceful display of unity with each other and autonomy from the Soviet Union.

In Poland, the pact and the anniversary have figured prominently in the official war memory. The complexities of interwar Poland's role in the events of 1938–1939, however, are largely overlooked in favor of a focus on steps leading to Poland's victimization by both the Nazis and the Soviets. Maxim Samorukov interprets public opinion data in Poland about the war and its role as a "wronged nation" that "sees its sufferings in World War II as evidence of its righteousness and nobility" (2021). Comparing Poland and Russian perceptions of their identity as a result of their war roles, Samorukov says, "Both nations are certain of their exceptionalism and the debt due them from the rest of the world . . . Above all, both nations view any accusations over the roles of their ancestors in the war as the greatest sacrilege, deserving the harshest revenge ". Polish anger over President Obama's gaffe regarding "Polish death camps" would seem to support this idea. Another central element of official remembering of the pact in Poland is the equivalence made between communism and Nazism. In August of 2022, an outdoor exhibit in the capital city of Warsaw, which has marked the anniversary since 2011, featured large panels with photographs and text narrating the "pact of criminals," its context and, particularly, its consequences for Poland (Webber 2022). Karol Nawrocki of the Institute of National Remembrance (IPN), which sponsored the exhibit, said at its opening, "The interwar period saw the birth of two states built on the same foundation . . . of hatred towards certain social classes or ethnic groups, and of a constant drive for expansion . . . two kingdoms emerged— one to carry the revolution abroad and the other to gain the Lebensraum—and these two, the Soviet Union and the German Reich, were the realms of disdain, propaganda, lies and death" (Webber 2022).

Curiously, the memory of the Molotov-Ribbentrop Pact has not been revived in Romania. Alina Thiemann and Valentina Pricopie (2021) suggest this owes to mnemonic competition involving August 23, 1944, when Romania switched sides from Axis to Allies. August 23 became a national day of remembrance, in recognition of that switch, while memories of the pact between the USSR and Germany remained marginal, even after the Cold War ended and became the European Day of Remembrance. As a result, the Day of Commemoration for Victims of Fascism and Communism has neither received the same media attention, nor has it been commemorated through official events in Romania as it has in the Baltic states or in Poland. It is possible that the pact and the European Day of Remembrance may gain salience in Romania over time, particularly since the country has become a member of a transnational European memory actor.

Nonstate Memory Actors

"Recovering" national memory after the Cold War, the Molotov-Ribbentrop Pact has become central to efforts to interpret and make meaning of the war and its aftermath in Poland and the Baltics. National governments are not the only memory actors active in this effort, however, nor have they stopped at unilateral efforts to construct the memory of the pact. The European Network Remembrance and Solidarity was founded in 2005 to foster dialogue and greater understanding about difficult chapters of European history. Based in Warsaw, the ENRS receives funding from the governments of Poland, Hungary, Slovakia, Germany, and, since 2014, Romania. The impetus for its founding was a controversial proposal made by the German Union of Expellees to commemorate the twelve million Germans who fled or were expelled from Central Eastern Europe at the end of World War II. Governments in Central Eastern Europe were concerned that the expellees' campaign, which they saw as a distortion of the past, would become part of a memory war aimed at extracting reparations and the restitution of property in East European countries. The ENRS organizes symposia, workshops, makes short films, documentaries, and podcasts relating to memory of the war, and creates online content for educators. As the ENRS explains, its work is intended to "focus on the ideologies and totalitarian systems of power, wars and crimes, which all precipitated the tragedies that afflicted Europe in the last century."[6] The ENRS's use of the language of equivalence seems to normalize what is clearly an obscuring of the particular nature of ideologies, crimes, and afflictions in the twentieth century. Among the ENRS highlighted historical events

---

[6] https://enrs.eu/en/a-brief-history-of-the-enrs

is the Molotov-Ribbentrop Pact with its project "August 23: European Day of Remembrance for the Victims of Totalitarian Regimes."[7] While the organization does not offer an example of what I have called an antagonistic memory challenger, it is indicative of the Eastern Europeans' quest to define the Molotov-Ribbentrop Pact as pivotal to the region's identity and to show the harm done by ignoring its importance for so long.

The other actor worthy of mention is the Platform of European Memory and Conscience; initiated by the Czech Republic when it held the EU presidency, it gained support particularly among the Visegrad countries, Hungary, Poland, and Slovakia, in addition to the Czech Republic. The purpose was to create a pan-European effort to document and raise awareness concerning the history of twentieth-century totalitarianism. The PEMC counts as its members both EU and non-EU countries, as well as several national historical institutes (like the Polish IPN). It has organized conferences, mainly on the crimes of communism. Officially an educational project of the European Union, in practice it has become a tool for the Eastern EU members to integrate the history of suffering under communism into the European mnemonic landscape. Its activities are often aimed at youth, including a textbook for secondary students called *Lest We Forget: Memory of Totalitarianism in Europe*, efforts to create a pan-European memorial for victims of totalitarianism in Brussels, and a board game called "Across the Iron Curtain."[8]

While efforts by Eastern European countries to highlight and interpret the Molotov-Ribbentrop Pact and interpret it through a "double genocide" lens have not met with resistance by, or much interest in Western European countries, these memory moves have certainly become a point of contention between Eastern Europeans and Russia.

The Russian Perspective: A Memory Revised

Post-Soviet Russia's official memory of August 23, 1939, shifted from a long-overdue recognition of the pact between Stalin and Hitler to vehement defensiveness and even offensiveness, especially toward Poland. The timing of the

---

[7] The project includes six profiles and videos of individual "victims of Nazism, Stalinism and all other totalitarian ideologies," links to further information about the causes of the outbreak of World War II, and information about where to find the special "August 23." See https://enrs.eu/august23. See also the Hi-Story Infographic Lesson on the Molotov-Ribbentrop Pact at https://hi-storylessons.eu/events/23_august_molotov-ribbentrop_pact_concluded_by_the_third_reich_and_ussr/.

[8] For more on the boardgame, see Ana Milošević, "Playing Memory Games with Europe's Totalitarian History" in *The Balkan Insight*, February 6, 2019, https://balkaninsight.com/2019/02/06/memory-games-moving-the-iron-curtain-01-28-2019/.

narrative shift suggests it was a response to Eastern Europeans' efforts to raise awareness about their experiences under communism and, simultaneously, to place communism on the same footing as Nazism.

Until the late 1980s, the Hitler-Stalin Pact was ignored, while the steps leading to war were attributed to Germany alone. Beyond seeking to avoid the topic of cooperation with Nazi Germany, the official silence entailed other motives: During the Cold War, August 23, 1939, had served as a symbol used by refugees and anti-communist dissidents to criticize Soviet imperialism and the Soviet regime's failure to protect human rights. In 1989, it came to symbolize the illegal seizure of the Baltics in 1939, coupled with the loss of freedom and sovereignty, and was used to mobilize peaceful protest against Soviet domination. Following Gorbachev's encouragement of a more truthful accounting of the war and its aftermath, the pact became a subject of analysis among Soviet, then post-Soviet historians, though the document itself was not released until 1992.

Assuming the presidency in 2000, Putin characterized the pact as "immoral"—and continued to do so until 2009. In 2002, Putin and Polish President Kwasniewski discussed the creation of a Russian-Polish Group on Difficult Matters, which formed several years later, which began to examine "the most difficult problems in bilateral relations over ninety years, from 1918 to 2008, in a 'mirror' approach incorporating both the Polish and Russian perspectives."[9] This effort to sustain a dialogue about specific events in history—events that had not only been interpreted differently between the two countries but also suppressed, distorted, and weaponized—represented significant progress between countries with a long history of distrust. The joint team of historians, political scientists, and economists met together in several sessions eventually publishing a volume, *White Spots Black Spots* (2015), each of its fifteen chapters focused on a specific time period or theme, with each containing an essay from a scholar from each country.

Meanwhile, Putin's interest in "historical policy" began to intensify shortly after he assumed the presidency. An important vehicle for this policy is the State Programme of Patriotic Education of Russian Citizens with its five-year plans for implementing an official Concept of Patriotic Education. According to Bækken and Enstad (2020), the first plan began in 2001and entailed both policy content and financial support for specific projects, such as publications,

---

[9] Adam Daniel Rotfeld and Anatoly V. Torkunov (eds) *White Spots Black Spots: Difficult Matters in Polish-Russian Relations, 1918–2008* (University of Pittsburgh Press 2015) 2.

conferences, and festive events to "commemorate past military achievements" (333). In 2003 Putin met with professional historians at the Rumiantsev Library in Moscow where he signaled his desire that history books not become a source of political and ideological discord but rather they serve their core purpose: to encourage pride in Russia and its past. The meeting with historians, according to Pal Kolstø, was "a turning point in recent Russian history policy, away from laissez-faire attitudes under El'tsin, and towards stricter policy control" (2019, 752). While he has not (yet) issued a collected works of Soviet/Russian history, as Stalin had done, Putin has directed the publication of history textbooks. In 2007, he promoted a history text for teachers and advanced students, supporting the earlier, conservative Soviet narrative that "Russia faces a hostile international environment which requires the concentration of political and economic power in the Russian State." It justifies many of Stalin's draconian policies as necessary for modernization in the face of German and Japanese threats, and compares Stalin's acts to the United States' Patriot Act after 9/11 (Sherlock 2011, 96–7). Putin has called for a "united" history textbook for schools and has overseen the closing or curbing of access to historical archives (Bernstein 2016, 426). This powerful memory actor insists on a monist memory narrative, emphasizing heroism in the face of external threats.

In reaction to the Prague Declaration and the promulgation of the Double Genocide Theory by Eastern European leaders, Sergei Lavrov has argued, "The victory came at too high a price to allow it to be taken away—for us, it [the Prague Declaration's equivalence of Nazi and Soviet roles in World War II] is a 'red line'" (Roth 2019). President Putin began to push back vigorously on the pluralization of World War II memory, doubling down on an interpretation that emphasized Russian valor and pride in the victory over Nazism. In so doing, Putin refuted Gorbachev and Yeltsin's willingness to allow and even encourage memory narrative pluralism. He also sought to counter what he has characterized as "attacks" by Eastern European countries exploiting narratives about World War II, the Red Army, the meaning of August 23, 1939. At the center of this effort was the status of August 23 in the history and memory of the war. In the interpretation endorsed by Putin, the Munich appeasement of September 1, 1939, marked the onset of war, not the non-aggression pact of August 23, 1939, as Eastern Europeans argued. Nor has Putin accepted that the pact rendered the Soviet Union an accomplice of Germany or its war crimes (Kolstø 2019, 754). Sergei Lavrov, now foreign minister, declared in 2009 that in making the deal with Germany, "the Soviet Union . . . acted in line with the usual diplomacy for this time" (Koposov 2018, 256).

When Putin assumed the prime minister position in 2008, as Dmitry Medvedev became president, his mnemonic agenda continued unabated. On May 15, 2009, then-President Medvedev issued a decree creating the Commission against the Falsification of History. The twenty-eight-member body was chaired by Sergey Naryshkin, who was Medvedev's chief of staff at the time. The Commission was comprised of representatives from the Duma, the armed forces, the security service (FSB), and the army, including only a handful of historians.[10] Prominent Russians, including former leader Mikhail Gorbachev, criticized the commission. Strong objections to the political nature of the commission also came from historians outside of Russia. Perhaps best known for his biography of Stalin, Robert Service, a British historian of the Soviet Union, observed in 2009: "President Medvedev, following in the footsteps of his predecessor Vladimir Putin, wants to control history. He wants to control the past in order to control the present. This is the classical scenario of George Orwell."[11] The commission's purpose was to report to the President about alleged attempts to falsify history, as well as to advise him on how to counter such falsifications. The commission was dissolved in February 2012, shortly before Putin returned to the presidency. In 2014, Russian lawmakers passed a memory law that criminalizes the expression of certain opinions about the Soviet past. Part of the law criminalizes Holocaust denial or approval; the crux of the law, however, criminalizes "lies" about the activities of the Soviet Union in World War II (see chapter 5). The timing of the law, passed by the Duma in 2009 but not signed into law until 2014, is significant; in 2008–2009 the European Union adopted the Prague Declaration with its focus on communist crimes; in 2014 Russia moreover annexed Crimea, provoking a great deal of criticism from the international community (Edele 2017, 109). Such criticism was especially irritating to Russia coming from Eastern European countries, where the removal of Soviet-era monuments and the establishment of new anti-communist memorials and museums had become more common.

The politics of history and memory in post-Soviet Russia has not been uniform. There have been moments when a more pluralistic, critical exploration of the past was permitted. That period came to end when Putin returned to the presidency in 2012, following an election marred by irregularities that sparked significant protests in Russia. Since then, Putin has intensified the harassment

---

[10] Kolstø posits that Medvedev's creation of the commission was intended to forestall harsher legislation that would criminalize the "falsification" of history, particularly the rehabilitation of Nazism. Once Putin returned to the presidency, he oversaw the enactment of "memory laws," starting in 2014.

[11] Cited in Pål Kolstø, "Dimitrii Medvedev's Commission Against the Falsification of History: Why Was It Created and What Did It Achieve? A Reassessment," *Slavonic and East European Review*, Vol. 97, No. 4 (2019): 746.

of critical and independent media, civil society, and others who would point out the distortions in his construction of reality.

By the pact's seventy-fifth anniversary in 2014, Putin had bent the history of war to serve his purposes of strengthening Russian unity and his own legitimacy. The hardening of a particular narrative about the past also served his foreign policy goals: to create the sense that Russia had to defend itself— chiefly from the West—and to offer a cultural and geopolitical alternative—a pole in a multipolar world—to the decadent West. Putin amplified this narrative following Russia's annexation of Crimea in 2014: The move on Crimea and the Donbas (and then in 2022 the whole of Ukraine) was a reaction to Western overtures to a region that Putin considers part of Russia. According to this narrative, resting on nationalist and Eurasianist ideas, like those espoused by Aleksandr Dugin, the West has isolated Russia repeatedly in the past. Accordingly, the West is antagonistic, and Russia is merely reacting to it. In a March 2014 speech to the Duma and Federation Council, Putin explained Russia's move into Crimea as a necessary defense against Western influence in Ukraine:

> They are constantly trying to sweep us into a corner because we have an independent position, because we maintain it and because we call things like they are and do not engage in hypocrisy. But there is a limit to everything. And with Ukraine, our western partners have crossed the line, playing the bear and acting irresponsibly and unprofessionally. After all, they were fully aware that there are millions of Russians living in Ukraine and in Crimea. They must have really lacked political instinct and common sense not to foresee all the consequences of their actions. Russia found itself in a position it could not retreat from. If you compress the spring all the way to its limit, it will snap back hard. You must always remember this.
>
> (Putin, March 18, 2014)

This narrative finds parallels between the present and the 1930s; Putin's war, like the Molotov-Ribbentrop Pact, is a necessary response to the West's isolation of Russia.[12] At the center of Putin's narrative of Russian's struggle to chart its own path is the Great Patriotic War.

---

[12] Aleksandr Dugin is the Russian "political philosopher" who some have called "Putin's brain" because of his influence on the president's thinking about geopolitics and Russian influence in "Eurasia," which supposedly includes Ukraine. Dugin is believed to have been an important advisor to Putin in the 2014 annexation of Crimea and the 2022 attack on Ukraine.

The Great Patriotic War at the Center of Russian Identity

From the perspective of 2022, it is obvious that Putin's imposition of a singular interpretation of the war and of Soviet sacrifices and heroism is part of an effort to unify Russians around a shared, unambiguously positive understanding of the nation's roots, core values, its place in the world today and in the future. Since the 1991 collapse of the USSR, the re-narration of the Russian past has included a rediscovery of imperial historical figures like Peter the Great and Catherine the Great (actually a German). To some extent, Stalin has also been revived as a positive historical figure, although his accomplishments are selectively included in the official and public memory. That memory emphasizes that Stalin stood up to Hitler, making the decisive contribution to the Allied victory in Europe. Implicit in this interpretation is the debt owed by the West, which underappreciates the USSR/Russia's sacrifices. Stalin's brutal purges, the Gulag, and the Holodomor in Ukraine are forgotten elements of the official memory or, at least, not actively remembered. Lenin, the Russian Revolution, communist ideology and the founding of the USSR are also largely absent from official memory in Putin's Russia. Occasional circumstances call for drawing attention (usually negative attention) to elements of history that the Kremlin would sooner forget; in the context of the war against Ukraine, the Kremlin has faulted the USSR for having constructed an artificial system of ethnicities that is, according to the logic, the root of "confused" Ukrainian nationalism today.[13]

Putin frequently refers to the war to impart lessons to the Russian people, particularly youth, as well as to defend particular policy positions ranging from the glorification of veterans to the 2022 invasion of Ukraine; Putin claims the purpose of his "special military operation" was to denazify the country and return it to the Russian domain. He has given several speeches in recent years during which he embarks on long (selective) history lessons to rally Russians behind his policies and to vilify real and imagined enemies. Perhaps the most famous of Putin's speeches is that of February 21, 2022, in which he laid out his justification for war against Ukraine by offering a distorted history of Ukraine

---

[13] Soviet "nationalities policy," created by Lenin and meant to increase support for the USSR, had the unintended effect of institutionalizing national difference, strengthening the resolve of some republics to break away from the Union in the early 1990s. See Rogers Brubaker, "Nationhood and the National Question in the Soviet Union and Post-Soviet Eurasia: An Institutionalist Account," *Theory and Society*, Vol. 23 (1994): 47–78.

and Russia, claiming their inseparability.[14] He reiterated his claim that "modern Ukraine was entirely created by Russia or, to be more precise, by Bolshevik, Communist Russia." We will return to this speech and the war in Ukraine in chapter 6.

Over the years Putin has published several tracts outlining his interpretation of World War II and "plans" to write a book about it. Although not a historian by profession, he relishes defending his positions on Russian history with archival evidence. He receives information, including archival sources (he claims) and other historical documents from officials like Sergey Naryshkin of the Foreign Intelligence Service, who chairs the Russian Historical Society (RIO), and Vladimir Medinsky, a former culture minister who chairs the Russian Military Historical Society (RVIO).[15] Putin played an active role in setting parameters for textbooks for history (re)education in Russian schools. In 2021, he ordered the creation of a commission on history education whose stated purpose was "to ensure a planned and aggressive approach to the matter of defending the national interests of the Russian Federation."[16] Chaired by Medinsky, this commission addresses history as interpreted by museums, culture, and entertainment.

Not satisfied with merely talking about history or shaping it through policy, Putin has increased the ferocity with which the state opposes purported "falsifiers" of the history of the Great Patriotic War. To combat alleged falsifiers he has promised, "we will stuff their filthy mouths with documents, so that they learn their lesson."[17] Since the dissolution of the Commission against the Falsification of History in 2012, Putin's memory politics have been supported by memory laws, including Article 354.1 of the Criminal Code, that criminalize the exoneration of Nazism or the "dissemination of false information about the activities of the Soviet Union during the Second World War" and/or "the desecration of symbols of military glory."[18] This law (discussed chapter 5) fixates on the Nuremberg Trials having set the limits for examinations of wartime

---

[14] Putin's speech of February 21, 2022 can be found at http://en.kremlin.ru/events/president/news/67828. Two days later, he went on television to announce the "special military operation" in Ukraine. That address can be found at http://en.kremlin.ru/events/president/news/page/130.

[15] For more analysis of the historical interpretations of these advisers to Putin, see Julie Fedor, "'Historical Falsification' as a Master Trope in the Official Discourse on History Education in Putin's Russia," *Journal of Educational Media*, Vol. 13, No. 1 (Spring 2021) 107–35.

[16] Putin cited in Mikhail Sokolov and Robert Coalson, "'A Dangerous Commission': Russian Historians Alarmed as Putin Creates State Body on 'Historical Education,'" *RadioFreeEurope/RadioLiberty*, August 10, 2021.

[17] Cited by Sergei Radchenko, Foreign Policy, January 21, 2020.

[18] A Russian blogger, Vladimir Luzgin, posted the following in 2014: "The Communists and Germany jointly invaded Poland, sparking off World War II. That is, communism and Nazism closely collaborated." For this he was tried, convicted, and fined 200,000 Rubles.

activities and motives. In other words, only parties found guilty by the International Military Tribunal can be criticized or held responsible for perpetrating war crimes. Since the USSR was not on trial at Nuremberg, the implication of the memory law is that no one can claim that either Russia or its military were anything but heroic. Hence, atrocities committed by the Red Army are forgotten. Logically, the only way to interpret the Molotov-Ribbentrop Pact is to see it as having been defensive and unavoidable. In 2016, the Russian Supreme Court upheld the conviction of a man for stating that Nazi Germany and the Soviet Union had cooperated and attacked Poland in 1939.

We have already seen how significant anniversary years can provide memory challengers with opportunities both to draw attention to their interpretation of the past and to instrumentalize commemorations for new purposes. Putin has seized on anniversaries to make strong statements about the war and his country's role in it. Addressing a joint press conference with German Chancellor Angela Merkel on the occasion of the seventieth anniversary of the end of World War II, in May 2015 Putin defended the Molotov-Ribbentrop Pact, insisting it "made sense for ensuring the security of the Soviet Union" and suggesting that Stalin had previously made numerous attempts to form a coalition with Western countries against Nazi Germany but that such efforts had been rebuffed (Coalson 2015).

Timothy Snyder called out Putin's audacity in endorsing the Molotov-Ribbentrop Pact in 2015 this way:

> In claiming that Stalin was behaving as a reasonable statesman in 1939, Putin is saying that at the moment Hitler should not have been resisted. This is not only a problematic assessment of Soviet foreign policy. It is also a direct challenge to the fundamental myth of the establishment of the postwar Federal Republic of Germany, which is that Hitler should have been resisted in 1939. And there were of course European states that did make the opposite decision at the time: France and Great Britain and most significantly Poland did resist Hitler in 1939. Hitler had courted Poland as an ally for a war against the Soviet Union for five years, between early 1934 and early 1939, and was refused. He courted Stalin for a war against Poland for three days in August 1939, and was accepted with enthusiasm.
>
> (2015, 2)

Putin has used "what about-ism" on numerous occasions to suggest that the Munich Appeasement, not the Molotov-Ribbentrop Pact, led to the war. Radchenko points out, however, that "In making a comparison between the Munich Agreement and the 1939 Soviet-German Pact, [Putin] fails to acknowledge that the former did not see Britain and France help themselves to parts of a sovereign country. Stalin, by contrast, did exactly that in Poland" (2020). Sergei Radchenko also questions Putin's claims about the pact/appeasement comparison, noting that "it is naïve to argue that Stalin, for his part, would have jumped at the chance to join France in a war against Germany in 1938. Indeed, none of the evidence [Putin] cites shows that the Soviet Union was genuinely committed to Czechoslovakia's defense. Even as he accuses the British and the French of "cynicism," he seems unwilling to see Stalin as a cynical operator who would have been overjoyed to see Germany and the West at each other's throats (2020).

In addition to the shift in Putin's interpretation of the Molotov-Ribbentrop Pact as "immoral" to "inevitable," it is important to highlight how he has weaponized the pact's memory against Poland. In contrast to earlier efforts to learn from each other's memories of the war, Poland and Russia increasingly diverged in their remembrances. This divergence became more acute with the Law and Justice Party's re-nationalized memory politics featuring equivalence of the two totalitarianisms. In reaction, Putin publicly blamed Poland's actions in the 1930s for escalating the aggression that led to war. In 2019, the year of the eightieth anniversary of the Molotov-Ribbentrop Pact, Putin made several public comments about Polish authorities' cooperation with the Nazis. At an event late that year, Putin described the Polish ambassador to Nazi Germany, Jozef Lipski, as a bastard and an anti-Semitic pig, claiming that Lipski had approved of persecution of the Jews in 1938.

Another of Putin's lengthy reinterpretations of history was published in *The National Interest* in June 2020, marking the seventy-fifth anniversary of V-E Day.[19] In that essay, Putin picks up the earlier Soviet interpretation that ignored the destructiveness of Stalin's policies and cast the country as Europe's savior, primarily responsible for the victory over Nazi Germany. To resurrect the Soviet interpretation, Putin elaborates on the narrative that Polish actions made the pact unavoidable. Rather than seeing the Molotov-Ribbentrop Pact as leading to the invasion of Poland and hence the war's onset, he focuses on the appeasing of Hitler at Munich and Poland's role in dismembering and occupying Czechoslovakia, which preceded the pact.

[19] "Vladimir Putin: The Real Lessons of the 75th Anniversary of World War II," *The National Interest*, June 18, 2020, https://nationalinterest.org/feature/vladimir-putin-real-lessons-75th-anniversary-world-war-ii-162982, accessed June 7, 2021.

In the run-up to the eightieth anniversary, pact memory became a weapon in hybrid warfare against the West, which now includes post-communist Eastern European countries. Russian state media launched a disinformation campaign, also carried out in social media, with the slogan #TruthAboutWWII; Also involving Russian diplomats outside of the country, the disinformation campaign amplified justification for the Molotov-Ribbentrop pact by blaming Poland for provoking the war and by distorting the facts about the circumstances under which the Baltic states were brought into the Soviet Union in 1939. In this campaign, Putin's memory challenge echoes the earlier, conservative Soviet narrative about the past with an important modification: The older narrative cast Russia as peaceful and not inclined to interfere with other countries. James V. Wertsch contends that one of the Soviet conservative narrative templates interpreted the country as being "treacherously and viciously" attacked—without provocation—by foreign enemies bent on defeating it totally and destroying its civilization, however, the great and heroic Russian nation ultimately triumphs and expels foreign enemies (Wertsch 2008, 66). Putin's narrative shifting blame is consistent with the conservative Soviet approach, but he modifies it by making Poland the antagonist in the Russian memory of August 23, 1939. During Soviet times, Poland was an ideological ally, as part of the Soviet bloc, and thus not associated with Western imperialists. That sense of kinship is completely gone; Poland is, once again, viewed by Russian nationalists as a foreign enemy intent on besmirching, if not destroying if it could, Russia's heroic history and culture.

At his annual news conference in December 2019, Putin said:

> Yes, the Molotov-Ribbentrop Pact and its secret protocols were signed. That's true. Is it good or bad? I'll draw your attention—this is important now—to the fact that the Soviet Union was the last, it was the last state in Europe, that signed a nonaggression pact with Germany. Everyone else had already signed one. So what was the Soviet Union supposed to have done? Take on [Germany] by itself?

He stressed further:

> You see, I mean to write an article about this event. I will definitely have it published because I asked my colleagues to select archive materials for me. When I read some of them, everything becomes clear: everything in the process of appeasing Hitler is sorted out by year, month, and almost by day.
>
> (Putin, December 19, 2019)

Although he claims to be setting the record straight by pushing back against critics of the Soviet role in the war, Putin has articulated a revisionist history of the Molotov-Ribbentrop Pact in several speeches, interviews, official statements and various publications. One such pamphlet, "75th Anniversary of the Great Victory: Shared Responsibility to History and Our Future," was published as a challenge to the European Parliament's September 19, 2019, resolution, which contained references to the Molotov-Ribbentrop Pact. The EP resolution held that the Soviets and Nazis shared blame for starting the war, calling for the removal of Soviet war memorials from Europe. In reaction, Putin's pamphlet made several questionable claims, among them:

> In the autumn of 1939, the Soviet Union, pursuing its strategic military and defensive goals, started the process of incorporation of Latvia, Lithuania and Estonia. Their accession to the USSR was implemented on a contractual basis, with the consent of the elected authorities. This was in line with international and state law of that time.
>
> (Cartwright 2021 n.p.).

The pamphlet also suggests that, by invading Poland, Stalin helped to save "Jews living near Brest and Grodno, Przemsyl, Lvov and Wilno, [who] would be left to die at the hands of the Nazis and their local accomplices—anti-Semites and radical nationalists." Yet, Stalin was certainly no savior of European Jews; he was well aware that his cooperation with Nazi Germany would result in the destruction of much of Eastern European Jewry. This statement also ignores the treatment of Jews in territories occupied by Stalin, as well as the treatment of Jews in Stalin's USSR.

From Revision to Denial

President Putin is a memory challenger like no other examined here in that he holds the most powerful office in his country. Through the state apparatus he controls, a significant portion of the media, access to historical archives, and the spaces needed to debate and publish views about, and authoritative accounts of, the past inside his country. With such vast power concentrated in the president and state, prospects for distortion of the facts, along with the production and dissemination of disinformation by historians, diplomats, news media, and social media, are almost limitless. At various times, Russian official bodies have claimed that the USSR was never allied with Nazi Germany, something easily refuted by official documents pertaining to the German-Soviet Frontier Treaty, the German-Soviet Commercial Agreement 1940, and about NKVD-Gestapo cooperation. After nearly two decades of conceding that the pact and secret protocols existed and were "immoral," Russia's leadership, chiefly Putin, has led the effort to deny the fact that the Molotov-Ribbentrop Pact played a central role in launching the war. Consistent with the earlier official Soviet narrative, Russia insists that the war only began for the USSR in 1941 with the Nazi invasion of its territory. It denies that the Soviet Union participated in the start of the war by cooperating with Nazi Germany and even joining it in attacking Poland. Many Russians believe the narrative that Putin has been articulating for several years: It's "all the West's fault" (Wesolowsky and Luxmoore 2019, n.p.).

Yet, the fact is that the Soviet NKVD and the German Gestapo "promised each other to suppress any Polish resistance." This resulted in half a million Poles being sent to the Gulag and thousands of Polish officers, "[m]any of whom were fresh from combat against the Wehrmacht," being murdered by the Soviets (Snyder 2015, 3). Other facts the Russians deny include the joint Soviet-German assault on Brest-Litovsk, followed by a military parade of German and Soviet soldiers there. Finally, Russia denies that the Soviet Union occupied the Baltics in 1940, claiming that these countries were, instead, liberated by the USSR from Germany. The three states were forced to sign mutual assistance treaties with Moscow. In 1940, Moscow claimed the Baltic states were conspiring against the USSR, using that argument as a basis for forming new, Soviet-backed governments there and initiating a military build-up of Soviet troops there.

In Soviet times, and now again in Russia, the official Great Patriotic War narrative attests that the war commenced in 1941 when Germany invaded the USSR. However, the Soviets were involved in the war from 1939–1941, fighting in the eastern theater and supplying Nazi Germany with "the minerals, oil and food needed to make war against Norway, Denmark, the Netherlands, Belgium, Luxembourg, and most importantly France and Britain. During this stage of the war Stalin was eager to please Hitler" (Snyder 2015, 5). According to Snyder, there was "one major exception" to the Soviets' enthusiasm for aiding Germany at that time: it refused to accept the transfer of two million of Poland's Jews to the USSR, an offer made by Adolf Eichmann in early 1940. This stark reality, like many others related to the Soviet–German relationship before June 1941, is still ignored in the official Russian memory.

A "Defensive" Weapon against the West

Where the memory of August 23, 1939, is concerned for the Baltic countries and for Poland, the claim that the Soviet Union was the savior of Europe is a gross distortion built on glaring omissions. But Putin does not merely seek to set the record straight about the Soviets' role in the Molotov-Ribbentrop Pact, he seeks to use this "defense" of the Soviet/Russian honor in the war to unify his country on the basis of pride and shared fate but also, importantly, on the basis of what he suggests is an ongoing campaign by the West, indeed a conspiracy, to emasculate and humiliate his country. In pushing back on the Eastern European commemoration of the Molotov-Ribbentrop Pact and its anniversary's place in the European Union's calendric memory, Putin casts himself as the defender of his country from outside enemies bent on maligning it. In 2020, for example, Putin announced that an archive of historical materials on World War II would be established and open to anyone in Russia or abroad, claiming:

> It is our duty to defend the truth about the Victory; otherwise, what shall we say to our children if the lies, like a disease, spread all over the world ... we must set facts against outrageous lies and attempts to distort history. This is our duty as a winning country and our responsibility to the future generations.
>
> (cited in Zima 2020).

The Molotov-Ribbentrop Pact has been repurposed to help Vladimir Putin create a historical narrative that supports his conservative-nationalist neo-imperialist agenda. One of the main objectives of his memory challenge is to strengthen national patriotism and unity, both of which suffered mortal blows when the USSR collapsed and as a result of the chaotic Yeltsin years. In his annual address in 2005, Putin famously said:

> Above all, we should acknowledge that the collapse of the Soviet Union was a major geopolitical disaster of the century. As for the Russian nation, it became a genuine drama. Tens of millions of our co-citizens and compatriots found themselves outside Russian territory. Moreover, the epidemic of disintegration infected Russia itself. Individual savings were depreciated, and old ideals destroyed. Many institutions were disbanded or reformed carelessly. Terrorist intervention and the Khasavyurt capitulation (an accord that ended First Chechen War in 1996) that followed damaged the country's

integrity. Oligarchic groups—possessing absolute control over information channels—served exclusively their own corporate interests. Mass poverty began to be seen as the norm. And all this was happening against the backdrop of a dramatic economic downturn, unstable finances, and the paralysis of the social sphere.

(Putin, April 25, 2005)

Memory politics have been used by Putin to unify a country that he saw as too fragmented, to bolster the confidence of Russians in the context of growing competition, including in narratives about their own past, from outside the country. He also harnessed memory politics to legitimize a neo-imperialist foreign policy toward former Soviet Republics. Disinformation campaigns inside Russia but also in Georgia (which Russia invaded in 2008) and in Ukraine (which it first invaded in 2014) emphasize Russia as a defender and savior of Europe in World War II—painting it as a friendly, peace-loving society that is, once again, threatened by external enemies. This narrative aims to neutralize domestic Russian opposition to aggression against neighboring countries. It is intended to create a sense of common fate among Russian citizens, who will be relied upon to sacrifice again in the course of current and future military campaigns. In that way, Evgenia Olimpieva suggests, "collective memory of WWII in Putin's Russia has turned into a geopolitical ideology."[20]

Given the developments I have outlined here, it is not surprising that in July of 2020 the Duma adopted several amendments to the Constitution of the Russian Federation. Article 67, Paragraph 3 now states:

The Russian Federation respects the memory of the defenders of the Fatherland and protects the historical truth. It is not allowed to diminish the significance of the heroism of the people in defending the Fatherland.

(Constitution of the Russian Federation 2020).

In contrast to so many commemorations, Putin's memory politics were not put on hold during the global covid-19 pandemic. In the face of fluctuating oil prices, international condemnation of the poisoning of Alexei Navalny, and foreign challenges to Russian influence in Ukraine and Belarus, Putin remained sensitive to the need to strengthen his legitimacy as a leader who stands up for Russian interests in the international arena. Putin used the occasion of the eightieth anniversary of the war's end in Europe (V-E Day),

---

[20] https://cpb-us-w2.wpmucdn.com/voices.uchicago.edu/dist/a/107/files/2017/02/CPW_Olimpieva_02.08.15-2j1whpv.pdf

examined in the following chapter, to underpin his narrative that the West was engaging in "falsification" of Russian history. "Historical falsification," Julie Fedor observes, has become a master trope in the official memory in Putin's Russia (Fedor 2021). On the eightieth anniversary of May 9, Victory Day in Russia, the government displayed documents from its archives, including those pertaining to the Molotov-Ribbentrop Pact, with interpretations repeating earlier claims about Stalin having no choice and Soviet sacrifices for Western missteps during the months prior to August 23, 1939.

While leaders and educators in other countries struggled to address the needs—logistical and emotional—of teachers and students in their countries, Putin used the beginning of the 2020–2021 school year to stoke young Russians' fears of historical falsifiers; he drew parallels between World War II and the present. In a September 1, 2020, address opening the Russian school year, warning pupils in an online video:

> People who collaborate with the enemy in wartime . . . are called collaborators. Those who agree with the initiators of the rewriting of history today can absolutely be called collaborators of the present day. There have always been such people everywhere, and there always will be. They have various motivations; we won't go into the details now. It's important only to understand that this is very relevant today.
>
> (cited in Fedor 2021, 108)

Putin's suggestion that enemies are trying to undermine Russia and that people, especially young, impressionable people who consume international media, must be vigilant demonstrates conspiratorial thinking but also a unifying rallying cry. Younger Russians lack a lived, personal connection to the war, so Putin's memory politics include efforts to educate and mobilize them.[21] Russia, as is widely recognized, still feels the sting of the collapse of the Soviet empire and the political and economic instability that characterized the decade that followed. Its ontological insecurity is, arguably, more acutely felt than is the case in other countries that experienced the collapse of communism or the breakup of Cold War federations. As the most populous and powerful

---

[21] In July 2022 a new law in Russia required history classes to include new topics, such as "the rebirth of Russia as a great power in the 21st century," "reunification with Crimea," and "the special military operation in Ukraine." It also stipulated that Russian students must learn to defend historical truth and "uncover falsifications in the Fatherland's history." A new patriotic youth movement is to be formed, presided over by the President himself. Reported by Anton Troianovski, "Putin Aims to Shape a New Generation of Supporters through Schools," *The New York Times*, July 16, 2022.

republic in the USSR, Russia experienced those transformations as profound losses rather than as liberations.

Putin's interventions in memory construction in post-Soviet Russia are, he claims, a defense against distortions of the past by Eastern European countries and, I would add, what he perceives as a lack of appreciation for Russia's sacrifices in the war and the isolation of his country by the European Union, NATO, and the governments of Western European countries. Putin's memory politics, however, employ many of the same tools that far-right memory challengers in Europe, Western and Eastern, use: distortion and exaggeration, obfuscation and what-aboutism, false equivalence (although *not* the comparison of fascism and communism), as well as insider-outsider dichotomies and denialism. Elements of Putin's and European far-right narratives align, namely the emphasis on sovereignty, freedom, conservatism, and cultural and ethnic nationalism. While Putin has expressed an affinity for far-right parties in Western Europe, offering some of them financing and oil deals, his relationship with such parties in Eastern Europe is less cordial. Putin's relationship with Viktor Orban (despite the latter's staunch anti-communism) is a glaring exception. Putin sees support for nationalist-populist parties as a tool to divide Europeans, specifically as a means to sow division within institutions like the European Union and NATO.

Timothy Snyder puts a fine point on this idea:

[I]t is the Kremlin's basic alignment with the European far-Right against the European mainstream that made the rehabilitation of the Stalin-Hitler pact inevitable, or at least predictable ... they are, for the time being at least, partners in the (*sic*) Putin's new Molotov-Ribbentrop pact ... Just as Stalin sought to turn the most radical of European forces, Adolf Hitler, against Europe itself, so Putin now attempts the same thing with his grab bag of right-wingers. His allies on the far-Right are precisely the political forces that wish to bring the European Union to an end, and return Europe to an age of nation states.

(2015, 6)

If the far-right in Western Europe were to become more electorally reliable and competent when in government, then Russian sponsorship could pose a serious threat to political stability in the region. The support for far-right leaders and parties is part of a broader strategy of hybrid warfare against the West, meant to weaken cohesion inside and among these countries. While other elements of Russia's hybrid warfare are of immediate concern, such as energy politics, election interference, and disinformation in social media, the distortion of the past has gained the attention of Western European leaders, intelligence agencies, and scholars.

The more serious conflicts over interpreting the past involve Russia and Eastern Europe. The manipulation of memory of the Molotov-Ribbentrop Pact, though partially for domestic consumption, is mainly a response to the thawing out of Cold War memory in the former East Bloc. It is a strategy for countering the renationalization of wartime memory in former Soviet republics and Eastern European satellite countries, particularly in its efforts to cast communism and the Soviet Union as just as evil and deadly as fascism and the Third Reich. Doing so, the memory challenger insists, devalues the sacrifices that Soviets/Russians made in the war, which debunks the idea at the center of Russian collective memory: that the country consistently stood against Hitler, saved Europe from fascism, and thus deserves respect from the West. The contents of the Prague Declaration and the adoption of a European commemoration that remembers the Molotov-Ribbentrop Pact as a symbol of Soviet duplicity and imperialism are perceived as threats to the Russian sense of national virtue, as well as to Putin's self-perceived image as heir to a heroic past. To counteract that, Putin has done more than deflect from Soviet blame by casting Poland as responsible for provoking war in Europe in 1939. He has cultivated a new cult of the Great Patriotic War, one that rehabilitates Stalin and places Victory Day on May 9 as the most important day of remembrance.

5

Commemoration of Victory Day

The Many Meanings of the War's End

One might assume that reflections on the war in Europe over seventy-five years ago would be settled memory, that postwar and now post-Cold War generations could find a common understanding of events in commemorating the end of the most devastating conflict in modern memory, and that national war memory could now be complemented by transnational European commemoration. Key anniversaries of the war's end in Europe, particularly the sixtieth in 2005 and the seventy-fifth in 2020, however, proved the opposite: memory was far from settled, and Victory-Europe Day, VE Day, became a platform for challenging dominant narratives and for demanding recognition of many forms of national suffering, including the war's aftermath. While Western and Eastern Europeans, as well as Russians agree that VE Day marks the conclusion of military conflict in Europe, there continues to be strong disagreement about whether that date marks the start of a period of liberation from fascism, allowing for democratic renewal, or the abandonment of Eastern Europe and the continuation of oppression there under a new ideological banner. Should VE Day be commemorated as heroic or tragic?

Efforts to construct either a purely heroic or tragic narrative deflect from the complexities of the war and stifle further thoughtful reflection about the range of wartime experiences and their legacies. In recent years, the anniversary of VE Day has been used by memory actors to achieve their domestic political goals while signaling to other countries the importance of the wartime experience to a nation's contemporary status as a regional and international actor. The rhetoric and rituals surrounding recent VE Day commemorations have become media events that occasionally spark controversy and have the potential to further divide mnemonic space, particularly between Europeans and Russians.

Stefan Troebst describes 1945 as "the European *lieu de mémoire*" (2012b, 58). In this chapter, I examine the unsettled character of VE Day, one aspect of that *lieu de mémoire*. This particular day of remembrance differs from other commemorations examined in this study in that it does not mark a single event

World War II Memory and Contested Commemorations in Europe and Russia. Jennifer A. Yoder, Oxford University Press.
© Jennifer A. Yoder (2024). DOI: 10.1093/oso/9780198894162.003.0005

that took place at a specific site, nor did it affect only a specific community or group of people.[1] Its transnational nature does not translate to a common impact nor a common interpretation and memory narrative, however. More than any day of remembrance discussed in this book, VE Day is significant to all countries across the three meso-regions, but its interpretation, meaning, and centrality to national identity vary greatly.

The date of the commemoration is the first disagreement discussed in this chapter. Depending on the meso-region, May 8 or May 9 marks VE Day; since the end of the Cold War, some countries have switched from one anniversary date to the other. We then turn to the various meanings attributed to VE Day and how they have evolved over the last eight decades; even within countries, the significance and interpretation of VE Day has changed over time. The final section examines diverging attempts to instrumentalize the memory of VE Day either to challenge the dominant interpretation of the war and its end, or to use the commemoration to project a particular image at home and abroad. As with the preceding chapters, we will pay close attention to the strategies of memory challengers and reactions to them.

May 8 or May 9?

The German Instrument of Surrender was signed in Reims, France on May 7, 1945, but the war's end was formally recognized a second time, at Stalin's insistence, on May 8, 1945, in Berlin. For Western Europeans, the day after the surrender in Reims, May 8, is commemorated as the end of World War II. For the East Bloc and now for Russia, the day after *their* German surrender, May 9, marks "Victory Day" as the end of *their* "Great Patriotic War," also referred to as the "Great Fatherland War." According to Nurit Schleifman, "Although initially a mere technicality, it eventually became another sign that distinguished World War II from the Great Patriotic War" (2001, 9). As an online memorial to Soviet veterans of the war observes, "Although the Great Patriotic War was certainly a part of World War II, the Russian (and many former Soviet) people perceive it as a separate war in which the very existence of their country and their national identity were at stake."[2] Since 1984, May 9 has been celebrated as Europe Day in the European Union to commemorate Robert

---

[1] Technically, the formal end to the war occurred at two sites: the Germans surrendered at Reims, France, and a day later they surrendered in Berlin.

[2] https://english.pobediteli.ru/faq.html

Schuman's declaration on that date in 1950, leading to the eventual creation of the European Coal and Steel Community, the first step in postwar European integration.

For decades, Soviet republics and Eastern European satellite countries recognized only May 9 as the final point of the war. That would change after 1989 in Eastern Europe; most countries now observe VE Day on the 8th. Today, most post-Soviet states, with the exception of Ukraine, still commemorate Victory Day on May 9, as do some countries formerly part of Yugoslavia, like Serbia and Bosnia Herzegovina.

In Western Europe, the day evokes pride and relief or shame and remorse, depending on whether a country was on the winning or losing side of the war as of May 8, 1945. May 8 has long been an official national commemorative day in the United Kingdom and France. In Germany and Austria, both vanquished countries, the day has had different meanings, though in both cases the meaning has shifted over time. More than seventy-five years later, the meaning of VE Day today depends less on whether a country was a victor or vanquished but more importantly on which side of the Iron Curtain a country found itself on in the late 1940s. For those on the western side, no matter the actual wartime role, the day now represents liberation from fascism, wartime loss, and dislocation, but it also marks a new democratic dawn. For those on the eastern side, however, May 8/9 serves a reminder of the long period of domination and suffering—for some, at the hands of the Nazis until 1945—and for all, at the hands of the Soviets after 1945. For post-communist states, the day is linked to the Molotov-Ribbentrop Pact of August 23, 1939, the secret and informal Percentages Agreement between Churchill and Stalin in October 1944, and the Yalta Conference of February 1945, all of which register on the calendar of betrayal by Western Europe, the beginning of communist mis-development and denial of freedom. In stark contrast, for Russia, May 9 is a defining moment and symbol of a great destiny in a narrative of the war constructed largely by Vladimir Putin over the last decade. While all of the countries discussed here display a will to keep the memory of the war alive, particularly for younger generations with no personal war experience, the extreme measures to center the war in the national collective memory in Russia suggest its unusual importance for national identity in that country today. Maria Mälksoo reminds us, "the victory of World War II is the only victory of the Russian people that is celebrated throughout the world today; indeed, it is the last event in which modern Russia can proudly claim something universal in its specificity" (2009, 664).

Changing Meanings of VE Day in Germany and Austria

The memory of VE Day has been consistently triumphant in the United Kingdom and generally stable in France and Italy, two countries where other aspects of wartime memory have been challenged, as analyzed in chapter 3. The memory of the war's end has been less stable in Austria and, in particular, Germany.

Heike Karge notes that in the immediate aftermath of the war in 1945, the Day of Remembrance for the Victims of Fascism was observed across occupied Germany, beginning on September 9, 1945, in Berlin. Initiated by concentration camp survivors, the commemoration reflected an early "anti-fascist consensus" among Germans in the occupied zones. When the two German states were founded in 1949, however, the common remembrance ended in the West German state, replaced by a Remembrance Sunday in November, which recognized all victims of war and tyranny. In the communist East German state, commemorations continued on May 8, eventually shifting to May 9, but the date celebrated only the communist anti-fascist resistance, "thus changing the whole character of the memorial from the remembrance of victims to that of resistance fighters" (Karge 2012, 142).

During much of the Cold War, May 8 was commemorated as a day of liberation from fascism in East Germany and as a day of defeat in West Germany. The first Federal President of the West German state, Theodor Heuss, said on May 8, 1949, "The fundamental fact is that for each of us May 8, 1945 remains the most tragic and questionable paradox of history. Why? Because we were, at one and the same time, redeemed and annihilated."[3] While both states saw May 8, 1945, as an occasion for a new beginning, it would be thirty years before a West German leader, this time Foreign Minister Walter Scheel would use the term "liberate" to describe the date: "We were liberated from a terrible yoke. From war, murder, subjugation and barbarity . . . but we have not forgotten that this liberation came from the outside. That we, Germans, were not capable of shaking off this yoke ourselves" (2020).

The meaning of May 8 in West Germany began to change along with the official memory culture, which as earlier chapters noted, experienced a relatively long and public debate resulting in a dominant memory culture of contrition. In an important speech in 1985, as the fortieth anniversary of the end of the war approached, Federal President Richard von Weizäcker reminded his

---

[3] Marcel Fürstenau, "May 8, 1945: Total Defeat or Day of Liberation?" DeutscheWelle, May 5, 2020. https://www.dw.com/en/may-8-1945-total-defeat-or-day-of-liberation/a-53340869

fellow citizens, "We must not regard the end of the war as the cause of flight, expulsion and deprivation of freedom . . . The cause goes back to the start of the tyranny that brought about war. We must not separate May 8, 1945, from January 30, 1933." He also memorably said, "Today, on May 8, let us as best as we can, look truth straight in the eye" (Weizäcker 1985). Thus, over four decades, the meaning of May 8 shifted from loss and occupation to liberation and a new start.

In Austria, likewise occupied by the victorious Allies in 1945, May 8 was celebrated squarely as a liberation day. Unlike West Germany, postwar Austria focused on positive days of remembrance, such as its declaration of independence (it regained full sovereignty when occupation ended in 1955) and the proclamation of its neutrality (Pirker et al. 2019, 442). In addition, Austria commemorated its fallen Wehrmacht soldiers at the historic Heroes' Monument in Vienna's Heroes Square, something unimaginable in Cold War Bonn or even post-Cold War Berlin. Much later, when Austria became an EU member in the mid-1990s, the meaning of the day began to change. May 8 became a date for mourning victims of the Holocaust locally in Vienna but not nationally. The date had "scant significance in Austria's official culture of commemoration" until 2012, about which more is said below (Pirker et al. 2019, 442).

VE Day for Eastern Europeans: Liberation or Abandonment?

Throughout the Cold War, Eastern European satellite states and the republics of the Soviet Union were obliged to commemorate Victory Day on May 9 as proscribed by Moscow. After the 1989 collapse of communism in Eastern Europe and the 1991 break-up of the USSR, commemorations in the Baltics and other Central and Eastern European countries quickly shifted from May 9 to May 8. The meaning of the commemoration, once jubilant, also shifted. Most post-communist countries in the region (with the exception of Belarus) began to remember May 8, 1945, not as a symbol of liberation but of communist domination and Western betrayal (Mälksoo 2009; Onken 2007). Lithuanian President Valdas Adamkus said in 2009, "Unfortunately, this date is also a reminder of a forcefully disunited and divided Europe. For Lithuania, like many other eastern European nations, May 8 of 1945 did not bring victory over violence, but simply a change of oppressor. Once again, history was turned into the handmaiden of politics and ideology and thrust upon

Lithuania and its people to cover up injustice and crime, distort facts, slander independence and freedom-fighters."[4] Among Eastern European societies today, there is a clear desire to move away from Russian mnemonic influence and commemorative traditions. They prefer to commemorate August 23, 1939, over May 8, 1945, and to foreground their memory of Stalinist victimization alongside, or even above, that of the defeat of Nazism and the memory of the Holocaust.

Poland and the Baltic states used the occasion of the sixtieth anniversary of the war's end to make a clear distinction between May 8 and May 9, distancing their countries from the Soviet/Russian emphasis on liberation (the latter) and, instead, embracing the former as Europe Day. Mälksoo (2009) describes a kind of competition between Eastern European countries and Russia to set the record straight during the sixtieth anniversary of VE Day, to correct the West and the international community about Eastern interpretations of the war's end. Latvian President Vike-Freiberga was the only leader of a Baltic country to accept Russian President Putin's invitation to attend a commemorative event and military parade in Moscow on the occasion of the sixtieth anniversary, which the Russian president had extended to fifty heads of state/government. The Lithuanian and Estonian leaders declined to attend, stressing the negative Soviet/Russian role in their histories and collective memories. Joined by the Polish president, Vike-Freiberga did not stand quietly by and allow Putin to dominate the "collected" memory of VE Day in 2005. On several occasions, she made bold statements refuting the traditional Soviet narrative of the war, statements that "were explicitly intent on revealing the 'other side' of the Soviet participation in the war, as well as calling for Western support to encourage Russia to express its regret over the post-war subjugation of Eastern Europe as a direct ramification of the Molotov-Ribbentrop Pact" (Mälksoo 2009, 667). In doing so, Vike-Freiberga asserted an Eastern European, post-colonial memory of May 8 and boldly opposed Putin's memory politics.

Eastern Europeans' efforts inside the European Union to draw attention to the crimes of communism and their suffering during the Cold War were briefly discussed in the last chapter. Their efforts to downgrade the importance of VE Day commemorations and upgrade August 23, 1939, as the key date in the twentieth century make clear this meso-region's mnemonic priorities. On the occasion of the seventy-fifth anniversary of VE Day, the presidents of the three

---

[4] "History Based on Falsification Is No History," Opening address by Valdas Adamkus, President of the Republic of Lithuania, at the 22nd European Meeting of Cultural Journals, Eurozine May 20, 2009. https://www.eurozine.com/history-based-on-falsification-is-no-history/

Baltic countries issued a joint statement that made clear the meaning of the date—May 8, not May 9—to their countries:

> We, the Presidents of Estonia, Latvia and Lithuania, commemorate the 75th anniversary of the end of World War II in Europe, honour the sacrifice of all victims and the Allied soldiers who defeated the Nazi regime on 8 May 1945, thus liberating many European countries from occupation and ending the horrors of the Holocaust . . . However, the end of World War II does not mark freedom to the nations of Central and Eastern Europe. Instead, one totalitarian regime was replaced by another.
>
> (*Estonian World*, May 7, 2020)

Victory Day for Russia: Great, Greater, Greatest

Victory Day became the most important day of remembrance in the Soviet Union; that continues to be the case in post-Soviet Russia. Typically, there has been a military parade on May 9, viewed on television by three-quarters of the Russian public, a Victory Speech delivered by the Soviet, now Russian leader; people across the country observe a minute of silence at 6:55 MST.[5] People traditionally wear St. George Ribbons, a military symbol associated with patriotism, dating back to the Russian Empire. The Banner of Victory, representing the flag that the Red Army waved from the top of the Reichstag building in Berlin, is another symbol associated with this commemoration. Mass processions called Immortal Regiments which began as grassroots movements have been coopted by the state. This popular ritual is observed by carrying pictures of one's relatives who fought in the war.[6] Another relevant ritual associated with May 9 is the laying of wreaths at war monuments, including the Tomb of the Unknown Soldier in Moscow.

Victory Day symbolizes the heroism and bravery of the Soviet military, along with the sacrifice, suffering, and massive civilian losses required to defeat Nazi Germany. Its centrality for Soviet, now Russian identity lies in its "[p]rogress-glorifying messianism," as Mälksoo describes it (2009, 664). Elizabeth Wood calls it "[A] morality tale of suffering and redemption and a foundation myth" (2011, 173). The day of remembrance serves to remind Russians of their uniqueness among nations. As a commemoration that seeks to

---

[5] According to Andrei Kolesnikov, "Our Dark Past Is Our Bright Future: How the Kremlin Uses and Abuses History," Carnegie Moscow Center, May 5, 2020.

[6] The processions began by and featured ordinary citizens in 2012. In 2015, they prominently featured participation by senior political officials.

mobilize the mass public, it has been almost a founding day, much more significant to memory culture and national identity than the October Revolution was for the USSR or than any other date has become in post-Soviet Russia.

The day has not been uniformly or consistently observed since 1945. Its commemorative evolution illustrates the significance of political context and, often, the role of top executive leaders in framing memory. On May 9, 1945, the Supreme Soviet declared May 9 a work-free "Feast of Victory," with lavish celebrations across the USSR (Tumarkin 2003). Three years later, the commemoration was changed to a regular workday. Roman Serbyn explains the reason for the change: "the work-free Victory Day was not conducive to the development of a glorified image of war desired by Stalin. It gave the citizens time for unsupervised recollections of the horrors of war" (Serbyn 2007, 114). Thereafter, the commemoration was "supervised" by workplace and school discussions allowing for control over the narrative (Serbyn 2007, 114). Under Nikita Khrushchev (1953–1964), Victory Day was freed from the cult of Stalin, though the holiday remained a workday. Leonid Brezhnev (1964–1982) restored the holiday's importance and its status as a work-free day, starting in 1965. Under Vladimir Putin, Victory Day is not only commemorated as a sacred day, it is treated as the important public holiday in Russia.

The symbolic importance and political potential of Victory Day was not only expressed in terms of its status as a work-free holiday. Who was being commemorated was also contentious: was it the Soviet people who had sacrificed so much, or Stalin? May 9 was not initially a holiday from work for fear of suggesting the people had been at the center of the war and Victory Day, rather than Stalin. Because Stalin was so closely associated with the war, the memory of May 9 lost some of its potency under Khrushchev's destalinization and thaw. It is possible that political elites resented the legitimacy it accorded military leaders and soldiers, and saw the centering of Victory Day in the public imagination as a possible threat to their own legitimacy. Whatever the reason, Brezhnev reversed course on May 9, reconstructing a cult of the Great PatrioticWar around it. Rituals developed that brought school children and aging veterans together to educate new generations about the sacrifices of their elders. Nina Tumarkin describes the master-narrative that solidified under Brezhnev: "collectivization and rapid industrialization under the first and second Five-year Plans prepared the country for war, and despite an overpowering surprise attack by the Fascist Beast and its inhuman wartime practices, despite the loss of 20 million valiant martyrs to the Cause, our country, under the leadership of the Communist Party headed by Comrade Stalin, arose as one united front and expelled the enemy from our own territory and that of East Europe, thus saving Europe—and the world—from Fascist enslavement" (Tumarkin 2003, 601).

Under the leadership of Mikhail Gorbachev (1985–1991), the day of remembrance became more muted. *Glasnost* invited a closer look at Soviet history and, in particular, a more critical examination of the human toll of the Stalin years. Tumarkin says of Gorbachev's policies, they "demolished that sonorous combination of selfpity and self-congratulation that for so long had characterized the official memorialization of the 'Great Patriotic War.' An enshrined, idealized saga is being replaced with raw human memory" (1991, i). Moreover, the economic hardships confronting most Russians by the early 1990s challenged what had been a widely held consensus about the war and how it should be remembered. It is worth quoting Tumarkin, writing while Gorbachev still led the country, once more to underline the impact of *glasnost* on wartime memory:

> Can the Soviet Union find a social cement to replace the idealized memory of the Great Patriotic War? Until just a few years ago, memories and legendary recollections about the war years had created a cosmology that informed Soviet political culture, providing generations of Soviet citizens and their leaders with the fundamental lexicon they drew upon to explain themselves to the world. Now the loss of this shared memory has left the Soviet people in the throes of a spiritual crisis every bit as wrenching as the political and economic shocks that have sent their country spinning toward chaos
>
> (1991, iv)

Gorbachev's post-Soviet successor in Russia, Boris Yeltsin (1991–1999), saw the utility of the Great Patriotic War for building legitimacy for his regime and for fostering Russian, rather than Soviet, patriotism. Under Yeltsin, the project to refurbish Victory Park in Moscow was finally finished. The park at Poklonnaya Gora (Prostration Hill) was created following the victory over Napoleon's forces in the 1812 Patriotic War.[7] In the immediate aftermath of World War II, some, especially military leaders, favored adding to the park to commemorate the Great Patriotic War.[8] The project failed to take off for four decades, until the mid-1980s when work was resumed. In 1995, on the fiftieth anniversary of VE Day, many world leaders gathered in Moscow to join

---

[7] The name "Prostration Hill" recalls an old ritual whereby people arriving at that spot in Moscow from the west bowed down in homage.

[8] For an excellent analysis of the evolution of the park and its relevance to Soviet and Russian cultures of remembrance, see Nurit Schleifman, "Moscow's Victory Park: *A Monumental Change*," *History and Memory*, Vol. 13, No. 2 (Fall/Winter 2001) 5–34.

Russian President Yeltsin in solemn commemoration. In a move away from Soviet memory and toward Russian liberal-national identity, Yeltsin ended the practice of holding military parades in Red Square. During his presidency, central/official commemorations competed with those organized by local officials. To some degree, the dueling commemorations reflected political divisions between Yeltsin-supporters and opposition to his leadership (Smith 2002).

Today, the commemoration once again embraces the greatness of *Soviet* and, importantly, *Stalin's* victory and achievements. Putin has also overseen a remilitarization of the Victory Day commemoration, emphasizing the themes of Russian pride and defiance in a hostile world. In 2020, he added a legal dimension to his memory politics: the 1993 Russian Constitution was amended to ensure that the country "cherishes the memory of the defenders of the Fatherland and secures the defense of historical truth" (Laruelle 2020, n.p.). The commemoration gatherings for the sixtieth anniversary in 2005 and the seventieth anniversary in 2015 were the largest in Russia since the end of the Soviet Union. They were used by Putin to consolidate a particular interpretation of VE Day at home and to push back on more critical narratives in Europe, particularly in the Baltics and Poland.

With this overview of the evolution of the commemorations of May 8/9 across the three mnemonic regions, we now turn to the actors who attempt to instrumentalize the VE Day and the means by which they do so.

Memory Challengers and their Strategies

Germany

May 8 is not an official national holiday in Germany, though it has been recognized as an official day of commemoration in individual federal states.[9] In 2020, Esther Bejarano, a Holocaust survivor and chairwoman of the Auschwitz Committee in Germany proposed to make May 8 an official state holiday commemorating the liberation from fascism in all of Germany. The proposal found support among politicians of some political parties, namely the Greens, Left Party, and the Liberals, but was not endorsed by Chancellor Merkel or her

---

[9] It is an official day of commemoration but not a state holiday in Mecklenburg-Western Pomerania since 2002 and in Brandenburg since 2015. DeutscheWelle February 8, 2020.

government. Bejarano's online petition had collected 150,000 signatures by June 2021.[10] She died one month later.

Not everyone in the FRG agreed with Federal President Weizäcker's interpretation of May 8 as a day of liberation. The same year Weizäcker delivered his speech, in 1985, *Der Spiegel* editor Rudolf Augstein asked whether Germany's unconditional surrender invoked a collapse or a new beginning. As Tony Joel notes, Augstein's question was "clearly crafted for an 'either-or' rather than an 'as-well-as' answer" (Joel 2013, 1). Ten years later, on the fiftieth anniversary of VE Day, a group calling itself "Initiative 8. Mai" (May 8 Action Group) gave a clear answer. Comprised of prominent public figures, incumbent and former members of the federal and state parliaments, academics, editors and journalists, this group sought to downplay the liberation idea and shift the memory narrative to German suffering. One of the initiators was Alfred Dregger, a right-wing politician and leader of the Christian Democratic Union (CDU), who advocated the country "coming out of Hitler's shadow." The group took out large ads in the newspaper *Frankfurter Allgemeine Zeitung* (FAZ) in the weeks before the May 8 anniversary in 1995 with uppercase headlines warning "AGAINST FORGETTING" and stating:

> This day not only meant the end of the National Socialist reign of terror, but also the beginning of the terror of the expulsion and new oppression in the East and the start of the division of our country. A view of history that conceals, suppresses, or relativizes this truth cannot be the basis for the self-understanding of a self-assured nation.
>
> (quoted in Joel 2013, 2)

These early right-wing memory challengers sought to invert Germany's World War II role, from victimizer to victim—first of Hitler's "reign of terror," then of postwar policies and wartime narratives. This interpretation deliberately de-contextualized the suffering of Germans, failing to link it to the war of aggression, the destruction of much of Europe, and the Holocaust. About three hundred people signed the Appeal, most of whom were affiliated with the far-right Republikaner party, the CDU, its Bavarian sister-party the CSU, the FDP, right-wing publications like *Junge Freiheit*, or the military. On the sixtieth anniversary of VE Day in 2005, the Appeal was republished in the FAZ. The New Right think tank, the Institut für Staatspolitik (Institute for State Policy)

---

[10] See the petition at https://www.change.org/p/make-8th-may-a-public-holiday-needs-to-be-done-75years-after-the-liberation-from-fascism.

dedicated a conference to the Appeal that year, featuring speakers like Ernst Nolte, the conservative historian who had sparked the *Historikerstreit*.

The memory divide persists in Germany today. The left tends to view May 8 as a day of liberation, while the right sees it either as a "paradox" (like Federal President Theodor Heuss in the 1950s) or as a day of surrender. The far right is outspoken about its view. In 2005, for example, the NPD used the sixtieth anniversary of VE to stage a protest against the "cult of guilt" in Germany. Over 3,300 extremists gathered on the Alexanderplatz in central Berlin; they had planned to march through the Brandenburg Gate and past the Holocaust Memorial, but changed their route in the face of a large counter-demonstration. The main challenger today of Germany's memory culture of contrition is the far-right Alternative for Germany (AfD) party, discussed in chapters 1 and 2. In the days leading to the seventy-fifth anniversary in 2020, AfD leader Alexander Gauland argued against making May 8 a public holiday, saying its legacy was too ambivalent (DeutscheWelle May 6, 2020).

In direct response, German Foreign Minister Heiko Maas made a strong statement (co-authored with German historian Andreas Wirsching, released on May 7, 2020) warning of the dangers of forgetting over memory. In sharp rebuke of Gauland's claim pertaining to the legacy's "ambivalence," Maas declared "8 May 1945 shaped our recent past more profoundly than any other day." He then described the stakes for Germany:

> Those who now want to draw a line under this part of German history not only mock the victims but also rob Germany of its political credibility. Self-criticism and self-confidence are mutually dependent. This applies more to our country than to any other. We cannot conceive of politics without history. But conversely? How much politics is good for history?

In no uncertain terms, he criticizes attempts to distort history and invert wartime roles:

> 8 May thus shows one thing very clearly, namely that history shapes who we are, both as people and nations, thus making honesty in how we treat the past all the more important. German history demonstrates the danger of a revisionism that replaces rational thinking with national myths. That— and not a supposed moral superiority—is why we Germans in particular are called on to take a stand when those under attack are depicted as the assailants and victims are portrayed as the perpetrators. The repeated attempt in recent months to rewrite history so disgracefully requires us to speak up

loud and clear—something that should not actually be necessary in view of the irrefutable historical facts—and to leave no doubt whatsoever that Germany alone unleashed the Second World War by its invasion of Poland and Germany alone is responsible for the crimes against humanity of the Holocaust. Those who sow doubt about this and thrust other countries into the role of perpetrator do injustice to the victims, exploit history for their own ends and divide Europe

(Maas and Wirsching 2020).

Far-right parties, emboldened by their role outside parliament (NPD) or in the opposition (AfD), are outspoken in their desire to downgrade the dominant memory culture emphasis on contrition and responsibility and, instead, renationalize the narrative and invert Germany's role from perpetrator to victim. In contrast to the more conservative Kohl governments, the four Merkel governments, in which Maas served as foreign minister (2018–2021), were quick to call out revisionist rhetoric on the past of far-right actors and also emphatic in their articulation of a memory narrative of contrition.

Austria

Although Austria did not develop a nationwide commemoration of May 8, nor did it participate in any significant way in the Europe-wide fiftieth anniversary events, its commemorative practice began to change in reaction to a far-right-wing memory challenge that surfaced in 1996. That year on May 8, right-wing pan-Germanic fraternities (*Burschenschaften*), organized under the umbrella of the Wiener Korporationsring (Viennese Corporation Ring, WKR), held a *Totengedenken* (death-memorial) ceremony to mourn fallen Wehrmacht soldiers and members of the SS. Their commemoration of VE Day clearly involved a negative memory, not a day of liberation or even as a paradox. These traditionalist, ultra-nationalist fraternities, widely recognized as "the ideological and intellectual core of the FPÖ," the far-right Austrian People's Party, deliberately chose the crypt at the historic Heroes' Square in Vienna as the site for their commemoration (Pirker et al. 2019, 443). Built to honor the heroes of the Habsburg Dynasty, the Heldenplatz was the site where Hitler had announced the *Anschluss* (annexation) in 1938. The crypt under the Heroes' monument has also been controversial, since it held a book of honor for dead soldiers that contained a hidden message of support for National Socialism and the *Anschluss*. As Pater Pirker et al., attested, the message "disqualified the Heroes' Monument as an official place of remembrance, revealing the problematic practices of war commemoration in Austria after 1945" (448). Despite the obvious, problematic symbolism of the date and site of the *Totengedeken*, subsequent annual commemorative gatherings sponsored by the fraternities originally met with little media or public reaction. The WKR May 8 ceremonies grew more robust during the years when the FPÖ was politically powerful, as in 2000 when it entered into a governing coalition with the center-right People's Party (ÖVP), or in 2011 when it mobilized anti-immigration and anti-EU protest (443–4).

The appropriation of May 8 by the far-right was eventually met with resistance by political parties on the left, namely, the Social Democrats (SPÖ), the Greens, and by a host of civil society groups. These critical voices insisted on restoring the commemoration to its original meaning: liberation from war and Nazism. In 2012, the opposition began to mobilize against the right-wing appropriation of May 8. At the forefront was the Mauthausen Committee of Austria (MKÖ), representing survivors of Mauthausen concentration camp. Between 1938 and 1945, the camp inside Austria held 190,000 prisoners from all over Europe, of which more than 90,000 did not survive. On May 8, 2013, the MKÖ and several other civil society groups held the first Festival of Joy on May 8 at the Heldenplatz. The commemoration attracted 10,000 people, featuring speeches by Chancellor Werner Fayman of the SPÖ, Vice-Chancellor Michael Spindelegger of the ÖVP, representatives of the Viennese city government, Holocaust survivors and resistance fighters as well as a free concert by the Vienna Symphony Orchestra. The 2020 and 2021 commemorations, along with a free concert of the Vienna Symphony Orchestra, were held online due to restrictions on public gatherings during the covid-19 pandemic.[11]

In the Austrian case, the institutionalization of the May 8 as a positive, national commemoration occurred only after, and as a corrective to, far-right memory challengers' appropriation of the day for mourning soldiers who had fought for the pan-Germanic Nazi cause. Civil society actors played a crucial role returning the commemoration to its original meaning and pushing it into the public conscience. Speaking before the 2018 Festival of Joy, MKÖ Chairman Willi Mernyi characterized the commemoration's relevance for linking the past and the present this way: "People who have to leave their countries have lost everything. War and terror have turned their homeland into a for-

---

[11] https://www.festderfreude.at/en/the-festival/the-8-may, accessed March 26, 2021.

eign place. That was the case eighty years ago and so it is also the case today. That is something we may not forget."[12] The memory of the war should not be interpreted through the narrow lens of nationalism, nor should it foster the glorification of soldiers who fought for the Nazi regime. Instead, it should serve as a reminder of the fragility of freedom and the need to protect it, in standing against tyranny.

Eastern Europe

For the Baltic states and Eastern Europe, VE Day is first and foremost a reminder of Stalinization and decades of communist rule. Freed from one oppressor in 1945, they were abandoned by the West and subject to a new oppressor that, some claim, was worse than the Nazis. Having been left to languish behind the Iron Curtain, many wished to set the record straight about May 8/9 once they were free by pressing the European Union to focus on other days of remembrance that more powerfully symbolize Eastern European victimhood, namely August 23, 1939 or, perhaps, the Yalta Conference of February 4–11, 1945, the agreement that gave Stalin an unquestioned sphere of influence in Eastern Europe.

Several Eastern European countries have banned the public display of Soviet symbols; only Ukraine, however, under former president, Viktor Poroshenko, officially replaced the term "Great Patriotic War" with "Second World War" in 2015. Ukraine, Moldova, and Lithuania have banned display of the St. George Ribbon (discussed below). Such bans, along with the removal of Soviet monuments and memorials, increased in the context of Russian annexation of Crimea in 2014 and the Russian invasion of Ukraine in February of 2022. One site of Soviet wartime memory in Eastern Europe became the subject of a memory war between Latvia and its large Russian minority. The sprawling Victory Park in the Latvian capital city Riga included a number of imposing monuments, including the 80-meter Monument to the Liberators of Soviet Latvia and Riga from the German Fascist Invaders, erected in 1985. Victory Park and other Soviet sites of memory throughout the country came under the protection of a 1994 agreement made by Russia and Latvia to maintain and care for each other's war graves and memorials. As with

---

[12] Mauthausen Committee, "Fest der Freude am 8. Mai: Befreiung Österreichs vom Nationalsozialismus" (April 10, 2018), https://www.ots.at/presseaussendung/OTS_20180410_OTS0042/fest-der-freude-am-8-mai-befreiung-oesterreichs-vom-nationalsozialismus-bild.

the Bronze Soldier of Tallinn,[13] Victory Park became a site for ethnic Russians' commemoration of Victory Day on May 9. As George F. Sander puts it, "The government [of Latvia] wasn't happy about these celebrations, but it maintained a hands-off attitude toward them. That was before February 24"—the date in 2022 when Russia invaded Ukraine (Sander July 21, 2022). A few months later, on May 26, the Latvian Saeima voted for a new law, "On the Prohibition of the Display of Objects Glorifying the Soviet and Nazi Regimes and Their Dismantling in the Territory of the Republic of Latvia." The Monument to the Liberators was destroyed by the Latvian government in August 2022, in protest against Russia's war in Ukraine. The Riga city government defended the decision by saying it would not allow symbols that "justify and glorify aggression" (Kwai August 26, 2022).

Russia

"Happy Victory Day! The Victory had a colossal historic significance for the fate of the entire world. It is a holiday that has always been and will remain a sacred day for Russia, for our nation. It is our holiday by right, for we are blood relatives of those who defeated, crushed, destroyed Nazism. It is ours because we descend from the generation of victors, a generation we are proud of and hold in great honour. Our dear veterans, we bow before your courage and strong spirit and thank you for this immortal example of unity and love for our Motherland.... The Soviet people fulfilled their sacred oath, defended their Motherland and liberated Europe from the 'brown plague.'"
(Vladimir Putin, Victory Day speech on Red Square, May 9, 2021)

It is hard to exaggerate the significance of World War II for Putin's memory politics. The Great Patriotic War lies at the center of his increasingly active, potent memory politics. The domestic agenda clearly served by such memory politics is, first and foremost, the strengthening of national cohesion. The traumatic course set in motion by the break-up of the USSR and the political, economic, and social chaos of the 1990s weakened national unity. Restoring national unity, pride, and a sense of national mission have counted among Putin's priorities since he became president in late 1999. Their restoration

---

[13] For more on the memory war over this Soviet war memorial in Estonia's capital and its relocation, see Marko Lehti, Matti Jutila, and Markku Jokisipilä, "Never-ending Second World War: Public Performances of National Dignity and the Drama of the Bronze Soldier." *Journal of Baltic Studies*, Vol. 39, No. 4 (2008): 393–418 and Siobhan Kattago, "War Memorials and the Politics of Memory: The Soviet War Memorial in Tallinn." *Constellations*, Vol. 16, No. 1 (2009): 150–66.

helps to legitimize his leadership and the regime he has shaped. Before turn-ing to the role of Victory Day in Putin's mnemonic maneuvers, we explore the content and uses of the cult of the Great Patriotic War.

The Great Patriotic War is associated with the conservative values that Putin seeks to re-instill in Russian society: nationalism, militarism, obedience, and sacrifice. Those values are reflected in the many Red Army memorials, sym-bols, and stories told about the heroism of its soldiers. They are also associated with many millions of Russian civilians who sacrificed so much. The values embodied by the war generation are meant to inspire younger generations for whom sacrifice and obedience may be less familiar. The cult of war that Putin has revived fosters a belief in the uniqueness of Russians, their special virtues, character, and their sense of a mission, which today, as then, needs to stand up to threats to their culture and their vast territory. The Great Patriotic War rep-resents the pinnacle of Russians' bravery as the ultimate rescuers and restorers of peace. Unlike so many other Soviet memories, the war represents a "usable past," one that is presented as solely positive. Any questions as to whether the scope of death and destruction might have been less had another leader been in charge, much less public debate about the facts of the war and what came after, are not only criticized, they are not permitted. In contrast to criticisms of Stalin allowed by Khrushchev, Gorbachev, and Yeltsin, Putin has encouraged the rehabilitation of Stalin as a great war leader. In fact, the strength of Stalin as a leader is a motif that is useful to Putin; he has made a point of showing his admiration for authoritarian leadership during the war. Like Stalin, Putin wishes to be associated with heroism, the unity of the country, global power and respect.

Putin personally identifies with the Great Patriotic War and frequently meets with veterans, publicly venerating them. He also personalizes the war by repeatedly relating his own family's suffering during the siege of Leningrad. He makes frequent use of high profile, media-fueled visits to war memo-rials, in or near Orthodox churches, and relishes participating in military parades. Elizabeth Wood notes, "By making the war a personal event and also a sacred one, Vladimir Putin has created a myth and a ritual that elevates him personally, uniting Russia (at least theoretically) and showing him as the nat-ural hero-leader, the warrior who is personally associated with defending the Motherland" (Wood 2011, 198). His speech at the Victory Day commemora-tion in Red Square in 2021, particularly the lines quoted above, underscored the national values and sense of national unity that Putin prioritizes.

Putin uses the cult of the war to remind Russians of the need for military strength in a hostile neighborhood. His embrace of military parades, with daunting columns of soldiers and tanks, is meant to be a spectacle of military strength that both energizes his domestic audience and puts external actors on alert. In a similar way, Putin uses symbols of "martial masculinity" to mobilize societal engagement with wartime memory. In connection with the fiftieth anniversary of Victory Day (2005), his government launched the St. George Ribbon campaign. The orange and black ribbon of the Order of St. George dates back to the Russian Empire, formerly the highest military decoration awarded. It carried over to the Soviet Union, where it was accorded to soldiers who fought in the Great Patriotic War. In 2005, the government distributed free ribbons to Russians across the country. Irina Novikova holds that, "The Ribbon, which asks for individual performance or choice, has turned into a remarkably effective commemorative symbol of Russian martial/heroic masculinity, uniting Russian imperial and Soviet military histories" (2011, 595). According to Vladimir Jushkin of the Baltic Center for Russian Studies:

> In terms of its symbolic meaning and practical usage, wearing the Ribbon of St. George resembles wearing a cross around one's neck for Christians or wearing a yarmulke for Jews. In the first place, it points to identity as a "true patriot of Russia," and on the other hand, in this way it gives its wearer the chance to feel good and comfortable in society, and to participate in rites.
>
> ("In the Fog of Victory: Glorification of the Soviet Legacy in Russia," March 17, 2020)

The Ribbon has been banned in some other post-Soviet countries for the same reason.

Beyond rhetoric and symbols, the Putin regime has fostered martial masculinity through sites of nostalgia, heroism, and military might. One example, Patriot Park, opened outside of Moscow in 2016. The 123-acre park, often called Russia's "military Disneyland," offers visitors opportunities to see and even engage with Russian military technology and equipment. Putin has described the park as "an important element in our system of military-patriotic work with young people."[14] Please see Figure 5.1.

The park's key features include: an open-air display that stretches over twelve pavilions with tanks, armored vehicles, aircraft, and "game center" with a simulator of a T-80 tank; an interactive Guerrilla Village dedicated to partisan detachments formed in the Great Patriotic War against Germany and their

---

[14] Quoted in Shaun Walker, "Vladimir Putin opens Russian 'military Disneyland' Patriot Park," June 16, 2015. https://www.theguardian.com/world/2015/jun/16/vladimir-putin-opens-russian-military-disneyland-patriot-park

Figure 5.1 Patriot Park outside Moscow
Source: Photo 79822147 © Igor Dolgov | Dreamstime.com.

"everyday life and heroic deeds"; a Shooting Range, reportedly the largest in Russia, featuring twenty-nine shooting galleries, but "only blank shooting and air guns are available for foreign citizens"; a center of military tactical games, which includes airsoft and laser tag; an equestrian center; an extreme sports area; a Patriot EXPO for exhibits and forums, including ones that are "international"; and an area for historical reenactments (*RussiaEguide*, n.d.). Among the historical enactments was one of the Red Army's storming of the German Reichstag in May 1945 in Berlin. For that particular reenactment, which occurred in 2017, a model of the Reichstag was built, allowing 5,000 spectators to watch "Explosions send fire through the air, aircraft drone overhead, tanks rumble across the cratered ground, and machine guns chatter in murderous conversation on a chaotic battlefield" (Varangis 2017). Russian Defense Minister Sergei Shoigu proclaimed that the reenactment "will contribute to the patriotic education of young citizens and foreign guests" (Varangis 2017). The Reichstag event was geared specifically toward the Junarmija (youth army), or All-Russia Young Army National Military Patriotic Social Movement Association, created by Shoigu's Ministry in 2016 to train future military personnel and to instill patriotic values and remembrance of Russia's wartime past. It is open to youth between the ages of 8 and 17 and in 2020 had 718,000 members (CSIS September 22, 2020).

Putin's instrumentalization of war history has been aided by several efforts. The first measure centers on Putin's own attempt to cast himself as historical interpreter. Andrei Kolesnikov of the Carnegie Moscow Center observed that Putin's effort to change the historical narrative has developed in two stages. The first step was to draw attention away from events. For this he has utilized obfuscation or erasure, such as claiming to save Europe from Nazism, while ignoring crimes committed in the name of the USSR during the war and through a system of oppression that spread throughout Eastern Europe afterwards. The second stage has entailed filling the void with a new version of events.[15] This has included the rehabilitation of Stalin, a reinterpretation of the Molotov-Ribbentrop Pact, and the commissioning of new history textbooks for students.

To control the narrative about the Great Patriotic War, Putin has engaged historians, think tanks, and publishing houses. He has also used a range of other institutions, including the Russian Constitution and the national legislature, to construct a particular memory of war, silencing pluralistic or critical interpretations of the wartime past. A 2004 law closed historical archives that had been partially opened by the Yeltsin government in the early 1990s. Dina Khapaeva writes that the purpose of the law was to "protect" or rather prevent access to information about Russian citizens, "making it completely impossible to pursue any historical research—not to speak of any legal cases—against the perpetrators responsible for mass crimes against humanity under Stalin" (2016, 67).

A decade later, in May 2014, the Russia State Duma passed a law (Article 354.1 of the Criminal Code) that:

- prohibits the "exoneration of Nazism"
- penalizes the "dissemination of knowingly false information on the activities of the USSR during the Second World War," as well as the "desecration of symbols of military glory"
- prohibits "denying the facts recognized by the international military tribunal that convicted and punished major war criminals of the European Axis countries" as well as approval "of the crimes this tribunal condemned"
- prohibits the dissemination of "information on military and memorial commemorative dates related to Russia's defense that is disrespectful of society, and desecrating symbols of Russia's military glory publicly" (Wojcik 2020).

---

[15] Andrei Kolesnikov, "Our Dark Past Is Our Bright Future: How the Kremlin Uses and Abuses History," March 5, 2020.

The law's first application in 2014 focused on a Russian blogger named Vladimir Luzgin, who had posted the following statement: "The Communists and Germany jointly invaded Poland, sparking off World War II. That is, communism and Nazism closely collaborated." For this, he was convicted and fined 200,000 Rubles under the law.

In another act of official revisionism, the Perm Memorial Museum at the site of a former Soviet Gulag camp was closed in April 2014 and its employees harassed. The "reimagined" museum reopened in 2015 but focused on camp personnel rather than inmates. The original museum, which addressed the victims of Stalinism, was at odds with Putin's narrow view of the war and its aftermath and his narrative use of Stalin as a great leader. Together, these efforts to reintegrate "major pillars of Soviet propaganda" and to revive "Soviet demigods . . . into a state-sponsored historical narrative under Putin," create a fantasy of national unity (Khapaeva 68).

Victory Day plays a central role in Putin's conservative-nationalist project, by connecting the past, present, and future with one simple idea: Russia's special role. This idea fosters unity and pride in a country that feels ontologically insecure in a geographic region where former republics and satellites have joined or wish to join the European Union and NATO and where globalization makes it more challenging to insulate Russians from outside ideas and practices. The seventy-fifth Diamond Jubilee anniversary of the end of World War II provided a showcase for Putin's memory politics in action. While commemorative events in other countries were sharply curtailed to virtual modalities, due to the covid-19 pandemic, the show went on in Russia. Despite having the third highest (reported) coronavirus infection rate at the time (behind the United States and Brazil), the military parade through Red Square was massive. On display were 14,000 troops, 300 military vehicles and 75 war planes. Please see Figure 5.2.

Curiously, the parade was postponed from May 9 to June 24, the actual day that a parade at Red Square organized by the Red Army had taken place in 1945. A more logical reason for the postponement of the Victory Day celebration was the timing of a vote on sweeping constitutional changes.[16] As Vladimir Isanchenkov reported for the Associated Press at the time: "President Vladimir Putin's insistence on holding the parade reflects not only his desire to put Russia's power on display but also to bolster patriotic sentiments a week before a constitutional referendum that could allow him to remain in office until 2036."[17] The date for the plebiscite on the constitution, originally set for

---

[16] 206 changes to the Russian Constitution were included in the one yes/no vote.
[17] Vladimir Isanchenkov, "Putin Uses Parade to Boost Support before Vote," June 23, 2020, https://apnews.com/article/4ff118bcdd26bc59be06271bc3d31482.

Figure 5.2 2020 Moscow Victory Day Parade
Source: Mikhail Voskresenskiy, Host Photo Agency via AP.

April 22, was postponed until June 25–July 1, 2020. The constitutional changes allowed Putin to run for two more six-year presidential terms. They also put a number of conservative measures in place, including a ban on same-sex marriage, mandatory patriotic education in schools, and setting the Russian constitution above international law. The changes, moreover, include a direct reference to Putin's memory politics, making it illegal to criticize the role of the USSR in the Great Patriotic War or to disparage the heroism of the Russian people in defending the fatherland.[18] That amendment also contains a vague pledge to protect historical truth. Putin invoked the law to make an example of his most famous critic, Alexei Navalny who had been arrested for violating parole as soon as he returned to Russia from Germany in January 2021; he had sought medical treatment there after an attempted assassination in August 2020—likely by the Russian security service—by way of poisoning with the nerve agent Novichok. While in detention in Russia, Navalny was accused of defaming ninety-five-year-old World War II veteran Ignat Artemenko, who had appeared with other celebrities in a video supporting the constitutional change to remove presidential term limits.[19] Navalny, who had

¹⁸ Elizabeth Teague (2020). "Russia's Constitutional Reforms of 2020," *Russian Politics*, Vol. 5, No. 3, 301–28. doi: https://doi.org/10.30965/24518921-00503003.
¹⁹ The video: https://www.youtube.com/watch?v=Pmf-sZQ-fY4&feature=youtu.be&ab_channel=RT%D0%BD%D0%B0%D1%80%D1%83%D1%81%D1%81%D0%BA%D0%BE%D0%BC.

called people appearing in the video "traitors" and "corrupt stooges" on Twitter, denied the Kremlin's charge that he denigrated the honor and dignity of the World War II veteran.[20] In February, a Moscow court found Navalny guilty and fined him 850,000 Rubles ($11,481).[21] That episode offers an illustration of Putin's instrumentalization of the memory of World War II to enforce a national-conservative narrative and to snuff out any doubt about his role as the primary interpreter of the Russian past. The defamation and deprivation of human rights for an opposition figure, coupled with the use of aging veterans as fodder for tamping down dissent, are of far less consequence than controlling the memory narrative. The weaponization of the Great Patriotic War to foster a monist interpretation of the past, combined with the use of patriotism as his personal tool, to replicate the propaganda of Soviet times and with it, control of Russian society.

Putin's nationalistic memory politics also serve his foreign policy aims, pointing to a need to remain militarily strong and vigilant in a geopolitical neighborhood that is—as it has always been, he would argue—hostile. This narrative serves to justify neo-imperialism in Georgia, Ukraine, the Baltics, or in any other region or country that has sought or may seek independence or greater political, cultural, and strategic distance from Russia. In speeches leading up to and immediately after the invasion of Ukraine in February 2022, Putin warned of the West's aggression:

> Focused on their own goals, the leading NATO countries are supporting the far-right nationalists and neo-Nazis in Ukraine, those who will never forgive the people of Crimea and Sevastopol for freely making a choice to reunite with Russia.
>
>   They will undoubtedly try to bring war to Crimea just as they have done in Donbass, to kill innocent people just as members of the punitive units of Ukrainian nationalists and Hitler's accomplices did during the Great Patriotic War.
>
> (Putin February 23, 2022b)

Putin uses memory politics as an excuse to prepare the ground for a reassertion of Russian dominance in territories it considers strategically and/or culturally essential to Russian greatness, for example, Crimea. Putin repeatedly justified

---

[20] "Russia to Try Navalny on WWII Veteran Slander Charges," *Moscow Times*, February 5, 2021, https://www.themoscowtimes.com/2021/02/05/russia-to-try-navalny-on-wwii-veteran-slander-charges-a72841.

[21] DeutscheWelle February 20, 2021, https://www.dw.com/en/alexei-navalny-fined-for-defaming-russian-veteran/a-56635101.

his 2022 war against Ukraine in terms of fighting fascists and protecting the rights—the very lives—of ethnic Russians living there. In that famous speech justifying the "special military operation" in Ukraine, Putin proclaimed:

> The purpose of this operation is to protect people who, for eight years now, have been facing humiliation and genocide perpetrated by the Kiev regime. To this end, we will seek to demilitarize and denazify Ukraine, as well as bring to trial those who perpetrated numerous bloody crimes against civilians, including against citizens of the Russian Federation.
>
> (Putin February 23, 2022b)

As Jushkin observes, "The concept of 'fascist' is also filled with new meaning. It now includes the opposition that is outside the system, the leaders of those countries that do not consent to attend the victory parade, as well as the Ukrainian authorities. 'Holy war' carries over from the past into the present . . . In this light, the slogan '1941–1945. We can repeat it,' which is widespread among the people, becomes understandable" (2020). The slogan to which Jushkin refers became newly popular as a bumper sticker in Russia after the February 24, 2022 invasion and often features two stick figures: one with a swastika symbol for a head bent over and ostensibly being penetrated by another with a hammer and sickle head.[22]

Given that the Great Patriotic War narrative hinges on the defeat of Nazism and the rescue of Europe from fascism, it is ironic that, Putin, the new central figure in the cult of war, has himself cozied up to far-right parties and leaders in Europe. Russian loans and energy deals with the Austrian Freedom Party (Ibizagate), the Italian Lega, or the French Front National, now called Rally, have been leaked to media. Putin finds much to like about these nationalist-conservative, sovereigntist movements in Europe. He supports them as a way to destabilize liberal governments and undermine the European Union. Many of those far-right Western European parties have shifted their rhetoric about their admiration of Putin since Russia's attack on Ukraine. Former allies like LePen's National Rally, Meloni's Brothers of Italy, the German AfD, and Danish and Dutch far-right parties have adjusted their nativism and euroskepticism in response to softening public opinion, which has largely been sympathetic to Ukrainian refugees. The same is true of far-right parties in Finland, Romania, and Lithuania. Others, mainly in Eastern Europe, are critical of their countries' support for Ukraine, citing more pressing needs at home,

---

[22] See Ilya Kalinin, "The Broken Record Effect, or on the Advantage and Disadvantage of Historical Analogies for Life," Russia.Post. January 31, 2023, https://russiapost.info/politics/historical_analogies.

such as inflation and jobs. The Croatian HSP, Czech Freedom and Democracy Party (SPD), and Bulgarian Revival are among those using rhetoric of welfare chauvinism and economic protectionism to justify more pro-Kremlin positions (Ivaldi and Zankina 2023).

Russia Reborn

Russian political instrumentalization of remembrance of World War II supports the idea that mnemonic manipulations are most likely to emerge where and when the identity of the community or society is insecure. While Russia does not suffer from the ontological insecurity of a new country, or one that has suffered defeat and humiliation in war, it has suffered tremendous trauma from the implosion of the Soviet Union and the chaos of the early post-communist years. The loss of empire and its international standing is felt acutely by the regime and the population at large. Kolesnikov describes the memory challenge this way: "The new Russia defines its historical identity mainly in negative terms. If the breakup of the Soviet Union was 'the greatest geopolitical catastrophe of the century,' as Putin has said, then the Russian Federation that sprang up from its debris is not a full-fledged state. That means that Russia can only be reborn after it becomes great again. It must strike to resemble the Soviet Union, having inherited and officially blessed that country's historical myths and narratives" (2020). The reinstatement of Stalin as a positive figure in official memory is one manifestation of the desire to return to a position of strength and honor, to restore Russia's place in the world, while overlooking the tremendous violence and fear associated with Stalin's rule. The militarization of Victory Day commemorations and of the national identity, generally, can also be interpreted as responses to that trauma. Jushkin describes the Cult of Victory in Russia as Russia's popular religion, "like a secular Easter, by which a certain kind of resurrection is similarly celebrated" (2020). The importance of this commemoration and of mobilization of participation in its associated—and increasingly numerous—"sacred" rites are meant to strengthen social and national bonds. This popular religion, with Putin as high priest, is a dogmatic faith where non-believers can be fined or jailed.

Putin's memory politics have thus far been largely unchallenged. In comparison with memory challengers in other countries discussed here, Putin's manipulation of wartime memory faces far fewer obstacles. No external power exerts pressure on Russia to examine its past; there have been no sustained, endogenous efforts to reckon with the dark periods of Soviet and Russian history. An exception for some years was the NGO Memorial, but Putin has cracked down on its leaders and activities, leaving no significant civil society challenge to his instrumentalization of the past. In contrast to Eastern Europe, Russia has undertaken no trials of former communist leaders, no lustration, no truth-and-reconciliation-type exercise, and—with the exception of the early 1990s—no *Historikerstreit* among academics or public debate about the past. Russian protestors against the war in Ukraine have been neutralized by laws criminalizing independent news reporting and antiwar protests. Parents can even be arrested if their children speak out against the war in school or draw pictures that are deemed critical of the war (RFE/RL March 1, 2023).

Memory Entanglements, Memory as a Weapon of War

The VE Day commemorations across the three mnemonic meso-regions illustrate the various ways in which memory challengers use commemorations to advance domestic and foreign policy goals. In Germany and Austria, far-right memory challengers sought to obscure a memory of contrition for the war and the Holocaust by emphasizing their own victimhood and sacrifice. This counter-narrative targeted a mainly domestic audience, however; it found little resonance, indeed, it sparked official and public support for a cosmopolitan memory of the war. Eastern Europe has witnessed no controversy surrounding the meaning of VE Day for the region: it is generally viewed as a negative memory of occupation, dictatorship, and missed opportunities to share in European freedoms and prosperity. If the date is recognized, it is used largely to remind Western Europeans that they need to recognize and integrate the fate of Eastern Europeans during and after the war into Europe's mnemonic institutions and practices.

For Russia, May 9 marks its greatest historical moment. The date is inspiring, sacred, and unifying. Its commemoration creates an annual opportunity for Putin to link his leadership to the heroic past and to remind the West that Russia was and remains a formidable military power. Russia's most recent celebrations of Victory Day have also sent the message to the West that it deserves to possess a sphere of influence, rooted in history, and that it intends to defend it by any means necessary.

As previous chapters have demonstrated, eighty years on, many disagreements have arisen about the meaning of the war and its lessons for the present. The war in Ukraine supplies glaring evidence that there are no shared strategies for ensuring "never again war." Using memory of the war as a weapon,

Putin has cast his country as the righteous defender of honor and truth against the distortions and bellicosity of the West, which has come to include the Baltic countries, former satellites in Eastern Europe, and many Ukrainians who Putin, in a twist of his mnemonic knife, calls "Nazis." The Russian memory of the Great Patriotic War and of Victory Day have no limits. This chapter on the meanings of VE Day, like the preceding chapters on commemorations across the three mnemonic meso-regions, demonstrates that the wartime past is, now more than ever, used to distract, distort, and redirect in ways that divide countries and undermine the prospects for transnational dialogue.

6

The Present Meanings of the Wartime Past

This investigation of memory challenges at wartime commemorations assumed that the discourses, symbols, and rituals associated with the past vary across time and space. The framework for analyzing contested commemorations took as its starting point the three mnemonic meso-regions that emerged at the end of World War II and solidified during the Cold War. While the mnemonic patterns in Western European countries appeared, on the surface, to have been relatively stable and convergent on the Holocaust-centered narrative of the war and its lessons, the mnemonic landscapes in Eastern Europe and Russia were assumed to have been far less stable and subject to manipulation. The cases examined here suggest that, after the Cold War, rather than a sustained flourishing of *glasnost*, of open archives and openness to dialogue about the multiple experiences, perspectives, and meanings associated with World War II and its aftermath, mnemonic divisions have not disappeared and, in some cases, they have again hardened.

The end of the Cold War in 1989/90 did open up space for transnational mnemonic interactions. This study noted instances of cooperation across national boundaries among networks of memory actors, such as the short-lived cooperation between Russian and Polish historians or ongoing projects on the part of the European Network of Remembrance and Solidarity. Cooperation among memory *challengers* also occurred, for example, between veterans' organizations and far-right political movements and parties, as well as between the Kremlin and far-right parties in Western Europe. More often than not, memory challenges to commemorative practices in one area sparked negative reactions in another, occasionally escalating to a "memory war" between countries or regions.

The hardening of memory divides has been most visible in the mnemonic tug-of-war between Russia and Eastern European countries. Eastern European societies have moved away from the hegemonic Soviet memory of the war in favor of re-nationalized, victim-centered narratives, while Russia has clung to the Soviet narrative of heroism. Clashes between these antagonistic memories were bound to happen, particularly where ethnic Russians comprise a

World War II Memory and Contested Commemorations in Europe and Russia. Jennifer A. Yoder, Oxford University Press.
© Jennifer A. Yoder (2024). DOI: 10.1093/oso/9780198894162.003.0006

significant minority. Mnemonic tension also persists, however, between Eastern and Western Europeans. Old members of the European Union assumed that new members in post-communist Eastern states, who joined between 2004 and 2007, should and would adopt the Holocaust-centered narrative. There has been resistance to this and other forms of imitation, with Eastern Europeans insisting on integrating their national memories of victimhood under the "other totalitarianism," that is, communism, shaping pan-European discourses and practices of remembrance. Russia, meanwhile, has returned to the Soviet-style practice of constructing a narrative of greatness from the top down. Vladimir Putin has nonetheless departed from the future-oriented, internationalist narrative of the USSR, while cultivating a hyperbolic nationalist narrative that selectively invokes the tsarist past and rehabilitates Stalin.

In this concluding section, we begin by reflecting on the distinctive characteristics of mnemonic contestation in each of the three meso-regions. While important differences remain, we must recognize that across the case studies discussed in the previous chapters, there were some common characteristics in the emergence of memory challenges and the strategies of memory challengers. What are those differences and what are the implications of their shared features? Are there common circumstances that have produced similar grievances in the three meso-regions? Finally, this chapter will consider the potential that memory contestation holds within and between mnemonic regions for producing misunderstanding, animosity and, in the extreme, the deterioration of relationships; but memory contestation could also be potentially harnessed to foster more complex, pluralistic understandings of the difficult past.

The Durability of Differences between the Three Mnemonic Regions

The commemorations examined in the preceding chapters suggest the persistence of certain differences between the three mnemonic meso-regions, first, in terms of the memory actors that seek to instrumentalize the past; second, the contextual factors, including objectives of memory challenges and the cultural and institutional constraints they face; and, finally, the strategies that memory challengers employ.

We first consider core actors driving the reconfiguration of memory. In the four cases of wartime commemoration in Western Europe discussed in chapter 2, the memory challengers tended to be far-right parties operating outside of government, though there have been periods in Italy and Austria where memory challengers shared power. These antagonistic actors are often supported by right-wing media and intellectuals associated with the New Right (Minkenberg 1997). In Eastern Europe, memory challengers also come from right-wing groups and parties, but in Hungary and Poland, such groups are affiliated with or are themselves in the governing parties with the state apparatus at their disposal, not small fringe parties with few resources. In cases where powerful parties and leaders are the core memory challengers, national memory institutes, new museums, and ministries of education assist in the construction of national memory narratives that often reject or supplant the Holocaust-centered narrative. In Russia, the main memory actor has been the powerful president, aided by a largely compliant media, legislature, and judiciary.

Turning to the context in which wartime memories are challenged, recall that in Western Europe, generations have been exposed to Holocaust education and efforts to draw lessons from the war, particularly regarding human rights, protections for minorities, tolerance for and appreciation of difference. Strong civil society networks have pushed back against revisionist narratives of the past, as happened in the case of attempts to instrumentalize the commemoration of the Dresden bombing. The organizations in which Western European countries have long been members, that is, the Council of Europe, NATO, and the European Union, have all internalized Holocaust-centered memory and thus reinforce the norms, practices, and policies of reflective contrition. As a consequence, exclusivist, nationalistic groups and discourses have been taboo in Western Europe; since 1990, however, the cordon sanitaire that kept far-right parties from political power has weakened and even fallen in places like Austria and, most recently, Italy, as demonstrated in the election of a far-right coalition, led by Georgia Meloni of the neo-fascist Brothers of Italy party in September 2022.

Paradoxically, it was precisely those cultural and institutional constraints that became targets of memory challengers in Germany, France, Italy, and Austria. They oppose cosmopolitan memory and contrition because it has purportedly weakened national culture, identity, and law and order. Its analogue in the United States is the right-wing assault on the supposedly "woke agenda" of the Biden Administration, public school teachers and curricula, and many writers, librarians, and journalists. Far-right actors in Western Europe seek to transcend or "normalize" the past so that it is no longer a psychological or reputational burden that limits their discursive and policy choices. Rather than be reminded of the lessons of the past represented by the Holocaust-centered narrative, they seek to downplay, trivialize, or deny the Holocaust. They seek to fundamentally change the memory culture, often by reversing the roles of victim and perpetrator, casting their nations or the wartime actors they identify with as innocent victims in need of recognition. More significantly, they want to displace mainstream parties and their memory narratives of contrition, replacing them with exclusivist, that is, anti-immigrant, racist, homophobic, and sexist rhetoric and policies reminiscent of the dark past.

In the four Western European cases considered here, memory challenges emerged in reaction to the official memory taking new or additional steps to become more contrite, conciliatory, and inclusive. The latest memory challengers resemble the neo-conservatives of West Germany in the mid-1980s who sparked the *Historikerstreit*. Challenging the narrative of culpability that had begun to crystalize in the Federal Republic, they insisted on relativizing Nazism, advocating for the normalization of German identity and memory culture. More recently, the far-right Alternative for Germany (AfD) sought to politicize the wartime past to challenge Chancellor Merkel's "Open Door" policy and "Welcome Culture" toward migrants in 2015. Merkel justified her country's humanitarianism in historical terms, arguing its appropriateness given Germany's past as creator of refugees during World War II, as a destination for co-ethnic refugees from the East (*Aussiedler*) during the 1970s and 1980s, and following the fall of the Wall. In embracing a memory culture of contrition and in connecting it to a universal imperative to protect human rights, Merkel became emblematic of values and associations rejected by the AfD and other far-right groups. For those memory challengers, German leaders and mainstream political parties failed to put "German interests" first. That fundamental critique extends to far-right parties in Austria, France, and Italy, although there has been far less international media attention paid to those memory challenges.

The countries of Eastern Europe have had a shorter, less intensive engagement with the Holocaust-centered narrative. That narrative developed outside of the Eastern European mnemonic region, rendering it less welcome among communities whose leaders have long denied, or fostered their ignorance regarding, atrocities committed in their midst or in their name. In the opinions of some actors in this region, Holocaust memory is ill suited for societies for whom the experiences of Soviet domination and Stalinization/communization are most prominent in their personal and collective memories. Here, anti-communism is the hegemonic memory narrative, inseparable from anti-imperialism and nationalist sovereigntism. The grievances that motivate memory challengers in Eastern Europe stem from frustration with Western Europe's neglect of their renewed victimhood after the war, when they were abandoned by the West and colonized by the USSR. Beyond frustration, which might have been resolved through efforts like the Prague Declaration and the adoption of August 23 in commemoration of both victims of Nazism and communism, the grievances of memory challengers often go further and deeper, in search of transcendence of the fascist past. Their own roles in the crimes of fascism and the domestic roots of anti-Semitism and racism are, at the most, given lip service, while their own national suffering is prioritized and accorded almost religious status, as with Poland's commemoration of Cursed Soldiers or the Bleiburg commemoration of Croatian fascists.

In Russia, the primary contextual framework centers on humiliation, attributed to the collapse of the Soviet Union and the chaos, corruption, and deprivation of the immediate post-Soviet years. Compared to the other two regions, there are far fewer and weaker cultural or institutional constraints to temper the highly nationalistic and selective memory narrative being (re)constructed from the top-down. Russia is the mnemonic meso-region where the search for stability and maybe even for an escape from burdens of the immediate past are the greatest. Putin is a product of a society that was traumatized by the Soviet empire, then by the vacuum left by the collapse of the monist ideology that proscribed all aspects of life in it (Langdon and Tismaneanu 2019). Putin himself was traumatized by what he witnessed as a KGB officer in Dresden, East Germany, where his headquarters was mobbed by protestors in 1989 and where he and his colleagues burned intelligence documents, fearing they would be overrun and, perhaps, worse. The instability of 1990s was a second trauma for Russians, and Putin's reintroduction of centralized power and reassertion of influence in Russia's "near abroad" can be viewed as responses to that trauma. Adding to Russia's insecurity is its deep suspicion of the West, including the latter's alleged role in the Color Revolutions in former Soviet states and later the Euro Maidan protests of 2014. The Kremlin also fears further enlargement of the European Union and NATO into what it sees as its sphere of influence, especially Ukraine, Georgia, and Moldova. Putin's mnemonic politics have thus been shaped by a perception of threat from the West.

Putin has sought to deflect from Stalinist crimes and the weaknesses of the Soviet system, redirecting attention to the "screen memory" of the wartime heroism of USSR and its role as the savior of Europe. Dmitri Trenin has called this self-perception the "defender complex" (Trenin 2007, 55). Instances of the weaponization of the memory of the Great Patriotic War were discussed in earlier chapters, such as the revisionist narrative about the Molotov-Ribbentrop Pact and Poland's role in the onset of war, or using the worship of war veterans to silence political opponents. These strategies are meant to unify Russians and strengthen the regime's own legitimacy by focusing on continuities between Soviet military might and heroism, the country's present conditions, and its future as an exceptional nation: it offers an alternative model to the decadent culture, misguided economic and political systems, and "aggressive" security arrangements of the European Union and NATO. Despite these contextual factors, their sum total is not an effort to change the memory of the war fundamentally, as is often the case with far-right memory challengers in Western Europe or with memory challengers in Eastern Europe. Instead, the discomfort caused by the trauma and losses of the 1990s requires a balm, a nationalistic and heroic memory narrative flanked by rituals that invoke unity, strength, and exceptionalism. In the process, it must be noted, the Kremlin has used denialism, as when it silences critics, harasses organizations like Memorial, or redevelops a site of memory like the gulag museum Perm-36.

Another important component of Russia's memory complex is its frustration with the West for not properly acknowledging the Soviet Union's immense wartime sacrifice and its heroic defense of Europe. What is more, there is a sense that Russian exceptionalism is owed a debt; but instead of being paid the respect it deserves, the country's security interests are threatened by European Union and NATO expansion. The grievance most visible in Putin's memory politics, however, is the offense taken to Eastern European countries' blackwashing of the communist past and the USSR and their narration of that past not as part of a glorious experiment in the ashes of Nazi destruction, but, impudently, as imperialism.

Putin's memory manipulations appear formidable, owing certainly to his ability to use media and other institutions for propaganda purposes as well as to the intensity and scale of his revival of the cult of the Great Patriotic War. His efforts, though, represent a continuity with earlier Soviet methods of indoctrination and legitimation; in that, they are a restoration rather than a new challenge.

Figure 6.1 is a simple depiction of memory challengers and their goals across the three meso-regions. The top of the triangle shows areas of convergence of far-right actors in Western Europe and nationalist-populists in Eastern Europe. At the lower left are areas of convergence between far-right Western European actors and Putin's Russia. The clash of mnemonic challenges

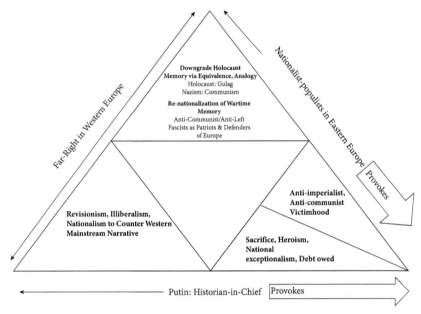

Figure 6.1 Mnemonic goals across three regions: shared features, provocations

Source: Author.

by Eastern European nationalist-populists and Putin's Russia are noted in the lower right corner.

In Western Europe, blinding or deflecting from the dark past, recasting the causes and consequences of World War II, and distorting facts about who did what to whom in the war are typical mnemonic moves meant to sow doubt about the established political actors' allegiance, courage, and independence from "internal" and "external" influences seeking, supposedly, to subvert the nation. Instead of anti-Semitism and explicit racism, deemed unacceptable both culturally and legally, Western European memory challengers speak of cultural integrity, while stoking fears of Muslim invaders. In doing so, they involve tropes reminiscent of their fascist forefathers in the 1930s: foreign invaders threaten the health of the nation with alien diseases, ideas, and behaviors. In these cases, memory politics are part of a larger strategy to push back against liberal democratic values, such as openness, respect for human dignity, and tolerance for difference.

Eastern European memory challengers seek to deflect from a dark past colored by culpability by whitewashing local anti-Semitism, racism, fascist movements and leaders, on the one hand, and by blackwashing the communist past and linking it to present-day leftists, on the other. Often attempting to blind their target audiences to crimes committed by their parents' and grandparents' generations during the war, Eastern European memory challengers are most concerned about isolating the national community from any residues of communism. Whitewashing and blackwashing are used to unify the nation through construction of simple dichotomies of "us," including former fascists and war criminals who opposed communism/the Soviets/the Partisans—and "them"—the Soviets/communists/anyone whose victimhood sheds a negative light on "us" (which often includes Jews, living or dead). Under this strategy, the Holocaust-centered memory of Western Europe is problematic in that it invites reflection on the complicity of Eastern Europeans in the dehumanization of groups and individuals. The ethos of the Holocaust-centered narrative moreover sits uncomfortably with the simplistic logic of the Us/Them dichotomy. Mainstream political elites and state historical institutions prefer the language of equivalence (Double Genocide, Two Totalitarianisms) over a careful examination of their countries' relationships to fascism, Nazism, and the Holocaust. Parties and groups on the far-right do not even bother to recognize victims of fascism; they celebrate only the patriotism and anti-communism of their countrymen and women. In addition to the twin strategies of distortion, whitewashing and blackwashing, memory challengers in Eastern Europe employ a "sovereigntist" narrative against neo-imperialism, an enemy primarily attributed to Russia but also selectively used to push back against EU integration. These revisionist strategies share a common goal: to create a sense of past, present, and future national, cultural, and historical distinctiveness and independence.

In Russia, wartime memory is used to create regime legitimacy by strengthening national pride and cohesion and by asserting distinctiveness from the West. Russian citizens are repeatedly told of (and legally required to respect) their country's heroic role in the war; Russians today are bound to those brave heroes of the past. Victory Day commemorations are an essential part of strengthening Russian identity and memory. The scale of the festivities, the symbols, rituals, and rhetoric of the leadership all remind Russians of their exceptional past, present, and future. Memory actors like President Putin and his advisors seek to construct a Russian identity that both sets it apart from the liberal-democratic West (now including Eastern Europeans), projecting strength and defiance to outsiders. Victory Day commemorations, but also anniversaries of the Molotov-Ribbentrop Pact, have been used to put former Soviet Republics and Eastern European satellite countries "in their places" and on alert. Putin's reinterpretation of the Molotov-Ribbentrop Pact, for example, sent a warning to Poland and the Baltic states regarding their renationalized narratives of victimhood. Putin's memory politics aim to remind Europeans, Western and Eastern, that they owe Russia for having defended them from fascism, and for that, it demands respect.

Finally, memory challengers in Western and Eastern Europe prefer a "normalization" of the past that refocuses on heroism, victimization, or innocence. They view the institutions and policies of the European Union as instruments of enemies—Jews and, lately, Muslims—and as existential threats to the nation. Across Europe, the memory challengers oppose notions of a common European identity based on "cosmopolitanism, transnationalism and universalized memories" of World War II and the Holocaust (Blacker, Etkind, and Fedor, 2013, 13). For Russians, however, Holocaust memory was never part of the *Soviet* narrative about the war. This remains absent from the cult of the war revived by Putin.

Recall in chapter 1 the discussion of grievances thought to motivate memory actors to contest the dominant interpretation of the wartime past. We suggested that certain types of grievances were likely to be associated with particular approaches, corresponding to how little or much memory actors sought to manipulate the past. Table 6.1 revisits the grievances that motivated contestation of wartime commemorations, noting some, but certainly not all, of the memory actors that employed particular strategies. One of the surprising findings of the case studies of was the similar breadth of approaches used, even if deployed in particularistic ways.

Emotional manipulation was universal among memory challengers. Across the three meso-regions, memory actors engaging in wartime commemorations performed rituals, such as marching, lighting candles, or laying wreaths, meant to bind participants to one another and, especially, to the victims, martyrs, or heroes being honored. Clothing, symbols, and often religious imagery signified belonging, reverence for fallen heroes or victims, and continuity with the past.

All of the cases and regions discussed here employed tactics that blind as well as bind, and many memory challengers moved well up the ladder of obfuscation to revision, engaging in competitive strategies to lift their own status and downgrade that of others. Memory challengers in Western and Eastern Europe share a desire to avoid a careful and critical examination of the fascist and collaborationist past. In every case in those two regions we saw efforts to downplay wartime roles and/or association with fascists. Deflection of blame as well as using the excuse that the other side also committed crimes (e.g., what about the Chetniks? Yes, but the communists . . .) were commonplace.

Table 6.1 Memory challenges and the grievances that motivate them

Approach	Features	Motivating grievances	Select examples
Manipulation of emotions	Performative identity, rituals. Emphasis on trauma, victimhood, martyrdom, or heroism and glory Use symbols, tropes to signify belonging	Desire for a usable past, one that is heroic and entitled to gratitude or one that is tragic and entitled to recognition for suffering Desire for national unity, particularly in face of perceived threats	**All.** Clothing, flags, banners with emotional appeals Rituals, religious or secular Social and other media calls to feel emotional attachment to past, often to stand against injustices or slights
Obfuscation	Whitewashing of homegrown fascism and anti-Semitism and/or collaboration with Nazis Use of a screen memory What-aboutism; Yes, but	Discomfort with unflattering wartime roles and associations. Confusion or humiliation caused by dissonance between self-perception and official record	**Italian Right**: Mussolini and fascism as great or benign, all blame on Germany. Attempt to abolish Liberation Day, replace with foibe screen memory **Bleiburg**: distract from Ustaše's collaboration with Nazis, crimes by pointing to Serb and communist crimes
Construction of binaries	Binaries to distract from complexity, critical thinking	Frustration with dominant narrative, desire to "correct the record"	**Siege of Budapest**: pure Hungarians against impure outsiders
Construction of symmetries	Construction of equivalence. Competitive martyrology or victimhood Use of metaphor and analogy. Appropriation of terminology, symbols	Frustration with dominant narrative, desire to "correct the record" Sense that own group or nation is unfairly judged and deserves recognition—or that another does not deserve recognition	**Dresden**: in GDR between Nazis and capitalist Allies; after unification, between German casualties and Jewish victims of Shoah **Eastern Europe**: equivalence of August 23/M-R Pact and Holocaust **Bleiburg**: Way of the Cross **Ulrichsberg**: Europastone of Peace **Dresden** and **Bleiburg**: "Bombenholocaust," "Holocaust of Croatian Martyrs"

Continued

Table 6.1 Continued

Approach	Features	Motivating grievances	Select examples
Revisionism	Whitewashing Blackwashing Inversion Distortion Conspiracy thinking/theorizing	Seek to significantly change the wartime narrative by upgrading own group or nation and downgrading others, by reinterpreting events or their meaning, by casting doubt on the veracity of other accounts or other groups' motives	**Ulrichsberg:** veterans as defenders of Europe. **Latvian Legion:** ignore affiliation with Nazis **Ukrainian Waffen-SS:** ignores homegrown fascism, collaboration with Nazis **Cursed soldiers:** Polish right's blackwashing of entire communist past; moderate right and political left as traitorous **Ulrichsberg:** veterans cast themselves as victims of neglect by memory culture of contrition **Putin:** campaign against "falsifiers of history" **Dresden:** facts of bombing, casualties, context. **Putin:** M-R Pact not responsible for start of World War II, instead "saved" Baltics and Poland **Putin:** rehabilitation of Stalin in memories of M-R Pact and Victory Day, cult of war **Putin:** rhetoric about M-R Pact memory falsifiers
Denialism	Trivialization Exculpation	Seek to fundamentally change or replace a narrative to erase an unflattering past, to marginalize an unflattering narrative or political opponents	**Russian** and **Polish** laws against criticism of nation in war **Putin:** silencing of Memorial, repurposing of Perm memorial **Vél d'Hiv:** France not responsible for roundup of Jews

Source: Author.

The use of simplistic binaries of Us and Them, hero or villain, was also similarly widespread across all three regions. Putin's rhetoric about Russia against the West infused much of his memory politics. The construction of an equivalence between fascism and communism and Nazism and Stalinism was a particularly blunt weapon in the toolkit of Western and Eastern European memory challengers, sparking further grievance on the part of Russia. Competitive victimhood was occasionally a part of contestation at commemorations, as with far-right groups in Dresden, Italy (with the foibe, also used as a screen memory) and Croatia (competing with Serb victimhood). The most egregious examples of appropriation were the labels "holocaust" and "genocide" used by far-right groups in Dresden and Croatia, places where Jews were deliberately targeted for extermination.

Revisionism, including whitewashing to significantly change the wartime narrative and extensive blackwashing of the communist past, were common approaches at Eastern European commemorations of the Waffen-SS or resistors of communism. These commemorations also embraced inversion as a strategy for claiming the mantle as heroes or victims but not as perpetrators or collaborators. Distortions of facts were not frequent in all cases; it was a tactic Putin used particularly aggressively to reinterpret the Molotov-Ribbentrop Pact and to rehabilitate Stalin. Memory challenges across the former Cold War divide infrequently used blatant exculpation; exceptions were memory laws to limit critical speech. The denial of crimes was unusual, except in the case of Vél d'Hiv where memory challengers revived the myth of innocent France.

Conditions That Facilitate Memory Contestation

The cases of contested wartime commemorations raise the question, why now? Or, at least, why in recent years? I wish to briefly highlight several factors or conditions that may have given rise to mnemonic contestation across the three regions: the roles of generational change, structural change, cultural backlash, shocks, and an unsettled mnemonic landscape. Other studies have examined one or more of the conditions in greater depth (Kattago 2012; Subotic 2018; Subotic 2019; Tismaneanu 2009). While simplifying more complex processes, my aim is to suggest how and why the last two decades have fostered similar kinds of anxiety and sources of insecurity in Europe and Russia that have been conducive to the instrumentalization of the past by memory challengers.

Generational change: We turn, first, to a basic condition that applies to all countries, regardless of their wartime roles: the passing of time and, with it, the passing of generations who were eye-witnesses to the atrocities of the first half of the twentieth century. The fact that there are few people alive today with personal experiences of those traumatic events signals a shift from communicative memory to cultural memory; they depend on information passed down from survivors of the war, interpretations filtered through memorials, education, or on other societal traditions that are at a distance from the events (Assmann 2008). It is now up to historiography and cultural production to keep memories of the past alive through representations.

With each new generation, the process of meaning-making can open space for reinterpretation and a reconstruction of the past (Schuman et al. 1997). Greater temporal distance from the wartime events may weaken the awareness of those events and the reflection on their meaning, making subsequent generations susceptible to reinterpretations of the past through memory challenges. In addition, generations may possess distinctive concerns, values, attitudes, and "needs" in the present, all of which affect their relationship to the past (Schwartz 1982). It is plausible that the conditions that foster the politicization of memory are rooted in present needs, fears, insecurities, cultural clashes, and political battles. While the precise nature of the memory challengers' grievances may differ from country to country or, as has been argued, from mnemonic meso-region to mnemonic meso-region, it is possible that generational change across countries and regions has unsettled the mnemonic landscape, rendering it more conducive to attempts to modify dominant narratives of the past.

Structural change: To one degree or another, the three mnemonic regions have experienced comparable social and cultural changes associated with late or post-industrialism. In an age of late or "liquid" modernity, the accelerated and disorienting pace of change, its non-linear and unfamiliar nature and its uncertain outcomes are ripe for mnemonic politics (Kattago 2012). When the pace or extent of change increases a society's insecurity about its status or its identity, the politicization of the past can become a weapon in the arsenal of the insecure and aggrieved (Elgenius and Rydgren 2022). The changes that confront most late-modern societies are felt more acutely by those whose identity and social standing are unsettled or who face new competition. Across the three meso-regions, traditionally privileged groups—often working-class men of the dominant ethnic group—face increasing competition in the labor market, in the share of public spending, and in their social standing, all in a more demographically diverse context. The break-up of socialist federations (the USSR, Yugoslavia, and Czechoslovakia), and the simultaneous nature of their political, economic, and social transitions, compounded the sense of dislocation and disorientation for many people. Where vulnerability in the present and uncertainty about the future are linked by mnemonic actors to grievances rooted in the past, the situation is particularly ripe for an eruption of memory.

Cultural backlash: As a source of potential grievance, this category of conditions conducive to memory challenges has been attributed to the emergence of populism; some have called this an "authoritarian revolt" (Weiss 2017), others a "cultural backlash" (Norris and Inglehart 2019). Indeed, many of the movements and parties associated with culturalist-populist backlash have looked to the past for reassurances that affirm myths, symbols, and tropes, in order to challenge what they see as confusing, complicated, and even unpatriotic representations of their group or country-related wartime roles. While nostalgia for "the good old days," a fascination with national heritage, and efforts to reenact events of the past are not by definition manifestations of cultural backlash, they often go hand in hand with an instrumentalization of memory for ideological purposes. Of course, this is true outside of Europe and Russia as well. The Tea Party in the United States, obsessed with the 1773 political protest in Boston, tricorn hats, and Gadsden flags, was a prime example of "historical fundamentalism" in the service of a conservative political agenda (Lepore 2010, 16).

In Europe, culturalist-populists have seized upon traditional ethnic costumes, dance, music, and rituals to underline the importance of distinctive identity rooted in the past. Van der Laarse describes the politicization of nostalgia as a strategy for constructing boundaries between an in-group and others. His work describes a "heritage crusade against multiculturalism, refugees, and Islamism on behalf of Europe's 'original,' white *Leitkultur*" (2019, 106). This construction is not new; it is a "progressive culturalist discourse . . . hijacked and step-by-step turned into its opposite," which has been used by the New Right in Europe since the 1970s to denigrate the social activism sparked by students in 1968 by "defending an *essentialist* notion of cultural diversity . . . *against* the universalist, Western multicultural human rights discourse and the threat of globalization" (emphasis van der Laarse's, 107). Along similar lines, Dominique Renyié, writing about "heritage populism," addresses the vertical and horizontal divides stoked by memory challengers:

> Previously, populists aroused mass protests by opposing liberal democracy. Today, they present themselves as the chief protectors of liberty, blaming the elite and the mainstream parties for failing to uphold the values and rules of liberal society and for being complacent about the rise of multiculturalism and Islamism—trends that populists trace to irresponsible immigration policies.
>
> (2016, 51)

The culturalist-populist concern derives from structural economic changes and is often directed at European integration and globalization, both of which are blamed for challenges to traditional identities and ways of life. The European Union offers "four freedoms" of movement of goods, services, people, and capital as well as norms and policies that affect citizens' everyday lives; globalization facilitates the spread of ideas, products, and, especially, people, including migrants. The processes of European integration and globalization opened societies up to other cultures and new norms like anti-racism, feminism, LGBTQ+ rights, and environmentalism. Populism, nativism, and other exclusionary ideologies and movements have reacted defensively and often aggressively to these changes (Elgenius and Rydgren 2022). In each of the three meso-regions, the instrumentalization of World War II memory often aims to alleviate anxiety, as part of "psychological need for continuity" (Steele and Homolar 2019, 216). Memory challenges are often efforts to unify traditional (if imagined) communities by defending the boundaries of who belongs; memory challengers seek to distinguish between insiders from outsiders, authentic from artificial, pure from complex, and innocent from corrupting.

For Russian memory challengers, cultural backlash entails an additional dimension. Beyond the usual national-conservative themes of nativism, patriarchy, and patriotism, there is also an assertion of an alternative developmental path, an eastern or Slavic cultural tradition (sometimes called "Eurasianism"), and an ancient and heroic identity that must be protected from the cultural pathologies and aggressive policies of the West (Van Herpen 2015).

Shocks as catalysts for memory challenges: Another category of facilitating conditions for memory challenges are abrupt policy or environmental changes. External shocks, such as contagion from the global financial crisis, a sudden wave of migration, instability and unrest in bordering counties, or a pandemic can exacerbate existing insecurities and provide further fuel for, or an opening for, the politicization of the past. Internal shocks, such as high-stake elections or significant policy changes like the inclusion of historically excluded groups, can also provide a catalyst to inflame the politics of memory. Each of the countries and regions examined here has been affected by one or, typically, multiple shocks. Memory challenges may not be a direct result of such shocks, however; mnemonic actors may see an opportunity to discredit established elites in their wake by attacking dominant memory narratives. This was true of far-right memory challengers in Germany and France following the migration wave of 2015 and, perhaps, in Eastern Europe after the 2008/09 financial crisis. It was also true in Russia after the Color Revolutions in several former Soviet Republics since 2004, countries that Putin considers part of Russia's sphere of influence, and certainly after the eastward expansion of the European Union and NATO.

Unsettled mnemonic landscape: The instrumentalization of the past may face fewer obstacles in societies where the wounds of past traumas have not healed and where the past has not been truthfully reckoned with and reflected in education and socialization processes. Where taboo subjects are discouraged or even prohibited from discussion and debate, pressure may build to revisit the past in ways that are extreme, exclusivist, and perhaps socially and polit-ically destabilizing. Truthful reckoning with the fascist and collaborationist past came relatively late to France, Austria, and Italy, often sparked by con-troversies such as the trials of collaborators (Touvier in France in 1994) or revelations about public figures (the Waldheim Affair in Austria in 1986). Such reckonings unsettled the mnemonic landscape, possibly motivating memory challengers to pushback on a more contrite, more pluralistic memory of the war.

In Eastern Europe and Russia, the traumas of wartime suffering, Stalinist oppression, and the collapse of federations—violently in the case of the former Yugoslavia—combined to create an acutely unsettled mnemonic landscape. To that, we must add the decades of indoctrination into a Soviet dominant narrative and the unsettling encounter with a more cosmopolitan, Holocaust-centered narrative in the 1990s. Russia's humiliation at the collapse of its empire was compounded by the chaos of the Yeltsin years. For the two post-communist mnemonic regions, the examination of the difficult past was much belated and scattershot, leaving societies ill prepared to counter memory challengers when they arose.

Memory challenges over wartime commemorations seemed to arise where new perspectives countered, neglected, or crowded out a dominant memory frame by seeking to expand it, by becoming more pluralistic and inclusive. In other words, memory challengers sought to oppose a more complex and "troubled" mnemonic landscape. The right-wing backlash in Poland regard-ing Jan Gross's revelations about Jedwabne and the growing complexity of representations of Poland's past (perpetrator and collaborator, as well as vic-tim and bystander) is an example. Others include the nationalistic backlash to remembrance of the Vél d'Hiv roundup in Paris or against Liberation Day in Italy.

The conditions described above unsettle relationships and identities. In response, memory challengers seek to construct or defend a memory narrative that is integral to their own sense of self, their status, and the ways in which they make sense of the world. In both Western and Eastern Europe, veterans' organizations have sought to remove any stigma that prevents them from being seen as patriots who sacrificed for their country and defended Europe from communism. As they construct a particular narrative about the wartime past, veterans typically refrain from questioning the legitimacy of their governments, leaders, or mainstream parties; the radical youth and far-right parties that often attend their commemorations do not shy from doing so, however.

When the dominant memory narrative is discontinuous, when gaps or contradictions in the narrative of the wartime past cause doubt, shame, or discomfort in the present, the mnemonic landscape is unstable and ripe for memory challenges. So, too, is the mnemonic landscape disturbed when the dominant memory narrative is updated or made more inclusive, encouraging more critical, truthful, and pluralistic representation of past events and meaning-making in the present. In both situations, ontological insecurity motivates memory challengers who seek to resolve what they perceive as threats to their culture and identity.

In her examination of the politicization of the past in Croatia, Jelena Subotic argues that states (or groups) use political memory when fundamental questions about the state's identity occur that cause a rupture in the status quo, or official, narrative about the past. She explains that critical situations:

> Produce questioning of one's self-identity, one's view of the self, and most importantly, one's autobiography and biographical narrative (the story about the biography). To resolve this incredibly destabilizing sense of ontological insecurity, actors "act out," often defensively, as "anxieties can no longer be controlled."
>
> (2018, 298).

Because of post-communist Eastern Europeans' "unsettled mnemonical map of their own role in the Holocaust," Subotic argues that actors in those societies feel a need for "narrative stability." This causes them to deny any local complicity and often reject the "perceived elevation of Jewish victimhood above other regional-majority ethnic groups" (300). A desire for narrative stability characterizes Western European and Russian memory challengers as well. In all three meso-regions, the strategies of memory challengers that dichotomize Us and Them and invert the roles of perpetrator-victim leave, in Subotic's terms, "almost no room for the incorporation of minority narratives" (300).

For Eastern European memory challengers, nationalization of the past was initially a reaction to Sovietization of the wartime narrative, coupled with a desire to reclaim their past and construct collective memory without external or ideological interference. Soon after embarking on this process of reclaiming wartime memory, many Eastern European countries lined up to join the European Union. While nothing in the formal process of EU accession and integration required official reckoning with the Holocaust, post-communist leaders and publics were aware of the liberal-democratic expectations, including tolerance of difference and upholding human rights, particularly of minorities. Resisting those values has become a way for some, particularly on the right, to reassert independence. Anne Applebaum attributes the "mood of post-colonialism" in Eastern Europe to their "humiliation to be expected to imitate the Western democratic project rather than develop one of their own" (2020, 50–1). Applebaum discusses the mindset this way:

> the nation is no longer great because someone has attacked us, undermined us, sapped our strength. Someone—the immigrants, the foreigners, the elites, or indeed the EU—has perverted the course of history and reduced the nation to a shadow of its former self. The essential identity that we once had has been taken away and replaced with something cheap and artificial.
>
> (2020, 75)

Part of their assertion of independence involves a reclaiming of a great national past, a defense against any attempts to include a more pluralistic and nuanced representation of that past, and a resistance to the cosmopolitan European Holocaust narrative.

It seems logical, then, that the representation of the wartime past is deeply intertwined with national post-communist efforts to assert cultural and identity autonomy after Soviet domination and, now, in the context of European integration. Jerzy Jedlicki points out that this sense of being confined to the periphery is much older than the post-World War II period. He contends that an asymmetrical relationship between Eastern Europe and the West produced "an inverted self" in the former as well as a lingering sense of humiliation, since "[t]he flood of its technical innovations and cultural patterns was for the most part uni-directional, from the West to the East" (2005, 44). He continues, "You are constantly reminded that you borrowed more than you are able to return, and that your culture is imitative by nature" (43). For many self-appointed defenders of national pride and identity, imitation is humiliating, but they also find liberal democracy, with its pluralism and frequent need for cooperation and compromise, to be deeply dissatisfying. Blaming post-communists, liberals, and other "Others" is a strategy to "restore" national pride and place and, in doing so, to find relief from humiliation.

For some of the same reasons, Western European nationalist-populist and far-right groups or parties exhibit ontological insecurity in their efforts to resist what they view as a homogenizing, hegemonic collective memory. For the nationalist-populist Right, "post-national" values and institutions are not only unsatisfactory as foci for activity and identity construction; they are also dangerous insofar as they are inclusive, pluralistic, and progressive. These actors view the consensual, "politically correct" politics of the mainstream in their own states and, certainly at the EU level, to be inauthentic and vacuous, threatening to the integrity of the national community. Similar to memory challengers in the post-communist context, far-right memory challengers in Western Europe use and misuse memory politics to resist the cosmopolitan memory narrative and to invigorate national culture and identity. Similarly, their project is both positive and negative: they seek to "consolidate a social bond" and "cement the community," while also stoking anxiety by claiming that the people, the national community, is under threat (Bull 2016, 5). Viktor Orban's style of mnemonic defensiveness shares much with the far-right movements in Western Europe:

> We hold that our traditions and history are exceptional, we celebrate our heroes, and above all we love our country. We do not want to, and indeed we will not, surrender it for the sake of any empire or global governance.
>
> (cited in Soroka and Krawatzek 2019, 168)

A similar dynamic can be detected in Russian/Putin's memory politics. Van Herpen (2013) identifies several similarities between Weimar Germany's "socio-psychological" conditions and post-Soviet ontological insecurity. For Russia, the humiliation of the loss of empire, the search for internal enemies to blame for turmoil and chaos, and the discomfort of guilt relative to Stalinist atrocities are factors that facilitated the emergence of Putinism, which for our purposes involves a memory politics that is highly selective and grandiose. Putin not only oversees an interpretation of the past in heroic terms, but he also takes the extra step of counteracting other interpretations. His regime has done so through ostensibly legal-bureaucratic means, such as setting up commissions, amending the constitution, and legislating speech about the Russian past. His regime has also instrumentalized the wartime past through extra-legal means, for example, by conducting hybrid warfare against Estonia for that country's relocation of a monument to the Soviet military in 2007, and against the Czech Republic for changing and eventually removing a statue of a Soviet general in 2019. One can see how Putin's Russia has sought relief from "post-imperial trauma" and the associated ontological insecurity by shaping a narrative about its heroic Great Patriotic War past and by linking that narrative to a policy agenda that contains elements of neo-imperialism and anti-Westernism (Van Herpen 2013, 15).

The wartime commemorations examined in this book offer both a warning and an opportunity. As a warning, the cases examined here concerning the instrumentalization of wartime commemorations demonstrated how memory can create a fog, a dreamlike quality that blinds and distorts reality. This leads to new conflicts and the continuation of old antagonisms, producing an inability to see historical patterns of intolerance and exclusion.

In the preceding chapters, we saw that repetition and rituals are important elements of commemoration. While these forms of calendric memory can be used to strengthen societal bonds and to create links between the past, present, and future, they are not modes of remembrance that typically invite careful, critical reflection. They focus attention on a single event or group of people just once a year, for a brief period of time viewed through a simplistic, usually single-angle lens. Such modes of remembrance rarely invite a reflexive stance, in contrast to some of the newer history museums, where professional curators and historians try to present multiple voices and perspectives, and invite visitors to reflect on the meaning of the past in the present. Because wartime commemorations marking five- and ten-year anniversaries invite the most media attention, they tend to become stages for national leaders to articulate a narrow, national narrative. There have been exceptions, such as the post-Cold War period of commemorations of V-E Day, bringing together leaders from numerous countries representing all sides of the war; but even this event has become more, not less, nationally focused, particularly since Putin's return to the presidency and his instrumentalization of that anniversary. Instead, recent wartime commemorations tend to produce exclusive remembering, mobilizing the public around patriotism rather than reflection on the causes and implications of war.

Could it be otherwise? Is it possible to get past a monist memory, avoid simplistic memes and tropes, and, instead, to engage across national borders and across wartime roles as victims or perpetrators, to learn from others about the past? Is it possible to use the occasion of wartime anniversaries to see humanity embedded in a range of experiences? The construction of wartime memory can provide an antidote to the exclusionary policies and behaviors

that led to war and also lead to forms of misunderstanding and even violence in the present. In theory, wartime commemorations could broaden the
scope of memory construction to examine roots and consequences of processes that preceded and paved the way for atrocities associated with World
War II and the Holocaust, including imperialism, colonialism, racism, and the
construction of identities in Europe and Russia. Rather than self-deception
and shifting blame for past injustices onto others, remembrance might become
a vehicle for understanding the range of experiences and choices that individuals and groups made in the past about whether to support an authoritarian
or totalitarian regime or whether to participate in acts and institutions that
harm or degrade others. Commemorations of World War II are, potentially,
a site for examining the problems of simplistic binary thinking. The commemoration of the bombing of Dresden, for example, has become a site for
competing narratives but also for more engaging a range of arguments about
the meanings of the past for the present. Not only politicians and cultural
elites but many civil society organizations and thousands of individuals participate annually in debates and rituals that are part of a larger process of
public construction of memory and identity in Germany. Broad-brush narratives about heroes and victims, winners and losers are weak bases for critical
thinking about the complex causes of conflicts and their legacies. It is possible that more contact or entanglement between national or group-centered
narratives of World War II could "shake-up" rigid mnemonic patterns and,
in doing so, help to confront denialism, revisionism, and other forms of distortion of the past. Mnemonic encounters might even facilitate conversations
about the persistence of racism, anti-Semitism, and other biases, making the
difficult past relevant to contemporary challenges, such as language politics
in heterogenous societies, immigration and citizenship policies, and relations
with neighboring countries.

I wish to note a couple of examples of efforts to facilitate an acceptance
of pluralism and an appreciation for complexity around wartime memory. These practices of remembering move beyond zero-sum, dichotomous
interpretations of the past, whereby antagonistic memory construction is
increasingly complemented or balanced by remembrance that allows for
other levels of memory- and identity construction than the national, and,
tries to open up new spaces of common ground. The European Association of History Educators, known as EuroClio, is such an effort. Founded
three years after the fall of the Iron Curtain, it has the support of the Council of Europe and the European Union and members from forty-six countries.
Its mission is

to inspire and empower educators to engage learners in innovative and responsible history and citizenship education. The vision of EuroClio is for all learners to become more responsible and contributing citizens through engaging in history and citizenship education for mutual understanding and peace. EuroClio supports the development of responsible and innovative history, citizenship, and heritage education by promoting critical thinking, multiperspectivity, mutual respect, and the inclusion of controversial issues.
(https://euroclio.eu/association/mission-and-vision/)

Much of the work of EuroClio is geared toward professional development of history teachers, including organizing conferences, offering webinars and online courses, and a young professionals program at the EuroClio Secretariat in The Hague. Among its several projects, I wish to highlight two. The Sharing European Histories project seeks to open up "a space to engage with the dissonant and often conflictual nature of European history" as "the first step in discovering common positions or overcoming divisions while acknowledging existing differences" (https://euroclio.eu/projects/sharing-european-histories/). It offers online teaching strategies for use in the classroom or for professional development workshops. Among the offerings are "Using commemorative practices to teach that history is a constructed narrative" and "Using stories of the past to teach students about its complexity." For the commemorative practices strategy, one possible lesson is an excursion with students to a local site of memory for which students will research the following background questions:

When was this commemoration created? Who created it? On whose initiative was this commemoration created? What circumstances led to this commemoration being created? What does it commemorate? Does the commemoration reflect a local, national, international event, or a combination of the aforementioned? What theme does this relate to (politics, culture, religion, etc.)? What historical periods are reflected in these commemorations? Has this commemoration changed over time?
(EuroClio "Using Commemorative Practices" n.d.)

The other project is "Contested Histories" in cooperation with the Institute for Historical Justice and Reconciliation (IHJR) and examines contestation over sites of memory. They also offer a wide array of tools "to educators and other stakeholders to better understand and address complex legacies of Europe's totalitarian past. By doing so, the aim is to highlight that historical complexity and contestation are universal themes across European societies and to motivate conversation surrounding histories" (https://contestedhistories.org/onsite/) In addition to numerous online publications and learning opportunities, the project hosts a podcast called "Past Times—Talking and Teaching History" with educators across Europe about topics ranging from teaching in the midst of a memory war to place-based history learning.

The working group "Historical Memory and Education" of the EU-Russia Civil Society Forum is another effort to engage in sustained dialogue about difficult aspects of history from pluralistic perspectives. The EU-Russia Civil Society Platform was founded in 2011 as a network of independent and civil society actors across Europe and Russia, although the shrinking space for such activity in Russia means that most Russian participants are living in exile. One of the primary objectives of the Historical Memory and Education project was to broaden multilateral dialogue on conflicting memories.[1] One effort to do so was a traveling exhibit "Different Wars," which aimed to reveal differences in narratives about World War II found in modern high school textbooks in the Czech Republic, Germany, Italy, Lithuania, Poland, and Russia.

Bull and Hanson describe a dialogic approach to memory that is "open-ended and does not aim at any specific conclusions" (2016, 396). Lähdesmäki, Passerni, Kaasik-Krogerus, and van Huis (eds) use the term "heritage dissonance" and advocate for challenging "authorized heritage discourses" and memory regimes from above and for an acceptance of dissonance—even as a method of thinking and collaborating (2019, 13). One such project is UNREST, Unsettling Remembering and Social Cohesion in Transnational Europe. A research project funded by the European Union, UNREST proposes an alternative to the top-down cosmopolitan EU memory and the antagonistic right-wing nationalist memory. It advocates for a "third memory way, which acknowledges and engages with widespread memory discontent without losing sight of fundamental EU ideals" and "embraces political conflict as an opportunity for emotional and ethical growth" (UNREST.eu). Relying on a consortium of several universities, museums, and research institutes, UNREST encourages transnational dialogue about remembrance practices across academia, the arts, and museums. The website includes a pedagogical package that can be downloaded by teachers and reports on transnational conversations around mass grave exhumations and war museums. Another

---

[1] The website for this forum https://eu-russia-csf.org/ is no longer functioning.

offering is an online course on research into agonistic memory with practical case studies.

As long as conservative nationalist parties and leaders impose antagonistic, monist memory on their societies, as has occurred in Russia, Hungary, and Poland, there is little hope of opening up memory practices to dialogic, open-ended, dissonant-accepting modes of remembrance. If and when those parties and leaders do give way to successors more accepting of reflective, critical engagement with the past, there will be examples of earlier projects, such as the White Spots/Black Spots work among Polish and Russian historians, as well as new generations of historians, museum curators, and educators prepared to facilitate teacher training and exchanges, innovative history curricula and pedagogies, and transnational conferences and projects.

As I write this conclusion, Putin's war against Ukraine just entered its second year. Reviving old tropes about "Nazi threats" and "genocide" against Russian ethnic minorities, his most lethal memory challenge yet aims to drive out the Ukrainian leadership, restore empire, and impose a monist, exclusivist culture and identity onto Ukraine. Since the February 2022 invasion, however, rather than further divide the West, a broad transnational alliance (including many conservative-nationalist and far-right leaders and parties in the Baltics and Poland) has emerged to stand against Russia and with Ukraine. European countries have opened the door to millions of Ukrainian refugees, increasing the potential for contact between mnemonic narratives. That Poland has welcomed almost a million and a half of those refugees is remarkable when one considers the bitter conflicts in the past between Poles and Ukrainians. Today, Ukrainian children learn in Polish classrooms and Ukrainian families reside in Polish neighborhoods, invariably creating opportunities to discuss the difficult past and, hopefully, to broaden remembrance and deepen understanding.

References

Allwork, Larissa. (2015). "Holocaust Remembrance as 'Civil Religion': The Case of the Stockholm Declaration (2000)," in *Revisiting Holocaust Representation in the Post-Witness Era*. London: Palgrave Macmillan. 288–304.

Anderson, Benedict. (1991). *Imagined Communities Reflections on the Origins and Spread of Nationalism*. London and New York: Verso Books.

Apperly, Eliza. (2019). "The far right is taking on cultural institutions." *The Atlantic*. 28.

Applebaum, Anne. (2020). *Twilight of Democracy: The Seductive Lure of Authoritarianism*. New York: Doubleday.

Ariely, Gal. (2019). "National Days, National Identity, and Collective Memory: Exploring the Impact of Holocaust Day in Israel," *Political Psychology*, Vol. 40, No. 6: 1391–406.

Arnold, Jörg. (2002). *Der Brand: Deutschland im Bombenkrieg 1940-1945*. München: Propyläen.

Arnold, Jörg. (2014). "After the Dresden Bombing: Pathways of Memory, 1945 to the Present." *GHI London Bulletin*. Vol. 36: 120–4.

Art, David. (2009). *The Politics of the Nazi Past in Germany and Austria*. Cambridge: Cambridge University Press.

Art, David. (2010). "Memory Politics in Western Europe." http://diana-n.iue.it:8080/bitstream/handle/1814/13248/MWP_2010_01.pdf?sequence=1&isAllowed=y

Assmann, Aleida. (2004). "Four Formats of Memory: From Individual to Collective Constructions of the Past," in Christian Emden and David Midgley, eds. *Cultural Memory and Historical Consciousness in the German Speaking World Since 1500*. Bern: Peter Lang. 19–37.

Assmann, Jan. (2008). "Communicative and Cultural Memory," in Astrid Erll and Asngar Nünning, eds. *Cultural Memory Studies: An International and Interdisciplinary Handbook*. Berlin: De Gruyter. 109–18.

Bækken, Håvard and Johannes Due Enstad. (2020). "Identity under Seige: Selective Securitization of History in Putin's Russia," *Slavonic and East European Review*, Vol. 98, No. 2: 321–44.

Ballinger, Pamela. (2004). "Exhumed Histories: Trieste and the Politics of (Exclusive) Victimhood," *Journal of Southern Europe and the Balkans*, Vol. 6, No. 2: 145–59.

Bazyler, Michael J. (n.d.) "Holocaust Denial Laws and Other Legislation Criminalizing Promotion of Nazism." https://www.yadvashem.org/holocaust/holocaust-antisemitism/holocaust-denial-laws.html

Behr, Valentin. (2022). "How Historians Got Involved in Memory Politics: Patterns of the Historiography of the Polish People's Republic before and after 1989," *East European Politics and Societies*, Vol. 36, No. 3: 970–91.

Benazzo, Simone. (2017). "Not All the Past Needs to Be Used: Features of Fidesz's Politics of Memory," *Journal of Nationalism, Memory & Language Politics*, Vol. 11, No. 2: 198–221.

Beniston, Judith. (2003). "'Hitler's First Victim'?—Memory and Representation in Post-War Austria: Introduction," *Austrian Studies*, Vol. 11: 1–13.

Berend, Ivan T. (2006). "The Revival of Anti-Semitism in Post-Communist Hungary: The Early 1990s," in Randolph L. Braham and Brewster S. Chamberlin, eds. *The Holocaust in Hungary: Sixty Years Later.* New York: Rosenthal Institute for Holocaust Studies Graduate Center of the City University of New York. 167–76.

Berger, Thomas U. (2012). *War, Guilt, and World Politics after World War II.* Cambridge: Cambridge University Press.

Bernardi, Marco. (2019). "Toponymy as Method: Official Italian Rhetoric, History and the Foibe." *Journal of Historical Sociology.* Vol. 32, No. 4: 478–91.

Bernhard, Michael H., and Jan Kubik, eds (2014). *Twenty Years after Communism: The Politics of Memory and Commemoration.* Oxford: Oxford University Press.

Bernstein, Seth. (2016). "Remembering War, Remaining Soviet: Digital Commemoration of World War II in Putin's Russia," *Memory Studies*, Vol. 9, No. 4: 422–36.

Bikont, Anna. (2015). *The Crime and the Silence: Confronting the Massacre of Jews in Wartime Jedwabne.* New York: Farrar, Strauss and Girouz.

Blacker, Uilleam, Alexander Etkind, and Julie Fedor. (2013). *Memory and Theory in Eastern Europe.* New York: Palgrave Macmillan.

Blutinger, Jeffrey. (2010). "An Inconvenient Past: Post-Communist Holocaust Memorial-ization," *Shofar*, Vol. 29, No.1: 73–94.

Braslava, Māra. (2017). "Ethnic Cleavage in Politics and Mnemonic Tensions: An Analysis of World War II Commemorative Practices in Latvia," Masters Thesis, University of Tartu.

Brubaker, Rogers. (1994). "Nationhood and the National Question in the Soviet Union and Post-Soviet Eurasia: An Institutionalist Account," *Theory and Society*, Vol. 23: 47–78.

Bull, Anna Cento. (2016). "The Role of Memory in Populist Discourse: The Case of the Italian Second Republic," *Patterns of Prejudice*, Vol. 50, No. 3: 213–31.

Bull, Anna Cento, and Hans Lauge Hansen. (2016). "On Agonistic Memory," *Memory Studies*, Vol. 9, No. 4: 390–404.

Caramani, Daniele, and Luca Manucci. (2019). "National Past and Populism: The Re-elaboration of Fascism and Its Impact on Right-Wing Populism in Western Europe." *West European Politics*, Vol. 42, No. 6: 1159–87.

Carli, Maddalena. (2015). "25 April 1994—17 March 2011: Symbolic Dates of the Past and Italy's Transition," *Journal of Modern Italian Studies*, Vol. 20, No. 2: 252–65.

Carrier, Peter. (2005). *Holocaust Monuments and National Memory-Cultures in France and Germany since 1989: The Origins and Political Function of the Vél d'Hiv in Paris and the Holocaust Monument in Berlin.* Oxford: Berghan Books.

Cartwright, Gary. (2021). "Molotov-Ribbentrop Pact: Vladimir Putin's Alternative History." *EU Today.*

Center for Strategic and International Affairs (CSIS). (2020). "Next-Generation Fighters: Youth Military-Patriotic Upbringing Bolsters the Russian Military's Manning and Mobilization Potential." September 22, 2020. https://www.csis.org/blogs/post-soviet-post/next-generation-fighters-youth-military-patriotic-upbringing-bolsters

Clifford, Rebecca. (2013). *Commemorating the Holocaust: The Dilemmas of Remembrance in France and Italy.* Oxford: Oxford University Press.

Coalson, Robert. (2015). "Turning Back Time: Putting Putin's Molotov-Ribbentrop Defense into Context." *Radio Free Europe/Radio Liberty.*

Constitution of the Russian Federation. (2020). https://rg.ru/documents/2020/07/04/konstituciya-site-dok.html

Czerwinski, Maciej. (2016). "Croatia's Ambivalence over the Past: Intertwining Memories of Communism and Fascism." *Cultures of History Forum.* https://www.cultures-of-history.uni-jena.de/debates/croatia/croatias-ambivalence-over-the-past-intertwining-memories-of-communism-and-fascism/

Danilova, Maria. (2013). "Ukraine Divided over Legacy of Nazi Fighters." *The Times of Israel.*

Darasz, Jan. (2018). "The History Men," in Jo Harper, ed. *Poland's Memory Wars: Essays on Illiberalism.* Budapest: CEU Press. 131–59.

Deutsche Welle. (2018). "Inside secretive fraternities of Germany and Austria." https://www.dw.com/en/inside-the-secretive-fraternities-of-germany-and-austria/a-42447338

Deutsche Welle. (2020). "AfD's Gauland Opposes May 8 Public Holiday in Germany." *Deutsche Welle.* https://www.dw.com/en/afds-gauland-opposes-may-8-public-holiday-in-germany/a-53349489

Dujisin, Zoltan. (2021). "A History of Post-communist Remembrance: From Memory Politics to the Emergence of a Field of Anticommunism," *Theory and Society,* Vol. 50: 65–96.

Eckersley, Susannah. (2020). "Between Appropriation and Appropriateness: Instrumentalizing Dark Heritage in Populism and Memory," in Chiara De Cesari and Ayhan Kaya, eds. *European Memory in Populism: Representations of Self and Other.* London: Routledge. 210–38.

Edele, Mark. (2017). "Fighting Russia's History Wars: Vladimir Putin and the Codification of World War II," *History and Memory,* Vol. 29, No. 2: 90–124.

Elgenius, Gabriella, and Jens Rydgren. (2022). "Nationalism and the Politics of Nostalgia," *Sociological Forum,* Vol. 37, No. S1: 1230–43.

Ellwood, D. W. (2005). "The Never-Ending Liberation," *Journal of Modern Italian Studies,* Vol. 10, No. 4: 385–95.

Estonian World. (2020). "Baltic Presidents: Attempts to Misrepresent the Events of the Second World War Undermine Europe." *Estonian World.* https://estonianworld.com/opinion/baltic-presidents-attempts-to-misrepresent-the-events-of-the-second-world-war-undermine-europe/

EuroClio (n.d.) "Using Commemorative Practices." https://www.euroclio.eu/wp-content/uploads/SEH-Using-commemorative-practices-2.pdf?_gl=1*1nezr46*_ga*NjIwNDExMDY4LjE2Nzk1MDcwMjU.*_ga_YVLRV8F5ZS*MTY3OTUwNzAyNC4xLjEuMTY3OTUwNzc4My4wLjAuMA..&_ga=2.242774210.1175941657.1679507026-620411068.1679507025

European Commission on Racism and Intolerance. (2018) "Report on Croatia." Council of Europe. https://rm.coe.int/fifth-report-on-croatia/16808b57be

Fedor, Julie. (2021). "'Historical Falsification' as a Master Trope in the Official Discourse of History Education in Putin's Russia," *Journal of Educational Media,* Vol. 13, No. 1: 107–35.

Focardi, Filippo. (2014). "Italy's Amnesia over War Guilt: The 'Evil Germans' Alibi." *Mediterranean Quarterly,* Vol. 25, No. 4: 5–26, DOI: 10.1215/10474552-2830836.

Focardi, Filippo. (2017). "The Dispute over the Past: Political Transition and Memory Wars in Italy, from the Crisis of the First Republic until the Present," *Observing Memories* https://europeanmemories.net/magazine/the-dispute-over-the-past/

Foot, John. (2009). *Italy's Divided Memory.* New York: Palgrave Macmillan.

"France not responsible for 1942 mass round-up of Jews, says LePen." (April 9, 2017). I24news. https://www.i24news.tv/en/news/international/europe/142295-170409-france-not-responsible-for-1942-mass-round-up-of-jews-says-le-pen

Freedom House. (2022). "Croatia." Freedom in the World 2022 https://freedomhouse.org/country/croatia/freedom-world/2022

Frei, Norbert. (2002). *Adenauer's Germany and the Nazi Past: The Politics of Amnesty and Integration*. New York: Columbia University Press.

Fürstenau, Marcel. (2020). "May 8, 1945: Total Defeat or Day of Liberation?" *Deutsche Welle*, https://www.dw.com/en/may-8-1945-total-defeat-or-day-of-liberation/a-53340869

Gerstenfeld, Manfred. (2007). "The Multiple Distortions of Holocaust Memory." *Jewish Political Studies Review*, Vol. 19, Nos 3–4: 35–55.

Ghiglione, Giorgio. (2021). "Mussolini's Heirs Equate World War II Killings of Italians with the Holocaust." *Foreign Policy*.

Ghodsee, Kristen. (2013). "Blackwashing History," *Anthropology News*.

Ghodsee, Kristen. (2017). *Red Hangover: Legacies of Twentieth-Century Communism*. Durham, NC: Duke University Press.

Gödl, Doris. (2007). "Challenging the Past: Serbian and Croatian Aggressor—Victim Narratives," *International Journal of Sociology*, Vol. 37, No. 1: 43–57.

Grgurinovic, Matea. (2021). "Croatian Anti-Fascists Criticise Memorial Graveyard for Nazi-Allied Troops," *Balkan Insight*, November 25, 2021. https://balkaninsight.com/2021/11/25/croatian-anti-fascists-criticise-memorial-graveyard-for-nazi-allied-troops/

Gross, Jan T. (2001). *Neighbors: The destruction of the Jewish Community in Jedwabne, Poland*. Princeton University Press.

Gross, Jan T. (2007). *Fear: Anti-Semitism in Poland after Auschwitz*. New York: Random House Trade Paperbacks.

Gudehus, Christian. (2008). "Germany's Meta-Narrative Memory Culture: Skeptical Narratives and Minotaurs." *German Politics and Society*, Vol. 26, No. 4: 99–112.

Harper, Jo (ed.). (2018). *Poland's Memory Wars: Essays on Illiberalism*. Budapest: CEU Press.

Hannah-Jones, Nikole. (June 30, 2020). What Is Owed. *New York Times Magazine*.

Himka, John-Paul and Joanna Beata Michlic (eds.). (2013). *Bringing the Dark Past to Light: the Reception of the Holocaust in Postcommunist Europe*. Lincoln: U of Nebraska Press.

Hollande, François. (2012). "The 'Crime Committed in France, by France." *The New York Review of Books*.

Hopkins, Valerie. (2018). "Croatia's Contested Commemoration." *Politico* https://www.politico.eu/article/croatia-contested-commemoration-world-war-ii-nationalists-catholic-church/

Hübscher, Monika. (2017). "The AfD's Attitude towards National Socialism, the Holocaust and Antisemitism: A Facebook Analysis." Unpublished thesis. University of Haifa.

Hurd, Madeleine and Steffen Werther. (2016a). "Waffen-SS Veterans and Their Sites of Memory Today," in Jochen Böhler and Robert Gerwarth, eds. *The Waffen-SS: A European History*. Oxford: Oxford University Press. 331–55.

Hurd, Madeleine and Steffen Werther. (2016b). "Retelling the Past, Inspiring the Future: Waffen-SS Commemorations and the Creation of a 'European' Far-Right Counter-Narrative," *Patterns of Prejudice*, Vol. 50, Nos 4–5: 420–44.

Isanchenkov, Vladimir. (2020). "Putin Uses Parade to Boost Support before Vote." https://apnews.com/article/4ff118bcdd26bc59be06271bc3d31482

"Italian Film Tells Uncomfortable Story of Partisan WWII Massacres." (2021). The Local Italy. April 25, 2021. https://jacobinmag.com/2021/04/italy-memorial-day-exiles-foibe-fascism-partisan-yugoslav-resistance.

Ivaldi, Giles and Emilia Zankina, eds (2023). *The Impacts of the Russian Invasion of Ukraine on Right-wing Populism in Europe*. European Center for Populism Studies (ECPS). March 8, 2023. Brussels. https://doi.org/10.55271/rp0010

Jedlicki, Jerzy. (2005). "East-European Historical Bequest en route to an Integrated Europe," in Wilhelm Spohn and Klaus Eder, eds. *Collective Memory and European Identity: The Effects of Integration and Enlargement*. London: Routledge. 37–48.

Jerzak, Claudia. (2015). "Memory Politics: The Bombing of Hamburg and Dresden," in Katharina Gerstenberger and Tanja Nusser, eds. *Catastrophe and Catharsis: Perspectives on Disaster and Redemption in German Culture and beyond*. Rochester, NY: Camden House. 53–72.

Joel, Tony. (2013). *The Dresden Firebombing: Memory and the Politics of Commemorating Destruction*. London: I. B. Tauris.

Jones, Sara. (2017). "Cross-Border Collaboration and the Construction of Memory Narratives in Europe," in Sindbæk Andersen, Tea and Barbara Törnquist-Plewa, eds. *The Twentieth Century in European Memory: Transcultural Mediation and Reception*. Leiden: Brill. 25–55.

Judt, Tony. (2005). *Postwar: A History of Europe since 1945*. New York: Penguin Books.

Jushkin, Vladimir. (2020). "In the Fog of Victory: Glorification of the Soviet Legacy in Russia." Website of the Museum for the Victims of Communism in Patarei Prison. https://communistcrimes.org/en/fog-victory-glorification-soviet-legacy-russia.

Kalinin, Ilya. (2023). "The Broken Record Effect, or on the Advantage and Disadvantage of Historical Analogies for Life," *Russia.Post*. January 31, 2023, https://russiapost.info/politics/historical_analogies.

Karge, Heike. (2012). "Practices and Politics of Second World War Remembrance: (Trans-)National Perspectives from Eastern and South-Eastern Europe," in Małgorzata Pakier and Bo Stråth, eds. *A European Memory? Contested Histories and Politics of Remembrance*. New York: Berghan Books. 137–46.

Karner, Christian. (2013). "Multiple Dimensions and Discursive Contests in Austria's Mythscape," in Karner and Mertens, eds. *The Use and Abuse of History: Interpreting World War II in Contemporary European Politics*. London: Routledge. 193–210.

Karner, Christian and Bram Mertens. (2013). "Introduction: Memories and Analogies of World War II," in Christian Karner and Bram Mertens, eds. *The Use and Abuse of History: Interpreting World War II in Contemporary European Politics*. London: Routledge. 1–21.

Kattago, Siobhan. (2009). "War Memorials and the Politics of Memory: The Soviet War Memorial in Tallinn." *Constellations*, Vol. 16, No. 1: 150–66.

Kattago, Siobhan. (2012). *Memory and Representation in Contemporary Europe: The Persistence of the Past*. Farnham: Ashgate Publishers.

Katz, Dovid. (2011). "Review Article: Detonation of the Holocaust in 1941: A Tale of Two Books," *East European Jewish Affairs*, Vol. 41, No. 3 (December): 207–21.

Khapaeva, Dina. (2016). "Triumphant Memory of the Perpetrators: Putin's Politics of Re-Stalinization," *Communist and Post-Communist Studies* Vol.49, No.1: 61–73.

Khromeychuk, Oleysa. (2012). "The Shaping of 'Historical Truth': Construction and Reconstruction of the Memory and Narrative of the Waffen SS 'Galicia' Division," *Canadian Slavonic Papers*, Vol. 54, No. 3–4: 443–67.

Kolesnikov, Andrei. (2020). "Our Dark Past Is Our Bright Future: How the Kremlin Uses and Abuses History." Carnegie Moscow Center. https://carnegiemoscow.org/commentary/81718.

Kolstø, Pål. (2010). "Bleiburg: The Creation of a National Martyrology," *Europe-Asia Studies*, Vol. 62, No. 7: 1153–74.

Kolstø, Pal. (2019). "Dmitrii Medvedev's Commission against the Falsification of History: Why Was It Created and What Did It Achieve?" *Slavonic and East European Review*, Vol. 97, No. 4: 738–60.

Kończal, Kornelia. (2020). "The Invention of the 'Cursed Soldiers' and Its Opponents: Post-War Partisan Struggles in Contemporary Poland," *East European Politics and Societies*, Vol. 34, No. 1: 67–95.

Koposov, Nikolay. (2018). *Memory Laws, Memory Wars: The Politics of the Past in Europe and Russia* (New Studies in European History). Cambridge: Cambridge University Press.

Korycki, Kate. (2017) "Memory, Party Politics, and Post-Transition Space: The Case of Poland," *East European Politics and Societies*, Vol. 31, No. 3: 518–44.

Kovács, Éva. (2016). "Overcoming History through Trauma: The Hungarian *Historiker-streit*," *European Review*, Vol. 24, No. 4: 523–34.

Krzeminski, Adam. (2005). "As Many Wars as Nations: The Myths and Truths of WWII," http://www.signandsight.com/features/96.html

Kucia, Marek. (2016). "The Europeanization of Holocaust Memory and Eastern Europe," *East European Politics and Societies*, Vol. 30, No. 1 (February): 97–119.

Kuljić, Todor. (2017). "Reflections on the Principles of the Critical Culture of Memory," in Oto Luthar, ed. *Of Red Dragons and Evil Spirits: Post-Communist Historiography between Democratization and New Politics of History*. Budapest: CEU Press. 87–114.

Kwai, Isabella. (2022). "Latvia Tears down a Controversial Soviet-Era Monument in Its Capital." *The New York Times*. August 26, 2023. https://www.nytimes.com/2022/08/26/world/europe/latvia-soviet-monument.html

Lähdesmäki, Yuuli, Luisa Passerni, Sigrid Kaasik-Krogerus, and Iris van Huis, eds. (2019). *Dissonant Heritages and Memories in Contemporary Europe*. Palgrave.

Langdon, Kate C. and Vladimir Tismaneanu. (2019). *Putin's Totalitarian Democracy: Ideology, Myth, and Violence in the Twenty-First Century*. Palgrave.

Langenbacher, Eric (2004). "The Anglo-American Aerial Bombing of Germany during World War Two," in Adam Jones, ed. *Genocide, War Crimes and the West: History and Complicity*. London: Zed Books.

Large, David Clay. (1987). "Reckoning without the Past: The HAIG of the Waffen-SS and the Politics of Rehabilitation in the Bonn Republic, 1950–1961," *The Journal of Modern History*, Vol. 59, No. 1: 79–113.

Laruelle, Merlene. (2020). "Russia's Constitutional Amendments Keep Some Futures Open for Putin." Russia Matters https://www.russiamatters.org/analysis/russias-constitutional-amendments-keep-several-futures-open-putin.

Lebow, Richard Ned, Wulf Kansteiner, and Claudio Fugo, eds. (2006) *The Politics of Memory in Postwar Europe*. Durham, NC: Duke University Press.

Lees, David. (2012). "Remembering the Vel d'Hiv Roundup," https://warwick.ac.uk/newsandevents/knowledge-archive/arts/roundups/

Leggewie, Claus (2010). "Seven Circles of Memory," *Eurozine* (December 20) https://www.eurozine.com/seven-circles-of-european-memory/?pdf

Lepore, Jill. (2010). *The Whites of Their Eyes: The Tea Party's Revolution and the Battle over American History*. Princeton, NJ: Princeton University Press.

Lichtner, Giacomo. (2015). "Italian Cinema and the Fascist Past: Tracing Memory Amnesia," *Fascism*, Vol. 4: 25–47.

Lind, Jennifer. (2008). *Sorry States: Apologies in International Politics*. New York: Cornell University Press.

Liphshiz, Cnaan. (2017). "6 Reasons Why Macron's Speech about the Holocaust Matters." *The Forward*, https://forward.com/news/377208/6-reasons-why-macron-s-speech-about-the-holocaust-in-france-was-groundbreak/.

Lipstadt, Deborah. (2020). "Holocaust Denial: An Antisemitic Fantasy," *Modern Judaism— A Journal of Jewish Ideas and Experience*, Vol. 40, No. 1: 71–86. https://academic.oup.com/mj/article-abstract/40/1/71/5698025

Loschberger, Alexander. (2013). "Flashpoints of Austrian Memory: A Critical Analysis of the Controversial Veterans' Meetings on the Ulrichsberg," Masters Thesis, Edmonton, Alberta.

Luthar, Oto. (Ed.). (2017). *Of Red Dragons and Evil Spirits: Post-Communist Historiography between Democratization and the New Politics of History*. Central European University Press.

Maas, Heiko, and Andreas Wirsching. (2020). "There Can Be No Politics without History." https://www.auswaertiges-amt.de/en/newsroom/news/maas-wirsching-end-second-world-war/2339620?fbclid=IwAR0rC2LfpWXIQeSQhnbvSckRaNXwqLhqjW8ZVXl2aoyl5AJ7tB0aXWRxt8o

Macron, Emmanuel. (2017). "Speech at 75th Anniversary of the Vel d'Hiv Roundup." *The Times of Israel*. https://fr.timesofisrael.com/discours-demmanuel-macron-a-la-75e-commemoration-de-la-rafle-du-vel-dhiv/.

Mälksoo, Maria. (2009). "The Memory Politics of Becoming European: The East European Subalterns and the Collective Memory of Europe," *European Journal of International Relations*, Vol. 15, No. 4: 653–80.

Manucci, Luca. (2019). *Populism and Collective Memory: Comparing Fascist Legacies in Western Europe*. London: Routledge.

Marples, David R. (2006). "The Resurrection of a Ukrainian National Hero," *Europe-Asia Studies*, Vol. 58, No. 4: 555–66.

Marples, David R. (2007). *Heroes and Villains: Creating National History in Contemporary Ukraine*. Budapest: Central European University Press.

Mauthausen Committee. (2018). "Fest der Freude am 8. Mai: Befreiung Österreichs vom Nationalsozialismus." https://www.ots.at/presseaussendung/OTS_20180410_OTS0042/fest-der-freude-am-8-mai-befreiung-oesterreichs-vom-nationalsozialismus-bild

Mcdonnell, Hugh. (2017). "The 'Grey Zone' of Vichy France: Understanding Marine LePen's Latest Comments on the Second World War." https://blogs.lse.ac.uk/europpblog/2017/04/12/the-grey-zone-of-vichy-france-understanding-marine-le-pens-latest-comments-on-the-second-world-war/

Miller, Alexei and Maria Lipman (eds.). (2012). *The Convolutions of Historical Politics*. Central European University Press.

Milošević, Ana. (February 6, 2019). "Playing Memory Games with Europe's Totalitarian History," *The Balkan Insight*. https://balkaninsight.com/2019/02/06/memory-games-moving-the-iron-curtain-01-28-2019/.

Mink, Georges. (2013). "Institutions of National Memory in Post-Communist Europe: From Transitional Justice to Political Uses of Biographies (1989–2010)," in Georges Mink and Laure Neumayer, eds. *History, Memory and Politics in Central and Eastern Europe*. New York: Palgrave. 155–70.

Minkenberg, Michael. (1997). "The New Right in France and Germany: Nouvelle Droite, Neue Rechte, and the New Right Radical Parties," in Peter H. Merkl and Leonard Weinberg, eds. *The Revival of Right-Wing Extremism in the Nineties*. London: Frank Cass.

Moorhouse, Roger. (2014). *The Devils' Alliance: Hitler's Pact with Stalin 1939–41*. London: Bodley Head. http://public.ebookcentral.proquest.com/choice/publicfullrecord.aspx?p=1681927.

Moorhouse, Roger. (2022). "Why We Should Remember August 23, 1939." https://enrs.eu/article/why-should-we-remember-august-23-1939

Moscow Times. (2021). "Russia to Try Navalny on WWII Veteran Slander Charges." *Moscow Times.* https://www.themoscowtimes.com/2021/02/05/russia-to-try-navalny-on-wwii-veteran-slander-charges-a72841

Müller, Jan-Werner, ed. (2002). *Memory and Power in Post-War Europe: Studies in the Presence of the Past.* Cambridge: Cambridge University Press.

Nedelsky, Nadya. (2016). "'The Struggle for the Memory of the Nation': Post-Communist Slovakia and its World War II Past," *Human Rights Quarterly*, Vol. 38: 969–92.

Neiman, Susan. (2019). *Learning from the Germans: Confronting Race and the Memory of Evil.* New York: Penguin Books.

Niven, Bill. (2006). *Germans as Victims: Remembering the Past in Contemporary Germany.* Basingstoke: Palgrave Macmillan.

Nolan, Mary. (2005). "Germans as Victims during the Second World War: Air Wars, Memory Wars." *Central European History*, Vol. 38, No. 1: 7–40.

Nolte, Ernst. (June 6, 1986). "Die Vergangenheit, die nicht vergehen will. Eine Rede, die geschrieben, aber nicht gehalten warden," *Frankfurter Allgemeine Zeitung.*

Norris, Pippa, and Inglehart, Ronald. (2019). *Cultural Backlash: Trump, Brexit and Authoritarian Populism.* New York: Cambridge University Press.

Novikova, Irina. (2011). "Renaming Men: The Politics of Memory and the Commemoration of War at the Baltic-Russian Crossroads," *Women's History Review*, Vol. 20, No. 4: 589–97.

Olick, Jeffrey K. (2013). *The Politics of Regret: On Collective Memory and Historical Responsibility.* New York: Routledge.

Onken, Eva-Claire. (2007). "The Baltic States and Moscow's 9 May Commemoration: Analysing Memory Politics in Europe," *Europe-Asia Studies*, Vol. 59, No. 1: 23–46.

Pakier, Małgorzata and Bo Stråth (eds.). (2010). *A European Memory: Contested Histories and Politics of Remembrance.* New York and Oxford: Berghahn Books.

Pavlaković, Vjeran. (2010). "Deifying the Defeated: Commemorating Bleiburg since 1990." *L'Europe en Formation*, Vol. 357, No. 3: 125–47.

Pavlaković, Vjeran, and Davor Pauković, eds. (2019). *Framing the Nation and Collective Identities: Political Rituals and Cultural Memory of the Twentieth-Century Traumas in Croatia.* London and New York: Routledge.

Pelinka, Anton. (2017). "Taboos and Self-Deception: The Second Republic's Reconstruction of History," in Günter Bischof and Anton Pelinka eds. *Austrian Historical Memory & National Identity.* London: Routledge. 95–101.

Petrović, Nikola. (2018). "Divided national memories and EU crises: how Eurosceptic parties mobilize historical narratives." *Innovation: The European Journal of Social Science Research*, Vol. 32, No.3: 363–84. DOI: 10.1080/13511610.2018.1523710

Petzold, Stephan. (2020). "Challenging the Politics of German Victimhood: Memory Activism and the Contested Anniversary of the Dresden Bombing since 2005," *German Life and Letters*, Vol. 73, No. 3: 441–63.

Pirker, Pater, Johannes Kramer, and Mathias Lichtenwagner. (2019). "Transnational Memory Space in the Making: World War II and Holocaust Remembrance in Vienna," *International Journal of Politics, Culture and Society*, Vol. 32: 439–58.

Preusser, Heinz-Peter. (2007). "Regarding and Imagining. Contrived Immediacy of the Allied Bombing Campaign in Photography, Novel and Historiography," in Helmut Schmitz, ed. *A Nation of Victims? Representations of German Wartime Suffering from 1945 to the Present.* Amsterdam: Editions Rodopi B.V. 141–59.

Prezioso, Stefanie. (April 25, 2021). "Stop Pretending Italian Fascists Were Innocent Victims," *The Jacobin*. https://jacobin.com/2021/04/italy-memorial-day-exiles-foibe-fascism-partisan-yugoslav-resistance

Pritchard, Gareth, and Desislava Gancheva. (2014). "Collaborator: No Longer a Dirty Word?" *History Today*, Vol. 64, No. 12 https://www.historytoday.com/archive/collaborator-no-longer-dirty-word

Prosser, Andrew Edwin. (2018). "Constructing 'the People' and the Past: The Alternative für Deutschland, Collective Memory, and Populism as a Repertoire." PhD. Dissertation, University of Victoria.

Pugliese, David. (2019). *Ottawa Citizen* https://ottawacitizen.com/news/national/defence-watch/canadian-officials-who-met-with-ukrainian-unit-linked-to-neo-nazis-feared-exposure-by-news-media-documents.

Puls24. (2023). "Wegen Ulrichsberg-Treffen abberufen: Nun wird ex-LVT-Chef erfördert." February 28, 2023 https://www.puls24.at/news/politik/wegen-ulrichsberg-treffen-abberufen-nun-wird-ex-lvt-chef-befoerdert/290324

Putin, Vladimir. (2014). Speech, March 18, 2014. http://en.kremlin.ru/events/president/news/20603

Putin, Vladimir. (2019). Annual News Conference. December 19, 2019. http://en.kremlin.ru/events/president/news/62366

Putin, Vladimir. (2020). "Vladimir Putin: The Real Lessons of the 75th Anniversary of World War II." *The National Interest.*

Putin, Vladimir. (2021). Speech "Victory Day," May 9, 2021 http://en.kremlin.ru/events/president/news/65544

Putin, Vladimir. (2022a). Speech, February 21, 2022. http://en.kremlin.ru/events/president/news/67828.

Putin, Vladimir (2022b), Televised Speech, February 23, 2022. http://en.kremlin.ru/events/president/news/page/130

Radchenko, Sergei. (2020). "Vladimir Putin Wants to Rewrite the History of World War II." *Foreign Policy*. https://foreignpolicy.com/2020/01/21/vladimir-putin-wants-to-rewrite-the-history-of-world-war-ii/

Rogulski, Rafał. (2020). "We Are All Victims of Totalitarianism." https://polishhistory.pl/rafal-rogulski-we-are-all-victims-of-totalitarianism/

Rehberg, Karl-Siegbert, and Matthias Neutzner. (2015). "The Dresden Frauenkirche as a Contested Symbol: The Architecture of Remembrance after War," in Marie Louise Stig Sørensen and Dacia Veijo-Rose, eds. *War and Cultural Heritage: Biographies of Place.* Cambridge: Cambridge University Press. 98–127.

Reynié, Dominique. (2016). "The Specter Haunting Europe: 'Heritage Populism' and France's National Front." *Journal of Democracy*, Vol. 27, No. 4: 47–57.

RFE/RL. (2023). "Russia Police Arrest Father of Sixth-Grader Who Drew Anti-War Picture." March 1, 2023. https://www.rferl.org/a/russia-police-arrest-father-moskalyov-girl-anti-war-picture/32294618.html

Richard, Nelly. (2019). *Eruptions of Memory: The Critique of Memory in Chile, 1990–2015.* Cambridge: Polity.

Rigney, Ann. (2012). "Transforming Memory and the European Project," *New Literary History*, Vol. 43, No. 4 (Autumn): 607–28.

Rotfeld, Adam Daniel, and Anatoly V. Torkunov, eds. (2015). *White Spots Black Spots: Difficult Matters in Polish-Russian Relations, 1918–2008*. Pittsburg: University of Pittsburgh Press.

Roth, Andrew. (2019). "Molotov-Ribbentrop: Why Is Moscow Trying to Justify Nazi Pact?" *The Guardian.*

Rudling, Per Anders. (2012). "'They Defended Ukraine': The 14. Waffen-Grenadier-Division der SS (Galizische Nr. 1) Revisited." *The Journal of Slavic Military Studies*, Vol. 25, No. 3: 329–68.

RussiaEguide.com. "Patriot Park and Kubinka Tank Museum." https://www.russiaeguide.com/patriot-park-tour.html

Samorukov, Maxim. (2021). "Can Russia and Poland Ever Overcome Their Historical Differences?" Carnegie Endowment for International Peace Commentary. https://carnegiemoscow.org/commentary/85115

Sander, George F. (2022). "Memory Wars in Latvia." *New York Review of Books* https://www.nybooks.com/articles/2022/07/21/memory-wars-in-latvia-gordon-sander

Schleifman, Nurit. (2001). "Moscow's Victory Park: A Monumental Change." *History and Memory*. Vol. 13, No. 2: 5–34.

Schuman, Howard, R. F. Belli, and K. Bischoping. (1997). "The Generational Basis of Historical Knowledge," in J. W. Pennebaker, D. Paez, and B. Rimé, eds. *Collective Memory of Political Events: Social Psychological Perspectives*. Mahwah, New Jersey: Lawrence Erlbaum Associates, Inc. 47–77.

Schwartz, Barry. (1982). "The Social Context of Commemoration: A Study in Collective Memory. *Social Forces*, Vol. 61, No. 2: 374–402.

Serbyn, Roman. (2007). "Managing Memory in Post-Soviet Ukraine: 'Victory Day' or 'Remembrance Day,'" in Stephen Velychenko, ed. *Ukraine, The EU and Russia*. Basingstoke: Palgrave Macmillan. 108–122.

Shafir, Michael. (2006). "Hungarian Politics and the Post-1989 Legacy of the Holocaust," in Randolph L. Braham and Brewster S. Chamberlin, eds. *The Holocaust in Hungary: Sixty Years Later*. New York: Rosenthal Institute for Holocaust Studies Graduate Center of the City University of New York. 257–90.

Shafir, Michael. (2012). "Denying the Shoah in Post-Communist Eastern Europe," in Robert S. Wistrich, ed. *Holocaust Denial: The Politics of Perfidy*. Berlin and Boston: de Gruyter. 27–65.

Sherlock, Thomas. (2011). "Confronting the Stalinist Past: The Politics of Memory in Russia." *The Washington Quarterly*, Vol. 34, No. 2: 93–109.

Shermer, Michael and Alex Grobman. (2000). *Denying History: Who Says the Holocaust Never Happened and Why Do They Say It?* Berkeley: University of California Press.

Sierp, Aline. (2014). *History, Memory, and Trans-European Identity: Unifying Divisions.* London: Routledge.

Sierp, Aline. (2017). "1939 versus 1989—A Missed Opportunity to Create a European Lieu de Mémoire?" *East European Politics and Societies*, Vol. 31, No. 3: 439–55.

Sindbæk Andersen, Tea and Barbara Törnquist-Plewa. (2016). *Disputed Memory: Emotions and Memory Politics in Central, Eastern and South-Eastern Europe*. Berlin and Boston: de Gruyter.

Siviero, Tommaso. (2022). "Italian Right Stirs Up Grievances about Yugoslavs' WWI 'Foibe Massacres.'" Balkan Transitional Justice. December 27, 2023. https://balkaninsight.com/2022/12/27/italian-right-stirs-up-grievances-about-yugoslavs-wwii-foibe-massacres/

Smith, Kathleen E. (2002). *Mythmaking in the New Russia: Politics & Memory during the Yeltsin Era*. Ithaca, NY: Cornell University Press.

Snyder, Timothy. (2009). "The Historical Reality of Eastern Europe." *East European Politics and Societies*. Vol. 23, No. 1 (February): 7–12.

Snyder, Timothy. (2015). "When Stalin Was Hitler's Ally." *Eurozine.* https://www.eurozine.com/when-stalin-was-hitlers-ally/

Sokolov, Mikhail, and Robert Coalson. (2021). "'A Dangerous Commission': Russian Historians Alarmed as Putin Creates State Body on 'Historical Education.'" *Radio Free Europe/Radio Liberty.* https://www.rferl.org/a/russia-history-commission-putin/31403236.html

Soroka, George, and Felix Krawatzek (2019). "Nationalism, Democracy, and Memory Laws," *Journal of Democracy,* Vol. 30, No. 2: 157–71.

Spillman, Lynette P. (1997). *Nation and Commemoration: Creating National Identities in the United States and Australia.* Cambridge: Cambridge University Press.

Steele, Brent J., and Alexandra Homolar. (2019). "Ontological Insecurities and the Politics of Contemporary Populism," *Cambridge Review of International Affairs,* Vol. 32, No. 3: 214–21.

Steinmeier, Frank-Walter. (2020). "Frank-Walter Steinmeier on the 75th Anniversary of the Bombing of Dresden during the Second World War, at Kulturpalast, Dresden, on 13 February 2020." https://www.bundespraesident.de/SharedDocs/Downloads/DE/Reden/2020/02/200213-Dresden-Gedenken-Bombardierung-Englisch.pdf?__blob=publicationFile.

Stone, Dan. (2013). *The Holocaust, Fascism and Memory.* London: Palgrave Macmillan.

Strickland, Patrick. (2018). "Thousands Attend Far-Right Commemoration in Southern Austria." *Al-Jazeera.* May 12, 2018. https://www.aljazeera.com/news/2018/5/12/thousands-attend-far-right-commemoration-in-southern-austria

Subotic, Jelena. (2018). "Political Memory, Ontological Security, and Holocaust Remembrance in Post-Communist Europe," *European Security,* Vol. 27, No. 3: 296–313.

Subotic, Jelena. (2019). *Yellow Star, Red Star: Holocaust Remembrance after Communism.* New York: Cornell University Press.

Szijaro, Imre, and Rosa Schwatzburg. (2020). "My SS Uniform Is Just My Heritage," Jacobin. https://jacobinmag.com/2020/03/day-of-honor-viktor-orban-hungary-neo-nazis-rally

Teague, Elizabeth. (2020). "Russia's Constitutional Reforms of 2020," *Russian Politics.* Vol.5, No.3: 301–28.

Teague, Elizabeth. (2020). "Russia's Constitutional Reforms of 2020," *Russian Politics.* Vol. 5, No. 3, 301–328.

Ten Dyke, Elizabeth A. (2001). *Dresden: Paradoxes of Memory in History.* London: Routledge.

The Budapest Times (2023). "Four Suspects Detained over Violent Attacks in Budapest." February 13, 2023. https://www.budapesttimes.hu/hungary/four-suspects-detained-over-violent-attacks-in-budapest/

Thiemann, Alina, and Valentina Pricopie. (2021). "Competing Regimes of Memory? The European Day of Remembrance in Romania," *Revue politique europeenne,* Vol. 71: 80–108.

Thomassen, Bjørn, and Rosario Forlenza. (2011). "Re-narrating Italy, Reinventing the Nation: Assessing the Presidency of Ciampi," *Journal of Modern Italian Studies,* Vol. 16, No. 5: 705–25.

Times of Israel. (2018). "Nazi Symbols, Salute on Display at Ukrainian Nationalist March." April 30, 2018. https://www.timesofisrael.com/nazi-symbols-salutes-on-display-at-ukrainian-nationalist-march/

Tismaneanu, Vladimir. (2009). *Fantasies of Salvation.* Princeton, NJ: Princeton University Press.

Trenin, Dmitri. (2007). *Getting Russia Right*. Moscow: Carnegie Endowment for International Peace.

Trillò, Tommaso, and Shifman, Limor. (2021). "Memetic Commemorations: Remixing Far-Right Values in Digital Spaces," *Information, Communication & Society*, Vol. 24, No. 16: 2482–501.

Troebst, Stefan. (2012a). "23 August: The Genesis of a Euroatlantic Day of Remembrance." *Remembrance and Solidarity Studies*, ENRS.

Troianovski, Anton. (2017). "The German Right Believes It's Time to Discard the Country's Historical Guilt," *The Wall Street Journal* (New York City), March 3.

Tumarkin, Nina. (1991). "Glasnost and the Great War: Report for the National Council for Soviet and East European Research." https://www.ucis.pitt.edu/nceeer/1991-804-07-Tumarkin.pdf

Tumarkin, Nina. (2003). "The Great Patriotic War as Myth and Memory," *European Review*, Vol. 11, No. 4: 595–611.

Uhl, Heidemaire. (2006). "From Victim Myth to Co-Responsibility Thesis: Nazi Rule, World War II and the Holocaust in Austrian Memory," in Richard Ned Lebow, Wulf Kansteiner, and Claudio Fugo, eds. *The Politics of Memory in Postwar Europe*. Durham, NC: Duke University Press. 40–72.

Uhl, Heidemarie. (2009). "Conflicting Cultures of Memory in Europe: New Borders between East and West?" *Israel Journal of Foreign Affairs*, Vol. 3, No. 3: 59–72.

Uhl, Heidemarie. (2011). "Of heroes and Victims: World War II in Austrian Memory," *Austrian History Yearbook*, Vol. 42: 185–200.

Uhl, Heidemarie. (2017). "The Politics of Memory: Austria's Perception of the Second World War and the National Socialist Period," in Günter Bischof and Anton Pelinka eds. *Austrian Historical Memory & National Identity*. London: Routledge. 64–94.

van der Laarse, Rob. (2019). "Europe's Peat Fire: Intangible Heritage and the Crusades for Identity," in Tuuli Lähdesmäki, Luisa Passerini, Sigrid Kaasik-Krogerus, Iris van Huis, eds. *Dissonant Heritages and Memories in Contemporary Europe*. Cham, Zwitzerland: Palgrave. 79–134.

Van Herpen, Marcel H. (2013). *Putinism: The Slow Rise of a Radical Right Regime in Russia*. Basingstoke: Palgrave Macmillan.

Van Herpen, Marcel H. (2014). *Putin's Wars: The Rise of Russia's New Imperialism*. Lanham, MD: Roman & Littlefield.

Varangis, Nicholas. (2017). "Storming the Reichstag in Russia's 'Military Disneyland,'" Warfare History Network. https://warfarehistorynetwork.com/storming-the-reichstag-in-russias-military-disneyland/

Verovšek, Peter J. (2016). "Collective Memory, Politics, and the Influence of the Past: The Politics of Memory as a Research Paradigm." *Politics, Groups, and Identities*, Vol. 4, No. 3: 529–43.

Vladislavljevic, Anja. (2020). "Austrian MPs Vow to Ban Croats' Ultranationalist Bleiburg Events." Balkan Transitional Justice. June 22, 2020. https://balkaninsight.com/2020/06/22/austrian-mps-vow-to-ban-croats-ultranationalist-bleiburg-events/

Volk, Sabine. (2020). "Commemoration at the Extremes: A Field Report from Dresden 2020," *Cultures of History Forum*. https://www.cultures-of-history.uni-jena.de/debates/commemoration-at-the-extremes-a-field-report-from-dresden-2020

von Weizsäcker, Richard. (1985). "Germany's Fortieth Anniversary: The End of the War in Europe." *SAIS Review*. Vol. 5, No. 2: 57–66.

Walker, Shaun. (2015). "Vladimir Putin Opens Russian 'Military Disneyland' Patriot Park." *The Guardian.* https://www.theguardian.com/world/2015/jun/16/vladimir-putin-opens-russian-military-disneyland-patriot-park

Webber, Alex. (2022). "'A Pact of Criminals': Commemorations Mark Anniversary of Molotov-Ribbentrop Pact." *The First News.* https://www.thefirstnews.com/article/a-pact-of-criminals-commemorations-mark-anniversary-of-molotov-ribbentrop-pact-32588

Weilandt, Ragnar. (2016). "Why Austria Almost Elected a Fascist President." Open-Democracy. June 13, 2016. https://www.opendemocracy.net/en/can-europe-make-it/why-austria-almost-elected-fascist-president/

Weiss, Volker. (2017). *Die autoritäre Revolte: Die Neue Rechte und der Untergang des Abendlandes.* Stuttgart: Klett-Cotta.

Wertsch, James V. (2008). "Blank Spots in Collective Memory: A Case Study of Russia." *Annals of the American Academy of Political and Social Science*, Vol. 617, The Politics of History in Comparative Perspective: 58–71.

Wesolowsky, Tony and Matthew Luxmoore. (2019). "Molotov-Ribbentrop What? Do Russians Know of Key World War II Pact?" *Radio Free Europe/Radio Liberty.* https://www.rferl.org/a/molotov-ribbentrop-what-do-russians-know-of-key-wwii-pact/30123950.html

Winter, Jay. (2010). "The Performance of the Past: Memory, History, Identity," in Karin Tilmans, Frank van Vree, and Jay Winter, eds. *Performing the Past: Memory, History, and Identity in Modern Europe.* Amsterdam: Amsterdam University Press. 11–34.

Wodak, Ruth and Anton Pelinka. (Eds.). (2002). *The Haider Phenomenon in Austria.* New Brunswick, New Jersey: Transaction Publishers.

Wojcik, Anna. (2020). "Memory Laws in Russia and Other Restrictions on Freedom of Expression." https://legal-dialogue.org/memory-laws-in-russia-and-other-restrictions-on-freedom-of-expression.

Wood, Elizabeth. (2011). "Performing Memory: Vladimir Putin and the Celebration of WWII in Russia." *The Soviet and Post-Soviet Review*, Vol. 38: 172–200.

Yoder, Jennifer A. (2019). "Angela Merkel's Discourse about the Past: Implications for the Construction of Collective Memory in Germany," *Memory Studies*, Vol. 12, No. 6: 660–76.

Yoder, Jennifer A. (2020). "'Revenge of the East'?: The AfD's Appeal in Eastern Germany and Mainstream Parties' Responses." *German Politics and Society*, Vol. 38, No. 2: 35–58.

Ziemann, Benjamin. (2013). *Contested Commemorations: Republican War Veterans and Weimar Political Culture.* Cambridge: Cambridge University Press.

Zima, Theodore. (2020). "Putin's Truth in the Era of Post-Truth." *Modern Diplomacy.* https://moderndiplomacy.eu/2020/02/12/putins-truth-in-the-era-of-post-truth/

Zuk, Piotr. (2018). "Nation, National Remembrance, and Education—Polish Schools as Factories of Nationalism and Prejudice," *Nationalities Papers*, Vol. 46, No. 6: 1046–62.

Index